A study of the 'romanticism' of Coleridge and Wordsworth. Their concern with creativity, and the conditions which helped or hindered their own artistic development produced a new concept of mental growth—a 'modern' view of the mind as organic, active, and unifying. In particular, we see how their aesthetics evolved from a personal and intuitional need to re-affirm 'value' in their own lives. Their discovery of the fundamental ambiguity of such intuitions is discussed in relation to some ideas of Empson Gombrich, and Ehrenzweig. 'Imagination' becomes a way of making conscious two levels of experience: its final expression is a view of the mind as a symbolic and symbolizing process— the means by which we create, perceive, and remember 'reality'.

As well as an essay in criticism, this is a contribution to the history of ideas: drawing together points in the background of philosophical and psychological theory from Hartley and Wesley to John Stuart Mill. Since many of our ideas about imagination, symbolism, and creativity are ultimately derived from Coleridge and Wordsworth, this is a book for students of romantic and modern literature. It will also interest the growing scholarly public concerned with the epistemological bases of literary, artistic, and historical studies.

COLERIDGE AND WORDSWORTH

The Poetry of Growth

COLERIDGE AND WORDSWORTH

❊

The Poetry of Growth

STEPHEN PRICKETT

Lecturer in English
School of English and American Studies
University of Sussex

CAMBRIDGE
AT THE UNIVERSITY PRESS
1970

Published by the Syndics of the Cambridge University Press
Bentley House, 200 Euston Road, London, N.W.1
American Branch: 32 East 57th Street, New York, N.Y. 10022

© Cambridge University Press 1970

Library of Congress Catalogue Card Number: 70–92253

Standard Book Number: 521 07684 6

Printed in Great Britain
by W & J Mackay & Co Ltd, Chatham

Contents

v

CONTENTS

Acknowledgements

I am deeply grateful to my colleague, Tony Nuttall, for his criticism of the early chapters; to Dr Margaret Leslie, of Lancaster University, for discussing with me my comments on Hartley in Chapter 2, and for giving me permission to quote from the Appendix on Hartley in her own unpublished dissertation, 'The Political Thought of Joseph Priestley'; and, above all, to Professor L. C. Knights, who shared with me his own enthusiasm for Coleridge, who encouraged and criticized the earlier drafts of this work, and without whom it would never have been written.

S.P.

Sussex, 1969

INTRODUCTION

The Rainbow and the Imagination

It seems widely agreed today that Coleridge and Wordsworth
stand at a critical point in the history of ideas of creativity. One
writer, for example, sees Coleridge as central to the transformation of 'imitative' into 'creative' theories of art.[1] For another,
the change is characterized by a tendency to 'pose and answer
aesthetic questions in terms of the relation of art to the artist
rather than to external nature, or to the audience.'[2] Yet a third
has described their Romanticism as a permanent and unalterable
revolution in human thought, analogous to a boiling-point,
where what follows is inevitably a change of state.[3] Others
again have transposed this change into a different key, and seen
it in terms of a new attitude to childhood and therefore to education.[4] With such a variety of convincing interpretations of the
shift of thought that we find in Coleridge and Wordsworth, it is
worth reminding ourselves that even the English Romantic
movement cannot be all things to all critics.

E. H. Carr once commented that 'the fact that a mountain
looks different when seen from different angles does not mean
either that it has no shape, or an infinity of shapes.' It is, I
believe, possible to find a unity in the complex of ideas evolved
over more than a decade by Coleridge and Wordsworth without our having to succumb to the temptation to clarify their
thinking into a spuriously attractive simplicity which it did not
actually possess. A. O. Lovejoy has doubted if there are any
common factors in what has been loosely termed 'Romanticism',

[1] Raymond Williams, *The Long Revolution* (Chatto, 1961), Pt I, Ch. I.
[2] M. H. Abrams, *The Mirror and the Lamp* (Oxford, 1958), p. 3.
[3] George Watson, *Coleridge the Poet* (Routledge, 1966), p. 22.
[4] For instance, see William Walsh, *The Use of Imagination* (Chatto, 1959); and
Peter Coveney, *The Image of Childhood* (Peregrine, Penguin Books, 1967).

and has warned us to speak rather of specific 'romanticisms'.[1] In this sense I think it may be helpful to see the work of Coleridge and Wordsworth—even when in disagreement—as part of the same 'romanticism'. For example, a cherished popular notion about 'Romantic' artists is that they believed themselves to be 'inspired'—in the sense of forgoing some conscious control of their work. But for Coleridge, as for Wordsworth, however much art may have reflected, at times, a transcendent vision, it was always the product of close conscious organization. For us, the unique quality of their collaboration lies in the peculiar extent to which both partners were, in their own ways, continually trying to account for what they felt was actually going on in their minds when they wrote a poem. Poetic creation and self-analysis were, for them, two sides of the same process. In volumes of notebooks; thousands of letters; books on criticism, philosophy, and religion; in lectures on drama, education and art; Coleridge has left us virtually a running commentary on the way his mind developed. From Wordsworth we have not merely the two Prefaces of 1800 and 1815, but *The Prelude*. What they have recorded for us in minute and scrupulous detail is the *structure* of creativity: how previous artistic schemata are matched with, or modified by new ideas; how the influence of method and tradition produces not repetition, but constant innovation and change; how symbol and myth tap responses deeper, if more ambiguous, than those of rational argument or conventional philosophy. If we have come to realize that major scientific or mathematical geniuses are 'creative' in the same sense that an artist is 'creative', we are, whether we know it or not, responding to a model of the way the human mind worked that comes to us from Coleridge and Wordsworth. It is that model of creativity that is the subject of this book. Coleridge called it 'Imagination'. It took him almost a lifetime to define what he meant by it—and even then his answer is not a fully consistent one. Nevertheless, it is this model—or to be exact, complex of symbols—that is 'the mountain' we must look at if we are to make sense of the revolution in ideas of 'creativity' that they initiated. But in

[1] A. O. Lovejoy, 'On the Discrimination of Romanticisms', *Essays in the History of Ideas* (John Hopkins Press, 1948).

order to do this, we must first of all try to understand why it was that, with a very few notable exceptions,[1] when the nineteenth century looked at Coleridge and Wordsworth they did not see any such revolution or 'boiling-point' of consciousness at all.

Over and over again, for example, we find that to nineteenth-century readers it was the 'incantatory magic' of Coleridge in *The Ancient Mariner*, *Kubla Khan*, and *Christabel* that appealed. What he seemed to offer them was a dream-world. It is significant that two of those three poems had been published as unfinished fragments. As a result, readers were able to respond to their beauty and—even more important—their 'feeling', while being free to interpret their structure in any way they chose, or even to ignore it altogether. The essential unity of Coleridge's thought was dismembered by the Victorians, who tended to carry off only such portions as were easy to digest. While the 'faerie' and 'dream' aspects of Coleridge influenced the poets, his philosophy and theology, disastrously severed from his poetry, had become the preserve of the 'Coleridgeians'—a small, if influential group of scholars such as F. D. Maurice and his Oxford tutor, Julius Hare. Once this divorce between his poetry and philosophy had been achieved, for whatever reason, Coleridge's concept of the Imagination could then be set aside as no more than a dictum of esoteric literary criticism.

The case of Wordsworth is parallel, and even more striking. We can see what has happened in Matthew Arnold's poem on the death of Wordsworth in 1850:

> Ah, since dark days still bring to light
> Man's prudence and man's fiery might,
> Time may restore us in his course
> Goethe's sage mind and Byron's force:
> But where will Europe's latter hour
> Again find Wordsworth's healing power?
> Others will teach us how to dare,
> And against fear our breast to steel:
> Others will strengthen us to bear—
> But who, ah who, will make us feel?

[1] For example, F. J. A. Hort's essay, 'Coleridge', *Cambridge Essays*, Vol. II (1856).

Wordsworth's distinguishing characteristic is his 'healing power'—and he is healing because he teaches us how to 'feel'. Arnold's view of Wordsworth here is, by and large, typical of Victorian England. As we shall see, John Stuart Mill in his *Autobiography* takes a very similar line when he recounts how Wordsworth helped him to recover from his breakdown. What is interesting is to see how, once Arnold and Mill have reached this view of Wordsworth, certain other conclusions about him follow almost inevitably. In his essay on Wordsworth, Arnold, like John Stuart Mill, has grave reservations about the quality of the *Immortality Ode*, and he dismisses *The Prelude* together with *The Excursion* as 'by no means Wordsworth's best work.' In confirmation of the popularity of this view, one common nineteenth-century edition of Wordsworth's *Poetical Works* omits *The Prelude* altogether, with the comment that it is 'not generally considered equal to his former poems.'[1] The poems Arnold singles out instead for special praise are, similarly, as representative of the best 'orthodox' taste of the period as we are likely to find. He writes:

If I had to pick out poems of a kind most perfectly to show Wordsworth's unique power, I should rather choose poems such as *Michael*, *The Fountain*, *The Highland Reaper*. And poems with the peculiar and unique beauty which distinguishes these, Wordsworth produced in considerable number...[2]

What Arnold has selected are short or medium-length lyric poems of 'feeling'. Nowhere does he suggest that they might form parts of a larger unity—that they are linked by a theory of human growth or creativity (and they are not, in any case, good examples of this). Though he sees Wordsworth as greater than Coleridge or Keats by vitue of his 'ampler body of powerful work', he makes it clear that 'ampler' is purely a measurement of quantity—not a qualitative assessment of any organic unity. Similarly Wordsworth's 'philosophy' is dismissed. In spite of Wordsworth's repeated stress on the essential unity of all his

---

[1] The 'Albion' Edition (Frederick Warne).
[2] 'Wordsworth', *The Portable Matthew Arnold*, ed. Trilling (Viking, 1949), p. 352.

4

work,[1] he has already been selected and anthologized into a succession of noble and feeling fragments.

We have noticed how similar John Stuart Mill's idea of Wordsworth was to Arnold's, but the philosopher in him drove him to be more explicit, so that the contradiction that is only latent in Arnold is brought out and formulated by Mill. In the *Autobiography* Mill acknowledges that it was Wordsworth who taught him to 'feel' again. In his earlier essay 'What is Poetry?', moreover, he explains that this 'feeling' is the essence of poetry—to be distinguished from its common companions 'eloquence' and 'narrative'. But in another essay, 'Two Kinds of Poetry', Mill comes out with the curious declaration that Wordsworth is not a 'natural' poet in the way that Shelley, for instance, is. 'In Wordsworth,' he writes, 'the poetry is almost always the mere setting of the thought.' What he means by this, he explains, is that Wordworth is almost always trying to enunciate a proposition, rather than express a 'feeling'. If Mill here is being inconsistent, it is only because he was being peculiarly honest. Both the propositions he makes about Wordsworth seem to him to be true. That Wordsworth had taught him to feel value once again, he could vouch for from his own experience; yet if the expression of deep emotion, undulterated by argument, be the purest poetry, then Wordsworth was not as 'natural' or as 'pure' a poet as Shelley. Yet so firmly was 'poetry' identified with 'feeling' in Mill's mind that he could not bring himself to question his premises. What was, for Wordsworth and Coleridge alike, a total affirmation of man's experience, became for the Victorians a 'mystical' assertion. The values asserted by poetry were not open to intellectual questioning. We find appearing in John Stuart Mill the doctrine of 'Two Truths': 'Poetry' he was forced to say, represented a different order of truth from 'science'; each could express truths that were not open to question by the other.

By and large, this was the view of poetry that prevailed in

[1] See, in particular, Wordsworth's description of his work as a 'gothic cathedral':
'Continuing this allusion, he may be permitted to add, that his minor pieces, which have been long before the public, being now properly arranged, will be found by the attentive reader to have such connexion with the main work as may give them claim to be likened to the little cells, oratories, and sepulchral recesses, ordinarily included in these edifices.' (Preface to *The Excursion*, 1814.)

the nineteenth century—with all the tenacity of a half-truth. To this climate of thought Wordsworth's own bold claim that poetry went hand-in-hand with science was simply incomprehensible:

If the labours of men of science should ever create any material revolution, direct or indirect, in our condition, and in the impressions which we habitually receive, the poet will sleep then no more than at present, but he will be ready to follow the steps of the man of science, not only in those general indirect effects, but he will be at his side carrying sensation into the midst of the objects of science itself. [1]

Yet Wordsworth, as almost always, is being quite specific here. To see what he meant by carrying 'sensation into the midst of the objects of science' we need look, for instance, no further than a short poem he wrote on 26 March 1802, the night before he started the *Immortality Ode*—and which, since he used the last lines as a motto for the *Ode*, was clearly linked with it in his own mind:

> My heart leaps up when I behold
> A rainbow in the sky;
> So was it when my life began;
> So is it now I am a man:
> So be it when I shall grow old
> Or let me die!
> The child is father to the man;
> And I could wish my days to be
> Bound each to each by natural piety.

The body is a changing, living, dying organism. If we are to find continuity in life we shall find it in the way we perceive the world. We exist as a network of relationships: how the child sees things will determine the kind of man he becomes. The child's joy at the rainbow modifies the entire way he grows up. As an example of perception Wordsworth chooses the rainbow, and in so doing enters a controversy that had been raging futilely and intermittently throughout the eighteenth century.

At the root of the problem lay Newton's *Opticks*. Though in fact this had not been published until 1704, Newton's simple experiments with a prism, and the discovery of the spectrum, had been known to Locke as early as 1690 when he re-drafted

[1] Preface to *Lyrical Ballads*, 1800.

his 'Essay Concerning Human Understanding'.[1] Newton did not, in fact, revolutionize the conception of the rainbow (most of his results were known or guessed already), but he came to stand for the eighteenth century as a profoundly ambiguous symbol of the whole scientific revolution of which he was only a part. It seemed at first sight that the epistemological implications of Newtonian science served to confirm Locke's model of the mind as a *tubula rasa*—totally passive in itself, and acted upon only by the external stimuli of the senses. That this was not the necessary conclusion from Newton's discoveries we shall see in a moment—yet, even assuming with most of the eighteenth century that this were so, the emotional responses to Newton within this thought-framework differed widely.

Broadly—and at the risk of over-simplifying—we can distinguish a polarization of reactions. For some, one apparent implication of Newton could be described in these terms:

The world that people had thought themselves living in—a world rich with colour and sound, redolent with fragrance, filled with gladness, love and beauty, speaking everywhere of purposive harmony and creative ideals—was crowded now into minute corners in the brains of scattered organic beings. The really important world outside was a world hard, cold, colourless, silent, and dead; a world of quanitity, a world of mathematically computable motions in mechanical regularity.[2]

We do not know if this was how Newton felt, but this was undoubtedly how it seemed to many near-contemporaries. Addison, writing on 'The Pleasures of the Imagination' in 1712 (*Spectator* 413) produces an image that was to become a classic expression of this aspect of man's new predicament:

Things would make but a poor appearance to the eye, if we saw them only in their proper figures and motions. And what reason can we assign for their exciting in us many of those ideas which are different from anything that exists in the objects themselves (for such are light and colours), were it not to add supernumerary ornaments to the universe, and make it more agreeable to the imagination? We are everywhere entertained with pleasing shows and apparitions, we discover imaginary glories in the heavens, and in the earth, and see some

[1] See Marjorie Nicolson, *Newton Demands the Muse* (Archon Books, 1963), p. 7.
[2] E. A. Burtt, *Metaphysical Foundations of Modern Science* (Routledge, 1932), pp. 236–7.

of this visionary beauty poured out over the whole creation; but what a rough and unsightly sketch of Nature should we be entertained with, did all her colouring disappear, and the several distinctions of light and shade vanish? In short, our souls are at present delightfully lost and bewildered in a pleasing delusion, and we walk about like the enchanted hero of a romance, who sees beautiful castles, woods, and meadows; and at the same time hears the warbling of birds, and the purling of streams; but upon the finishing of some secret spell, the fantastic scene breaks up, and the disconsolate knight finds himself on a barren heath, or in a solitary desert.

There is a sense in which *La Belle Dame Sans Merci* is not very far away from this idea of the imagination. Yet, at the same time, poets like Akenside and Thomson found in Newton a liberation. Science and beauty were revealed as coming together in a new and hitherto undreamed-of way. For those with understanding, a new beauty was created. The paradigm of this poetic rediscovery of colour was—inevitably—the rainbow. For Thomson, joy in the colours of the rainbow was inseparable from the intellectual joy of understanding how it was formed—in contrast to 'the swain' who tries to chase it:

> Meantime, refracted from yon eastern cloud,
> Bestriding earth, the grand ethereal bow
> Shoots up immense; and every hue unfolds,
> In fair proportion running from the red
> To where the violet fades into the sky.
> Here, awful Newton, the dissolving clouds
> Form, fronting on the sun, thy showery prism;
> And to the sage-instructed eye unfold
> The various twine of light, by thee disclosed
> From the white mingling maze. Not so the swain.
> He wondering views the bright enchantment bend
> Delightful, o'er the radiant fields, and runs
> To catch the falling glory; but amazed
> Beholds the amusive arch before him fly,
> Then vanish quite away.
>
> (*Seasons*, 'Spring', 203–17)

Similarly, Akenside in his *Pleasures of the Imagination* (1744) boldly took science into verse, finding in physics an even greater pleasure than in the mere appearance of the rainbow:

8

Nor ever yet
The melting rainbow's vernal-tinctur'd hues
To me have shone so pleasing, as when first
The hand of science pointed out the path
In which the sun-beams gleaming from the west
Fall on the watry cloud, whose darksome veil
Involves the orient; and that trickling show'r
Piercing thro' every crystalline convex
Of clust'ring dew-drops to their flight oppos'd,
Recoil at length where concave all behind
Th' internal surface of each glassy orb
Repells their forward passage into air;
That thence direct they seek the radiant goal
From which their course began; and, as they strike
In diff'rent lines the gazer's obvious eye,
Assume a diff'rent lustre, thro' the brede
Of colours changing from the splendid rose
To the pale violet's dejected hue.

(II, 103–20)

Akenside, like Thomson, could see in Newton's rainbow a marriage of visual and scientific sublimity; but neither this attitude, nor Addison's more ambiguous acceptance, went any further in solving the key problem of what actually happened in *perception* (as distinct from the mechanism of the eye). What was needed for this was not so much a scientific breakthrough— in the sense in which Newton's experiments with prisms had been—as a change in the way of thinking about the problem; and it is here that we return to Wordsworth.

Wordsworth's attitude towards Newton has for a long time seemed to puzzle commentators. Perhaps the most famous example of his apparently ambiguous attitude occurs in the accounts we have of the painter Benjamin Haydon's 'immortal dinner' which he gave on 28 December 1817. Haydon wrote in his diary afterwards:

The immortal dinner came off in my painting-room...Wordsworth was in fine cue, and we had a glorious set-to—on Homer, Shakespeare, Milton, and Virgil. Lamb got exceedingly merry and exquisitely witty, and his fun in the midst of Wordsworth's solemn intonations of oratory was like the sarcasm and wit of the fool in the intervals of Lear's passion...He then in a strain of humour beyond description,

9

abused me for putting Newton's head into my picture; 'a fellow', said
he, 'who believed nothing unless it was as clear as the three sides of a
triangle.' And then he and Keats agreed that he had destroyed all the
poetry of the rainbow by reducing it to its prismatic colours. It was
impossible to resist him, and we all drank 'Newton's health, and confusion to mathematics.'[1]

Wordsworth himself, however, had clearly had some hesitations
about the toast. Many years later, in October 1842, Haydon
wrote to Wordsworth reminding him of the dinner, and of his
reactions to Keats's proposal:

And don't you remember Keats proposing 'Confusion to the memory
of Newton', and upon your insisting on an explanation before you
drank it, his saying: 'Because he destroyed the poetry of the rainbow
by reducing it to a prism.'[2]

Was Wordsworth merely being pedantic, or did his demand for
an explanation stem from the fact that, unlike Keats, he admired
Newton? In Book III of *The Prelude* (1850) he paid tribute many
years later to his statue in Trinity College chapel:

> Newton with his prism and silent face,
> The marble index of a mind for ever,
> Voyaging through strange seas of thought alone.
>
> (60–3)

By 1817 Wordsworth had passed very much out of Coleridge's
orbit, and the creative side of their friendship was a thing of the
past. The Preface to his *Poems* of 1815 advanced a theory of the
Imagination that would have seemed conventional to many
eighteenth-century critics, and did scant justice to his own best
work—as Coleridge was quick to point out in his *Biographia
Literaria* published the same year as Haydon's dinner. But
during the great decade of their closest friendship, from the
publication of the *Lyrical Ballads* in 1798 to Coleridge's starting
The Friend in 1809, Wordsworth's theory of the Imagination
owed much to Newton as well as to Coleridge. Keats was
treading on dangerous ground in attacking Newton's rainbow.

---

[1] *The Autobiography of Benjamin Haydon*, ed. Elwin (Macdonald, 1950), pp.
316–17.
[2] *Correspondence and Table Talk of Benjamin Haydon*, Memoir by F. W. Haydon
(Chatto, 1876), Vol. II, pp. 54–5.

What distinguishes Wordsworth from the 'optical' poets of the eighteenth century, such as Akenside or Thomson, is not that he could propose a solution to the epistemological or psychological problems of vision, but that he could, and did, stand their problem on its head. For him, the job of the poet was not to record in verse the amazing technical developments of modern science, but to explore the new *relationships* that these suggested. His interest in *how* it happened led immediately— and in a way that was diffcrent in kind from the eighteenth-century 'Newtonians'—to *what* it implied about our experience. If we want to see what he meant by carrying 'sensation into the midst of the objects of science itself' we need to look at poems like *My Heart Leaps Up.* Here Wordsworth is by-passing both the problem of the 'reality' of the perception of the rainbow that had so disturbed Addison, *and* the technical questions of the refraction of light into the spectrum that had so delighted Akenside and Thomson. What interested him was the relationship between man and nature suggested by the act of perception—and as an example of this relationship the rainbow was peculiarly interesting. The Lockeian version of Newton had failed to stress that the rainbow is neither 'out there' in the sky, nor 'in' the mind of the beholder. It only exists when there are, on the one hand, certain specific conditions of atmosphere and light, and, on the other, the lens and retina of the observing eye. Nor is this all, for that favourite eighteenth-century toy, the camera-obscura, could imitate the eye so far as to produce the image of a rainbow; what it could not do was perceive. To 'behold', for Wordsworth, was a sentient act. Here, to behold a rainbow was an emotional experience. In other words, only when there is a co-operative interaction between the observer and the natural world does that 'thing' we call 'a rainbow' come into existence. That Newtonian optics implied this kind of two-sided relationship had been largely ignored by the eighteenth century, dominated as it was by Lockeian modes of thinking. As a result, we find that neither Coleridge nor Wordsworth was quick to acknowledge any specific debt to Newton. We find Coleridge, for instance, in a letter to Poole of 23 March 1801, sharply criticizing Newton as 'a materialist'—adding, significantly, that only Poole himself and Wordsworth know of his views. It is the word 'materialist' that gives us the clue to his attitude: Coleridge is here following Berkeley, and he seems to take no account of the extent to which Berkeley, too, makes use of Newton to attack Locke's materialism. How long Coleridge was a 'Berkeleian' is largely a matter of definition, and there is not much evidence to suggest that Wordsworth ever was; nevertheless, Berkeley's arguments, even while they carried him to a different conclusion, seem to have offered Coleridge and Wordsworth what they needed: a new and non-Lockeian way of assimilating Newton. What Berkeley had hoped to prove in his *Dialogues* was that all 'reality' is 'mental'; what in fact he had demonstrated was that we perceive not objects but *qualities*— such as colour, forms, and sounds—and that these are relative to the perceiver. The effect of Berkeley on Coleridge was to make him intensely conscious of light. *This Lime-Tree Bower My Prison* (1797) contains one of his finest overt references to Berkeley:

> So my friend
> Struck with deep joy may stand, as I have stood,
> Silent with swimming sense; yea gazing round
> On the wide landscape, gaze till all doth seem
> Less gross than bodily; and of such hues
> As veil the Almighty Spirit when he makes
> Spirits perceive his presence.
>
> (37–43)

'You will remember,' Coleridge wrote in a footnote on these lines to Southey, 'I am a Berkelyan.' For Berkeley, 'reality' lies not in the object itself, but in what you actually see. Within four lines of these Coleridge has turned back to nature with almost a painter's eye, looking not at forms, but at the sheer richness of light and shade:

> Pale beneath the blaze
> Hung the transparent foliage; and I watch'd
> Some broad and sunny leaf, and lov'd to see
> The shadow of the leaf and stem above
> Dappling its sunshine! And that walnut-tree
> Was richly ting'd, and a deep radiance lay
> Full on the ancient ivy, which usurps
> Those fronting elms, and now, with blackest mass

Makes their dark branches gleam a lighter hue
Through the late twilight...

Ignored by his own century, Berkeley was re-discovered by
the Romantics because, indirectly, he pointed to the way in
which such phenomena of light as the rainbow could be used as a
scientific model for the imagination as a perceptual relationship
between man and nature. It is this concept that underlies
Coleridge's idea of the Imagination as 'the prime instrument of
all human perception'. Though, for him, the final impetus
towards this revolutionary position was from Germany, it had
been prepared for in England by a century of speculation about
the connections between the mechanics of vision and perception
on the one hand, and a protracted discussion of the aesthetic
'pleasures of the imagination' on the other.

Again and again we shall find in the course of this book both
Coleridge and Wordsworth using the rainbow, in its various
forms, such as coronae, or 'glories', as a symbol of the Imagination. We shall be tracing a whole concept of 'Imagination',
and hence of creativity, in terms of this one image—and, as
we shall see, Coleridge's associated image of the Brocken-
Spectre. The subsequent ramifications of the rainbow and the
Imagination are no less interesting. One could, for instance,
base a claim for Gerard Manley Hopkins as Wordsworth's only
true successor as a 'nature poet' in the nineteenth century on a
poem that states the problem far more succinctly than my
critical analsysis:

> It was a hard thing to undo this knot.
> The rainbow shines, but only in the thought
> Of him that looks. Yet not in that alone,
> For who makes rainbows by invention?
> And many standing round a waterfall
> See one bow each, yet not the same to all,
> But each a hand's breadth further than the next.
> The sun on falling waters writes the text
> Which yet is in the eye or in the thought.
> It was a hard thing to undo this knot.

Hopkins wrote this when he was only twenty-one, in 1864.
Knowledge of the physics involved had not substantially
changed since Thomson wrote his *Seasons* nearly 140 years

before; what separates Hopkins from Thomson is a revolution in thinking that was primarily the work of Wordsworth and Coleridge. Yet Hopkins was one of the very few Victorians who was able to understand why Coleridge had linked Imagination with perception. For the rest, Arnold's idea of 'feeling' and Mill's associated doctrine of 'Two Truths' dominated nineteenth-century thinking about the Romantics, and without this framework what Wordsworth and Coleridge had to say about creativity and the human mind was incapable of being understood.

It is this that the rest of this book is about. What we are dealing with when we speak of their ideas of 'creativity' is a particular view of the growth of the mind. Corresponding to the change in the attitude to perception between Thomson and Hopkins is a second 'inner' revolution in attitude to the mind. As so often, we can trace this revolution in the change of meaning of a single word: 'symbol'. In his monumental psychological textbook, *Observations on Man, his Frame, his Duties, and his Expectations*, published in 1749, David Hartley, for example, defines the word 'symbol' indirectly like this:

When a Variety of Ideas are associated together, the visible Idea, being more glaring and distinct than the rest, performs the Office of a Symbol to all the rest, suggests them and connects them together. In this it somewhat resembles the first letter of a word.[1]

The real meaning of 'symbol' is made clear in the last sentence. It gathers up a number of distinct and related ideas in a particular rigid combination, and can be said to represent them like an initial letter. It is, basically, the sense of symbol meaning 'sign' as used by a mathematician. Its artistic equivalent is 'allegory': a direct translation of what one wishes to say into other terms. There is a simple one-for-one correspondence between the model and the thing that is being described—it is what I. T. Ramsey has called a 'picture model'.[2] Coleridge, however, distinguishes very carefully between an allegory in the above sense and *his* definition of the word 'symbol':

---

[1] Vol. I, p. 78.
[2] *Models and Mystery* (Oxford, 1964).

a symbol...is characterised by a translucence of the special in the individual, or of the general in the special, or of the universal in the general; above all by the translucence of the eternal in and through the temporal. It always partakes of the reality which it renders intelligible; and while it enunciates the whole, abides itself as a living part of that unity of which it is the representative.[1]

This, in Ramsey's terms, is a 'disclosure model'. Instead of there being demonstrated a simple one-for-one correspondence, what is shown is held to be only a glimpse of the whole, but this glimpse shares the nature of what is revealed. This is clearly a theory of art. *The Ancient Mariner*, for example, is not an allegory about man's spiritual progress in the way that Bunyan's *Pilgrim's Progress* is. What is shown to us, symbolically, is a particular experience of breakdown and regeneration—and to read the poem fully we must *share* the experience. What is important about a symbol, in this sense, is the way in which it alters us. Writing in *Theology of Culture* Paul Tillich declares:

Every symbol opens up a level of reality for which non-symbolic speaking is inadequate...But in order to do this, something else must be opened up— namely levels of the soul, levels of our interior reality. And they must correspond to the levels in exterior reality which are opened up by a symbol. So every symbol is two-edged. It opens up reality and it opens up the soul.

L. C. Knights takes up this idea of Tillich's in his essay 'Idea and Symbol: Some Hints from Coleridge'.[2] For Coleridge, a necessary part of the function of a symbol is personal *consent* to it. Romantic poetry works by means of symbols rather than analogies or allegories because it is concerned to change the way the reader experiences life. The growth of the mind was seen by Coleridge and Wordsworth as, among other things, a growth in *quality* of perception.

There is a good example of this in the oft-quoted (and correspondingly overlooked) Wordsworthian symbol of a flower. It has been pointed out how a Romantic poem was felt to reveal in its organization the way in which the poet's own mind has

[1] *The Statesman's Manual*, 'Works', ed. Shedd, Vol. I (New York, 1853), p. 437.
[2] In *Further Explorations* (Chatto, 1965).

developed.[1] Whether this applies to all 'Romantic' poems we may have leave to doubt, but it is certainly true of both *The Ancient Mariner* and the *Immortality Ode*. In this sense we can see such poems as an aesthetic summing-up, or climax, of the poet's development up to that point. But a recurring phenomenon we shall find in the poetry of both Wordsworth and Coleridge is the curious way that a poem, in stating a problem, seems to provide a solution *through* the very act of articulation. Saying what is wrong makes it better. For Wordsworth, in the *Immortality Ode*,

> A timely utterance gave that thought relief...

and similarly the Ancient Mariner finds that

> Forthwith this frame of mine was wrenched
> With a woeful agony,
> Which forced me to begin my tale;
> And then it left me free.

There is a parallel here with a flower. In one sense it is the aesthetic climax and completion of the plant's development, in another it is the source of new seeds and further growth. Nor do I think Wordsworth missed this parallel. There are places in his poetry where it seems clear that flowers are to him symbols of the regenerative effect of his own poems.

> For oft when on my couch I lie
> In vacant or in pensive mood,
> They flash upon the inward eye
> Which is the bliss of solitude;
> And then my heart with pleasure fills
> And dances with the daffodils.

What exactly is it that flashes upon Wordsworth's 'inward eye' when he is like this? The answer may not be as obvious as it appears. *The Daffodils* is of peculiar interest to us as an example of poetic creation, since we can put alongside it his sister Dorothy's account of the incident.

When we were in the woods beyond Gowbarrow Park we saw a few daffodils close to the water-side. We fancied that the lake had floated the seeds ashore, and that the little colony had so sprung up. But as we

[1] Abrams, *Mirror and Lamp*, Ch. IX.

went along there were more and yet more; and at last, under the boughs of the trees, we saw that there was a long belt of them along the shore, about the breadth of a country turnpike road. I never saw daffodils so beautiful. They grew among the mossy stones about and about them; some rested their heads upon these stones as on a pillow for weariness; and the rest tossed and reeled and danced, and seemed as if they verily laughed with the wind, that blew upon them over the lake; they looked so gay, ever glancing, ever changing. This wind blew directly over the lake to them. There was here and there a little knot, and a few stragglers a few yards higher up; but they were so few as not to disturb the simplicity, unity, and life of that one busy highway.[1]

By comparing this with the poem we can see how Wordsworth has modified and transposed the initial experience. This is not a question of what he actually 'saw'. We are not discussing here the action of Coleridge's 'Primary Imagination', but the 'Secondary Imagination'—the creative activity of the artist, which 'dissolves, diffuses, and dissipates, in order to re-create'. Wordsworth, we known, attached considerable importance to the precise words of the poem. In a letter to Sir George Beaumont early in 1808 he wrote:

Thanks for dear Lady B.'s transcript from your Friend's letter; it is written with candour, but I must say a word or two not in praise of it. 'Instances of what I mean,' says your friend, 'are to be found in a poem on a Daisy' (by the bye, it is on *the* Daisy, a mighty difference!) 'and on Daffodils *reflected in the Water*!' Is this accurately transcribed by Lady Beaumont? If it be, what shall we think of criticism or judgement founded upon, and exemplified by, a Poem so inattentively perused? My language is precise; and, therefore, it would be false modesty to charge myself with blame.

> Beneath the trees,
> Ten thousand dancing in the *breeze*.
> *The waves beside* them danced, but they
> Outdid the *sparkling waves* in glee.

Can expression be more distinct? And let me ask your Friend how it is possible for flowers to be *reflected* in water where there are *waves*? They may indeed in *still* water; but the very object of my poem is the trouble or agitation, both of the flowers and the Water.[2]

[1] *Dorothy Wordsworth's Journals*, ed. De Selincourt (Macmillan, 1941), Vol. I, p. 131 (15 April 1802).
Letters of William and Dorothy Wordsworth, ed. De Selincourt, Vol. I (Oxford, 1937), p. 170.

The sight of the daffodils was for Wordsworth a new revelation of harmony and order where he had previously supposed there to be mere haphazard confusion.[1] 'Trouble and agitation' are converted by them into a dance of delight. For Wordsworth, recollection has the power of converting aimless drifting into moments of insight and joy as he remembers his own change of mood under this revelation. The point is clearer if we remember that the poem as it was originally published in 1807 contained only three verses. The description of the daffodils went like this:

> I wandered lonely as a cloud
> That floats on high o'er vales and hills,
> When all at once I saw a crowd,
> A host of golden daffodils,
> Along the lake, beneath the trees,
> Ten thousand dancing in the breeze.
>
> The waves beside them danced, but they
> Outdid the sparkling waves in glee:
> A poet could not but be gay
> In such a jocund company!
> I gazed—and gazed—but little thought
> What wealth the show to me had brought.

We can say with some certainty, therefore, that here what Wordsworth is recalling in the final stanza is not the incident as it happened with Dorothy (when he was *not* 'lonely as a cloud') but how, in his poem, he found joy and harmony. The 'daffodils' he remembers are a symbol of the whole experience. In a letter to Coleridge in May 1809 Wordsworth explained that *The Daffodils* should be included among '...poems relating to natural objects and their influence on the mind either as growing or in an advanced state...by the life found in them, or their life given.'[2]

What follows in the rest of this book is an attempt to see in some detail how this idea of symbolism and a physical theory of perception are related to an idea of creativity which is, at the

---

[1] G. H. Durrant, 'Imagination and Life—Wordsworth's "The Daffodils"', *Theoria* (Journal of Studies of Arts Faculty, Natal University), No. 19, October 1962.
[2] *Letters*, Vol. I, p. 308.

same time, a model of growth. It is 'interdisciplinary' in the sense that it involves both literary criticism and a study in the history of ideas. We have described as a 'romanticism' this central concern which differentiates Wordsworth and Coleridge so sharply from other contemporary 'Romantic' poets. We shall see how almost every one of their distinctive traits can be traced back in one form or another to this preoccupation. At its simplest, it is very noticeable, for instance, that they stand almost alone among artists in their lack of any kind of élitism. As we have seen, in their attempts to understand themselves they were extremely unwilling to admit that a creative artist is different *in kind* from other men. In his Preface to the *Lyrical Ballads* of 1800, Wordsworth is writing on this point for Coleridge as well:

What is a poet?...He is a man speaking to men: a man, it is true, endued with more lively sensibility, more enthusiasm and tenderness, who has a greater knowledge of human nature, and a more comprehensive soul, than are supposed to be common among mankind; a man pleased with his own passions and volitions, and who rejoices more than other men in the spirit of life that is in him; delighting to contemplate similar volitions and passions as manifested in the goings-on of the universe, and habitually impelled to create them where he does not find them.

The poet shares with mankind—he is not cut off from it. It was partly the need to maintain this affirmation that led Coleridge to develop his theory of Imagination as essentially the same faculty by which *all* perception took place. It was no accident that he and Wordsworth were preoccupied first of all with optics, then theories of perception, and finally with psychology. Both poets seem to have held to the belief that in describing their own creative experiences, they were describing phenomena which, though 'poetic' in the sense that they were concerned with the perception of values, could be accounted for almost entirely in scientific or psychological terms. Their philosophy and psychology was grounded in the attempt to put into words and analyse the conditions that inhibited or fostered their own growth. As we shall see, Coleridge's movement from Hartley to Kant was motivated by this consistent psychological interest—always eclectic rather than systematic in the willingness to retain any elements of Hartley's structure that seemed to be useful. Nevertheless, we shall see too how neither simple vegetable analogies of growth, nor, finally, Kantian metaphysics fully answered to the complexity of the problem that he felt intuitively, but had such difficulty in articulating. Today, we can see how his creative experience involved him in ideas of 'value' and 'purpose' which are neither scientific nor strictly philosophical. But the reason is not necessarily that he gave too narrow or confused an account of himself in the terms of his own day. The process of compartmentalization which we have already commented upon has been at work in many of the later assessments of Coleridge, separating the 'great poet' from the 'bad philosopher'; it is we who have tended to over-simplify a vision that was both comprehensive and subtle.

We shall, therefore, go on to look at Coleridge's later view of perception as an interaction or relationship between 'projection' of mental or visual 'schemata', and an answering 'resonance' in nature. Such a model is implied from what we have already seen of Newton's optics and the rainbow. That it should also be strikingly similar to some modern perceptual theories should not surprise us: both Coleridge and this area of modern psychological theory owe, by different routes, a great deal of Kant as well as to Newton. It would be more surprising if there were not strong parallels. What was unique to Coleridge and Wordsworth, however, was the way in which they seemed to feel perception as a unifying and creative act in itself, involving a process of value-judgement and discrimination. Similarly, just as ambiguities of vision were interpreted and resolved by visual schemata, so poetry (involving ambiguities of human experience) relied upon previous verbal schemata. Even memory could be, and was, seen as subject to analogous laws. We shall try to see how mental growth was thus conceived as the product of a continual modification of perception: a dialectic in which, as in, for example, Coleridge's ode, *Dejection*, the articulation of dereliction and failure could provide the stimulus for new growth.

As I shall go on to argue, it seem to me that the crises and eventual failures of Wordsworth's and Coleridge's creativity must be seen against this background. Their interaction, development, and final divergence after the famous quarrel of 1810 can be seen as alternative responses to a common problem. Only in this way, I believe, is it possible to put Coleridge's late philosophy and poetry into a proper perspective.

There is a sense in which the argument of this book moves by a kind of 'insensible progression'. If this is irritating to the reader, I can only apologize in advance. The fact that the argument is cumulative rather than rigidly sequential is, as I hope will be apparent, imposed by the demands of the material itself. Coleridge was never capable of thinking along one line of reasoning without a corresponding modification taking place in the rest of his ideas. It is this, as much as any intrinsic esotericism in his thinking, that makes his philosophy so complex and difficult to follow. Yet to try and pursue one strand in rigorous isolation, as some commentators have attempted to do, runs the risk of falsifying his position by a corresponding over-simplification. For better or worse I have chosen the opposite vice and elected to follow Coleridge and Wordsworth together on a broad front. Only by doing this, it seems to me, can we do justice to their vision of man: a being who *creates*.

1

'An Image with a Glory round its Head'

Coleridge's poem *Constancy to an Ideal Object* ends like this:

> And art thou nothing? Such thou art, as when
> The woodman winding westward up the glen
> At wintry dawn, where o'er the sheep-track's maze
> The viewless snow-mist weaves a glist'ning haze,
> Sees full before him, gliding without tread,
> An image with a glory round its head;
> The enamoured rustic worships its fair hues,
> Nor knows he makes the shadow, he pursues![1]

The symbol is that of a Brocken-spectre. The shadow of a man is cast by the almost level rays of the rising or setting sun on to a bank of mist so that he sees what appears to be a giant figure whose head is surrounded by coloured rings of light, or coronae, called 'glories'. Coleridge himself had seen this phenomenon.[2] In May 1799 he had visited the Brocken in the Hartz mountains of Germany, from where the spectre takes its name, and he recorded two eye-witness accounts of it in this notebooks. The first, by a man called Jordan, tells how he caught a number of fleeting glimpses of the spectre during a walk on the Brocken:

In this mist, when the sun had risen, I could see my shadow, a gigantic size, for a few seconds as I moved, but then I was swiftly enveloped in mist, and the apparition was gone.[3]

Of the second account Coleridge noted:

---

[1] First published in 1828. E. H. Coleridge notes that the date 'now assigned (?1826) is purely conjectural'. J. D. Campbell believed that it was 'written at Malta'. See *Poems*, ed. E. H. Coleridge (Oxford, 1912), p. 455.
[2] *Ibid*. p. 456, n. 2.
[3] *Notebooks*, ed. Coburn, Vol. I (Routledge, 1957), 430.

A Mr Haue, on the 23rd. of May 1797, likewise observe[d] this Spirit of the Mountain—and wrote in the Stammbuch the following observation:

'Just after quarter past four I walked towards the inn...and turned round to see whether the air would clear to the Southwest to-day and permit me an undisturbed view. And behold! I saw towards the Achtermannshöhe, at a great distance, a human form of gigantic size, and as a gust of wind threatened to blow my hat off and I hastily seized it, making a movement of my arm towards my head, I saw the colossal figure make a movement too...I called the innkeeper...And it was not long before two such colossal figures took shape on the aforesaid mountain; we bowed to each other; they did likewise...'[1]

We can, I think, even in these excerpts feel something of the almost eerie ambiguity of the Brocken-spectre which so appealed to Coleridge. It made such a lasting impression on him that he reverted to it as an image of a certain kind of ambiguity at intervals throughout the rest of his life. In particular, we find him associating it with creativity. It is not difficult to see why. In or out of the mist the confrontation with the spectre is sudden, unexpected; it is both 'personal', and yet like that other German phenomenon, the *Doppelgänger*, or psychological 'double', the spectre stands projected as alien and in opposition to its creator. In Coleridge's poem this ambiguous confrontation is made even more abrupt. One minute he is striving after an apparently objective ideal; in the next, it has become his own shadow on the mist. There is a conscious echo here of Plato's cave-myth. But Coleridge, while playing on the echo, has transformed it into something much more ironic and baffling. Instead of the light throwing shadows on to the cave wall, here it is the rustic's own shadow which is projected on to the blank screen of mountain mist to create the spectre—now no shadow, but an aureoled giant.

What is Coleridge saying here about his 'ideal object'? Is he, as one critic has claimed, at last recognizing in despair that his poetic ideal is nothing but the 'self-generating illusion of the rustic'?[2] Such an interpretation appears at least to have a *prima facie* case. It assumes as its premise that this self-projection

[1] *Ibid.*
[2] James D. Boulger, *Coleridge as Religious Thinker* (Yale, 1961), p. 206.

symbolizes failure to break out of a personal and subjective world. Another critic, I. A. Richards, has argued that Wordsworth and Coleridge shared two attitudes to nature which he calls the 'Realist' and the 'Projective'.[1] In the 'Realist' attitude, he explains, the poet's mind sees through the outward appearances of things to 'reality' (in a Platonic sense) and reads nature as a symbol of this hidden reality. In the 'Projective', on the other hand, the poet's mind creates or invents (it is significant that the two words can be used synonymously) a nature into which he can read his own feelings—in a kind of all-embracing pathetic fallacy. So here, for example, the poet seeing his own shadow, and mistaking it for something objective, is turning his back on the 'reality' of the rising sun and chasing nothing but the misty shadows of his own unconscious creation. Such an account clearly supports the view we have quoted. Yet *is* this the whole story? The poem, we remember, is about creativity. It opens with just this question of what permanent value the artist's insight can have amidst change and decay:

> Since all that beat about in Nature's range,
> Or veer or vanish; why should'st thou remain
> The only constant in a world of change,
> O yearning Thought! that liv'st but in the brain?

The tone is pessimistic—even despairing. He is haunted by an 'illusion', a figment of his mind, yet without that illusion his life is waste and void. The most precious values of his life,

> The peacefull'st cot, the moon shall shine upon,
> Lull'd by the thrush and wakened by the lark,
> Without thee were but a becalmèd bark,
> Whose Helmsman on an ocean waste and wide
> Sits mute and pale his mouldering helm beside.

The parallel with *The Ancient Mariner* is deliberate. The Mariner's release comes through blessing 'unawares' the slimy and horrible water-snakes that until then had filled him with loathing and disgust. He had to learn to love and see beauty in what frightened and nauseated him. It was this very ambivalence in his own experience that he had to accept before he could be

[1] *Coleridge on Imagination* (Kegan Paul, 1934). Ch. II, and Ch. VI, pp. 143–6.

restored, cleansed, to the world of men. Similarly in this poem there is an abrupt change of tone as Coleridge suddenly turns to accept the illusion that until then had so frightened him. The dull resignation in the movement of the verse disappears with the question 'And art thou nothing?' and there follows a new sense of exultation and action. The image has a 'glory' round its head; the rustic is 'enamoured' and prepared to act: he 'pursues'. The effect of this is to suggest a new depth to the ambiguity we had noticed in the symbol. Is this the self-destruction of Narcissus, in love with his own reflection, or is it only by this very 'projection' that the vicious circle is broken and man's vision realized? Is this a paradox that underlies *all* artistic creativity?

In *Aids to Reflection* we find Coleridge applying this ambiguity of the Brocken-spectre to the individual's encounter with genius: 'The beholder either recognises it as a projected form of his own Being, that moves before him with a Glory round its head, or recoils from it as from a Spectre.'[1] Here it is the ambiguity which is the point of the image. Does deep call to deep so that the genius of, say, Shakespeare strikes us as if it were a projection of our own selves writ large, and endowed with a universal significance; or does it seem a spectre: gigantic, alien, and too self-revealing to leave us comfortable? The point is that the phenomenon allows both these possibilities. The encounter with Shakespeare involves coming to terms with ourselves. The basis of such an image of genius is traditional and obvious, what is new and uniquely 'modern' is the ironic complexity of Coleridge's symbol. Distinctions between 'realist' and 'projective' attitudes are hardly the relevant ones. Clearly the whole idea of self-projection is itself more ambiguous than Richards or the critic we quoted earlier would allow. Coleridge was at pains to insist that the mind was no 'lazy onlooker' at the world. Both the two attitudes suggested by I. A. Richards assume a kind of dualism, a fundamental gap between man and nature. They suppose either a 'mystical' approach (which, in this context, is usually taken to mean 'asserting as "poetry" what we all know to be untrue in fact'), or a straightforward delusion on the part of the poet. But neither Wordsworth nor

---

[1] *Aids to Reflection* (Grant, 1905), p. 200.

Coleridge at his most Platonic were mystics—nor were they prone deliberately to indulge in double-think or self-deception. Coleridge was quite explicit in his dislike of mysticism. In *Aids to Reflection* he wrote:

When a man refers to *inward feelings* and *experiences*, of which mankind at large are not conscious, as evidences of the truth of any opinion —such a Man I call A MYSTIC: and the grounding of any theory or belief on accidents and anomalies of individual sensations or fancies, and the use of peculiar terms invented or perverted from their ordinary signification, for the purposes of expressing these idiosyncracies, and pretended facts of interior consciousness, I name MYSTICISM...[1]

Let us look again at the rustic. Without him there would be no shadow. His shadow is not a matter of 'interior consciousness', but a particular configuration of light, there for anyone else in the right position to see—as in the second example quoted by Coleridge in his notebook. Yet it is one of the peculiarities of Brocken-spectres that, while it is possible to see the shadows cast by others, it is impossible to see a 'glory' round any but one's own shadow. Coleridge's 'ideal object' is, therefore, both 'objective' and, at the same time, uniquely personal. In *Tintern Abbey* Wordsworth describes sense-perception as 'both what they half create/And what perceive'; here, the rustic is perceiving what he half-creates. Like the rainbow, perception of the Brocken-spectre implies a relationship with nature. In other words, Coleridge seems to have chosen as his symbol a kind of experience where perception is in a peculiarly literal sense an act of creation. Now it is possible to reach this position from philosophical grounds, as Coleridge, following Kant, does elsewhere. Here, however, his approach is not philosophical but existential. The verbal ambiguity of the word 'glory' suggests the *value*, as well as the physical phenomenon of the corona. Perception depends on a co-operative interplay of the perceiver and the perceived—and is indivisible from the appropriate value-judgement.

I want to suggest that this symbol of the Brocken-spectre is central to Coleridge's thought about his own creativity. But to see this, we must first of all note that, even if we accept the rough analysis given above, it is still possible to interpret this

---

[1] *Ibid.* p. 349.

symbol in a variety of ways. The idea of the snow-mist as a 'screen', for instance, permits us to think of another meaning of the word: as something that hides or conceals. This brings us back to the Kantian philosophy mentioned above. According to Kant we can know nothing of objects in themselves, which, though they may exist, are always hidden from us.[1] All we can know through sense-experience are 'appearances', and it is the job of the 'imagination' to construct from those appearances the seemingly objective external world in which we all live. Coleridge was not a Kantian in any sense of the word a German philosopher would necessarily recognize, nor is his 'Imagination' Kant's, but he found in Kant's concept of the Imagination a solution to his own problem of how he might show an 'objective' value in human experience. It was through Kant that he came to think of perception as a creative act of the mind, which finds in external appearances (by just such an interplay as we have noted in the case of the rainbow) an answering resonance to the pattern already formed in his own mind. Like I. A. Richards's 'projection' theory with which we began this discussion, it is possible to see this new image of creativity in purely Kantian terms. But there is a danger in seeing such a major change in our sensibility too narrowly in terms of the history of ideas. Congruence of ideas does not, in itself, imply continuity of ideas. It is, for instance, equally easy to find English writers throughout the eighteenth century who apparently anticipate the ideas of Wordsworth and Coleridge. Joseph Warton, Abraham Tucker, and Alexander Gerard have all been put forward as sources of their theory of the 'Imagination'.[2] Undoubtedly greater in influence than any of these so-called forerunners of 'romanticism' is David Hartley's *Obervations of Man*—which cannot in any sense be considered 'romantic'.

[1] For this, and subsequent discussions of Kant, I am following Kemp Smith's abridged translation of the *Critique of Pure Reason* (Macmillan, 1934), his *Commentary* (Macmillan, 1923) and A. C. Ewing's *Short Commentary* (Methuen, 1938). In addition, I draw on the accounts and discussions of Kant in D. G. James's *Secpticism and Poetry* (Allen and Unwin, 1937), G. Mackenzie's *Organic Unity in Coleridge* (University of California Publications in English, Vol. vii), and Shawcross's Introduction to *Biographia Literaria*.

[2] See Abrams, *Mirror and Lamp*; Lovejoy's 'On the Discrimination of Romanticisms', *Essays in History of Ideas*; and Ch. 2 and 3 below.

Moreover, we have already seen something of the complications of their debt to Newton and Berkeley. We need to remind ourselves how much, in Lovejoy's words, 'the history of ideas is the history of confusion of ideas'. It is no more satisfactory to explain Coleridge's later development in terms of his reaction to Hartley, than it is to see Wordsworth's 1805 *Prelude* or the 'Letter to Mathetes' in *The Friend* as evidence of thoroughgoing Hartleianism—as one major critic has done.[1] Both poets tend to use the language they inherited from eighteenth-century thinkers with entirely new shades of meaning, and, as we shall see in some detail, Coleridge's theory of the Imagination remains in some ways curiously Hartleian. If we are to explain what happened in their idea of creativity we must step outside the realm of 'ideas' as such.

Lovejoy has remarked how much more revealing the bad or second-rate poetry of any period is than the great, since it displays the common ideas of its age in the least modified form. In enjoying what is a typically maverick paradox we tend to lose sight of its underlying assumption: that we can directly correlate the 'greatness' of poetry and the originality of its ideas. Once we have stated it as baldly as this it is obviously absurd, but the implications of the unspoken idea linger over the reputations of both poets. There are very few new ideas in the work of either Coleridge or Wordsworth. Nor is their thought necessarily even consistent. René Wellek, in *Immanuel Kant in England*, accuses Coleridge of lacking both system and originality in his thought.[2] In his righteous philosophic indignation he has, however, ignored a quality in Coleridge's thought that was to give him in the long run considerably greater influence than either virtue might have guaranteed him. The philosophers and critics he pillaged with such apparently wanton eclecticism, Schelling, the Schlegels, Fichte, etc., are to us now landmarks in the history of thought in the way that Coleridge is not; equally Coleridge is relevant to us today in a way that they are not. There is a tendency for this, perhaps rather obvious, fact to be hidden by the curious way in which Coleridge is often ostensibly

[1] A. Beatty, *William Wordsworth* (University of Wisconsin Studies, Madison, 1922).
[2] Princeton, 1931, Ch. III, pp. 65–136.

treated. Raymond Williams, for example, in *The Long Revolution*, as the excuse for a most interesting and sympathetic study of Coleridge, claims for him a central place in the transformation of 'imitative' into 'creative' theories of art.[1] Now this is a very dubious and insular argument. Coleridge was influential, certainly, in spreading some of these ideas in England, but if the aesthetic revolution Williams describes were fundamental to his interest in Coleridge, then he would do better to look to the Germans from whom Coleridge borrowed the ideas. The fact that he does not is not I think insularity. He is, rather, influenced by a total 'standpoint' or 'position' of Coleridge's that is not primarily philosophical. The very fact that Williams has some difficulty in saying what he finds so important in Coleridge should warn us of the problems involved. As we shall see, Coleridge's concept of 'Imagination' cannot be satisfactorily explained in terms of its origins in German philosophy—still less as a confusion of those ideas; it is a response to a particular need to affirm the value in human experience which was threatened by the prevailing climate of mechanistic thought in England. It is fatally easy to build up a picture of Coleridge through his sources, and lose sight of the creative mind at the centre. The symbol of the Brocken-spectre is a reminder that the problem of poetic creation—and in particular, of his own creativity—was for Coleridge an *existential* one. The sudden transformation from the desperately clung-to 'ideal object' to the acceptance of the ideal as a self-created spectre has all the characteristics of what a modern theologian (in a different context) has described as a 'disclosure in depth'.[2] The facts are not altered, yet the situation is completely changed. The rustic is not the passive spectator, he pursues, and *by his own act of pursuit* gives life to his ideal. . .

This was an affirmation that was to prove of immense importance to the nineteenth century. It has been argued that we must think of Romanticism as characterized by common problems rather than by common beliefs.[3] Yet the problem raised by Coleridge's poem of the Brocken-spectre takes us at once beyond

[1] Pt i, Ch. i.
[2] I. T. Ramsey, *Religious Language* (S.C.M., 1957).
[3] John B. Beer, *Coleridge the Visionary* (Chatto, 1959), p. 14.

the normal confines of 'Romanticism' to something that was common to the age, rather than to any particular movement. The case of John Stuart Mill is a classic one, but it is worth looking at in some detail since it focuses so clearly this problem of 'value'.

In Chapter Five of his *Autobiography* John Stuart Mill describes how, having been brought up by his father under one of the most rigorous and logical systems of education ever devised, at the age of twenty he lost all sense of purpose. Looking back in 1873 for words to describe his experience he turns immediately to Coleridge in *Dejection* (although, as he tells us, he had not at that time read it). He then goes on to write of his mental condition in terms remiscent of *The Ancient Mariner*:

I was thus, as I said to myself, left stranded at the commencement of my voyage, with a well-equipped ship and a rudder, but no sail; without any real desire for the ends which I had been so carefully fitted out to work for: no delight in virtue, or the general good, but also just as little in anything else.

The sense of value that Mill had lost was not *moral* value. He never lost the strong utilitarian ethical basis to his life. What he had lost was that something, over and above the normally definable facts of a situation, that gives meaning to it. A. N. Whitehead describes it like this:

Remembering the poetic rendering of our concrete experience, we see at once that the element of value, of being valuable, of having value, of being an end it itself, of being something for its own sake, must not be omitted in any account of an event as the most concrete actual something. 'Value' is the word I use for the intrinsic reality of an event.[1]

Whitehead, we notice, assumes that poetry is the natural vehicle by which that something he calls 'value' is incorporated into the description of an event. That 'something' Mill was to find satisfactorily expressed for the first time in the autumn of 1828 in reading the poetry of Wordsworth.

The *Autobiography* is not a record of the events of Mill's life, but, as he says, the history of his intellectual and moral develop-

[1] A. N. Whitehead, *Science and the Modern World* (Mentor Books, 1948), p. 89.

ment—in a sense not far removed from that in which *The Prelude* is Wordsworth's. Behind each is a theory of growth which came, in the first instance, from Hartley. Both, moreover, came to question, modify or reject Hartley in similar circumstances. Hartley's mechanical progression was, as we shall see in detail in the next chapter, an attempt by analogy from the physical sciences to account for the observed phenomenon of mental growth. Its corollary, that the meaning of the growth, so produced, was only to be found in the end-product, had not troubled either James Mill, John's father, or Hartley himself. Both were too unquestioningly certain of their ends. For the sensitive and more widely-ranging mind of John Stuart Mill, however, the tail appeared to wag the dog. Growth had become no more than the unresisting product of its own machinery. Here, in this crisis in his mental history, and at the turning-point of his *Autobiography*, he was confronted with a paradox that sooner or later besets any account of mental development, including Wordsworth's. Mill writes:

In this frame of mind it occurred to me to put the question directly to myself: 'Suppose that all your objects in life were realized; that all the changes in institutions and opinions which you are looking forward to, could be completely effected at this very instant: would this be a great joy and happiness to you?' And an irrepressible self-consciousness distinctly answered, 'No!' At this my heart sank within me: the whole foundation on which my life was constructed fell down. All my happiness was to have been found in the continual pursuit of this end. The end had ceased to charm, and how could there ever again be any interest in the means? I seemed to have nothing left to live for.

Purpose without value is meaningless. Unless mental growth can be felt to contain within itself at every stage a value that exists for its own sake, apart from the capacity for further growth, then ultimately the growth itself has no meaning. Just as Coleridge's account of dereliction in *Dejection* reflected Mill's own experience, so the affirmation of value—in particular in our response to nature—born of a similar crisis in Wordsworth himself, made an immediate appeal to Mill's altered sensibility.

Wordsworth describes his own crisis in Books x and xi of *The Prelude* (1805 version). In Book x, he tells how, in an impossible quest for proof of the values he had hitherto held, he lost all sense of them:

> Thus I fared,
> Dragging all passions, notions, shapes of faith,
> Like culprits to the bar, suspiciously
> Calling the mind to establish in plain day
> Her titles and her honours, now believing,
> Now disbelieving, endlessly perplex'd
> With impulse, motive, light and wrong, the ground
> Of moral obligation, what the rule
> And what the sanction, till, demanding *proof*,
> And seeking it in everything, I lost
> All feeling of conviction...

(889–99)

It was only through the influence of Coleridge and his sister, Dorothy, that he was restored by 'intercourse with Nature' to a sense of purpose and meaning in his life.[1] The memory of this crisis underlay Wordsworth's joy in the rainbow.

It was this experience of meaninglessness, not the answer to it, that Mill shared with Wordsworth. Mill writes that he could gain from Wordsworth 'perennial sources of happiness', but adds that there have 'certainly been, even in our own age, greater poets than Wordsworth.' He draws a sharp distinction between the 'grand imagery' and the 'bad philosophy' of the *Immortality Ode* in his *Autobiography*. *The Prelude* was not to be published for another twenty-two years after Mill first read Wordsworth, and he gives no sign that it ever made a great impression on him. But it is precisely because Mill does remain philosophically in opposition to Wordsworth that his testimony is so valuable to us. What he and Wordsworth held in common were neither specific attitudes (even, as we shall see, to nature), nor merely the need to feel a value in our existence independent of our purpose. It was rather a burning compulsion to try and see the development of their own minds in terms wide enough to include their intuitions of value—and so produce a total synthesis that would itself foster new growth. Mill tells us in the *Autobiography* that he wants to note the 'successive phases' of a mind

---

1 For a fuller account of this, see D. G. James, 'Wordsworth and Tennyson', *Proceedings of the British Academy*, Vol. xxxvi (1950).

that was 'always pressing forward'. In the essay on Coleridge what appeals most to Mill is his constant attempt to see things, however complex, as 'wholes'. Both Mill, in his *Autobiography*, and Wordsworth, in *The Prelude*, were trying to show in their own development the relationship they felt, but could not define in other terms, between value and growth. It was this, above all, that Mill found characteristic of Wordsworth. In his poems, Mill tells us,

> I seemed to draw from a source of inward joy, of sympathetic and imaginative pleasure, which could be shared in by all human beings; which had no connexion with struggle or imperfection, but would be made richer by every improvement in the physical and social condition of mankind.

Mill had read Byron before Wordsworth and found him no help. For Mill, like Wordsworth and Coleridge, growth depended upon a feeling of unity with the material world, and a sense of joy in it. As we have suggested, this 'source of inward joy, of sympathetic and imaginative pleasure, which could be shared by all human beings' did not depend upon intellectual agreement. For Mill, this feeling of unity was never more than an emotion; for Wordsworth and Coleridge, as in the case of the rainbow, it was a physical fact. Though Wordsworth like Mill had hoped, to begin with, that Hartley's 'mechanical' psychology would serve to explain his own development, when Coleridge wrote, that Wordsworth was capable of producing 'the FIRST GENUINE PHILOSOPHIC POEM'[1] he was not stressing that there were philosophic ideas in Wordsworth's poetry (Mill missed the point here with a half-truth), or even that one might be able to *extract* a coherent personal philosophy from it at all. He was saying that the accepted Lockeian empirico-mechanical philosophy had failed to offer a comprehensive and satisfying way of looking at human experience, and that the poetry of Wordsworth filled this gap. The sense of 'value' that Mill found in Wordsworth's poetry was not in any sense a rival 'philosophy' to that of Locke and Hartley; it was simply the way he responded to certain poems. Hartley had treated man as a 'thing', whose religious and intellectual growth could be

---

[1] *Biographia Literaria*, ed. Shawcross (Oxford, 1907), Vol. II, p. 129.

measured on the same mechanistic plane as his nervous system; Wordsworth, like Coleridge, saw that the mechanics of human development were meaningless unless persons were treated *as* persons. There is all the difference in the world between looking at somebody as a mechanism, and meeting them as a person. The difference has been described like this:

If you are sitting opposite me, I can see you as another person like myself; without *you* changing or doing anything differently, I can now see you as a complex physical-chemical system, perhaps with its own idiosyncrasies but chemical none the less for that; seen in this way, you are no longer a person but an organism. Expressed in the language of existential phenomenology, the other, as seen as a person or as seen as an organism, is the object of different intentional acts. There is no dualism in the sense of the co-existence of two different essences or substances there in the object, psyche and soma; there are two different experiental Gestalts: person and organism.[1]

The writer, we notice, for the purpose of this distinction, treats an organism as a mechanism—thus anticipating a problem Coleridge was later to face. Value can only be encountered at the personal level. When Coleridge found the mechanism of Hartley inadequate to describe his own insights into the growth of the mind, he repudiated it not with objections to it as a particular system to be replaced by a better, but as the *type* of all 'closed' systems that treated man as an object. His objection was to all closed systems *as such* as a means of qualitatively accounting for human life. It was not that Hartley had failed in his dream of being the 'Newton of the mind'; we did not, as Mill found, want a Newton of the mind at all.

Coleridge, even while he was still an avowed Hartleian had described a similar crisis to that of J. S. Mill:

> Beyond the shadow of the ship,
> I watched the water-snakes:
> They moved in tracks of shining white,
> And when they reared, the elfish light
> Fell off in hoary flakes.
>
> Within the shadow of the ship
> I watched their rich attire:

[1] R. D. Laing, *The Divided Self* (Pelican, Penguin Books, 1965), p. 21.

> Blue, glossy green, and velvet black,
> They coiled and swam; and every track
> Was a flash of golden fire.
>
> O Happy living things! no tongue
> Their beauty might declare:
> A spring of love gushed from my heart.
> And I blessed them unaware:
> Sure my kind saint took pity on me,
> And I blessed them unaware.
>
> The self-same moment I could pray;
> And from my neck so free
> The Albatross fell off, and sank
> Like lead into the sea.

The Mariner's restoration to a feeling of value comes in a spontaneous overflow of powerful feelings. It would be possible to explain the sudden 'spring of love' in Hartleian terms, but to do so would be to ignore the whole point of the experience. He repeats twice, for emphasis, the fact that it happened 'unaware'. The possibility of explaining it mechanistically—as stimulus and response—is not relevant. Coleridge is describing in the Mariner a different 'level' of event: what it actually felt like to be taken by surprise by an uprush of emotion, of 'blessing', in what had seemed a moment of utter despair. Hartley, it is true, sometimes allows for the mind being unaware of its own processes, but it would be nonsense to interpret this as in any sense a theory of the unconscious. At this turning-point of the poem, the Mariner, in blessing the water-snakes, is blessing not just the representatives of all life, but recognizing and blessing in himself things which had previously disgusted and repelled him. He had offended against some of the deepest layers of his being —the spirit 'nine fathom deep/From the land of mist and snow.'[1] Whether his recovery is seen as Divine Grace, or a force liberated from the Unconscious, it is only then, in recognizing beauty and value, that prayer becomes possible.

It is, indeed, the very closeness of the parallels between the

---

[1] For a fuller argument of this interpretation, see L. C. Knights, 'Taming the Albatross', *New York Review of Books*, 26 May, 1966.

experience of breakdown and renewal that Coleridge and Wordsworth have left us in their poetry, and John Stuart Mill's, that would warn us to tread carefully. What exactly *did* Mill learn from the two poets in his own crisis? He gives us in his *Autobiography* an interesting account of how he defended the 'reality' of the 'imagination' to his sceptical utilitarian friend, Roebuck:

It was in vain I urged on him that the imaginative emotion which an idea, when vividly conceived, excites in us, is not an illusion but a fact, as real as any of the other qualities of objects; and far from implying anything erroneous and delusive in our mental apprehension of the object, is quite consistent with the most accurate knowledge and most practical recognition of all its physical and intellectual laws and rela-tions. The intensest feeling of the beauty of a cloud lighted by the setting sun, is no hindrance to my knowing that the cloud is vapour of water, subject to all the laws of vapours in a state of suspension; and I am just as likely to allow for, and not on, these physical laws whenever there is occasion to do so, as if I had been incapable of any distinction between beauty and ugliness.

His argument seems, convincingly, to rest on a simple restate-ment of the distinction we have just noted between the personal and existential mode of existence, and the objective 'scientific' mode. Yet we become aware that over this very point he has parted company from Coleridge. The feelings of the observer, Mill argues, when looking at an object such as a cloud at sunset are as 'real' as the qualities it can be shown scientifically to possess. Nevertheless, such 'facts' as feelings remain of a different order from the 'facts' of physical science. Mill's joy at seeing beauty in the cloud is personal and subjective in contrast with the 'objective' physical phenomenon of the water vapour in suspension. Nature, for Mill, could provide an analogue for his feelings; it could not, in Coleridge's sense, be a symbol. His 'imaginative emotion' is a response to something that exists outside and beyond him. He is at pains to stress that whether or not he is capable of this aesthetic response makes not the slightest difference to the objective physical fact of the cloud itself. The word 'real' is applied to his feelings and to the cloud in two different ways.

For Coleridge this dualism did not exist. The clouds in

Dejection, for instance, are to him a symbol of his own mental turmoil. We recall that in his definition of a symbol in *The Statesman's Manual* he stresses that it partakes of the 'same reality' as the thing symbolized. In *Dejection* he continues:

> O lady! we receive but what we give,
> And in our life alone does nature live:
> Ours is her wedding-garment, ours her shroud!
>   And would we aught behold of higher worth,
> Than the inanimate cold world allowed
> To the poor loveless ever-anxious crowd,
>   Ah! from the soul itself must issue forth,
> A light, a glory, a fair luminous cloud
>   Enveloping the earth—

Clearly, Coleridge here is not saying the same thing as Mill at all. For Wordsworth the rainbow was neither 'in' the mind, nor 'out there' in the material world, but was created by the coalition of both. Here, at its simplest, Coleridge is saying the same thing. It is as if the 'glory' and 'fair luminous cloud' were the symbolic 'wedding-garment' of the mind's union with nature that occurs in every act of human perception. It is this union of perceiver and perceived that Coleridge means by the 'Imagination'. We can already see in his statement 'in our life alone does nature live' the idea of the Imagination as 'the living Power and prime Agent of all human Perception' which he was to make central to the *Biographia Literaria* fourteen years later. Even more important, perception and creativity are already inseparably linked in Coleridge's mind. The creative Imagination (later to be differentiated as the 'Secondary Imagination') is connected, in *Dejection*, with 'joy' in perception:

> This light, this glory, this fair luminous mist,
> This beautiful and beauty-making power.
> ...Joy, Lady! is the spirit and the power,
> Which wedding Nature to us gives in dower
>   A new Earth and new Heaven...

And here the strange problem of the Brocken-spectre is already foreshadowed.

In Book XIII of *The Prelude* (1805) Wordsworth creates a parallel symbol to that of the Brocken-spectre in the famous

description of the moonlight ascent of Snowdon. He describes
the view from the summit over a sea of clouds which almost
obscures the real sea beneath:

> Meanwhile, the Moon look'd down upon this shew
> In single glory, and we stood, the mist
> Touching our very feet; and from the shore
> At distance not the third part of a mile
> Was a blue chasm; a fracture in the vapour,
> A deep and gloomy breathing-place through which
> Mounted the roar of waters, torrents, streams
> Innumerable, roaring with one voice.
> The universal spectacle throughout
> Was shaped for admiration and delight,
> Grand in itself alone, but in the breach
> Through which the homeless voice of waters rose,
> That deep dark thoroughfare had Nature lodg'd
> The Soul, the Imagination of the whole.
>
> (50–63)

This passage, with its apparent echo of *Kubla Khan*, seems at
first glance to offer yet another interpretation of 'Imagination'.
The total image is worth looking at in detail. The vast bulk of
Snowdonia running right down to the sea is invisible under a
second 'sea' of clouds. Only the very summit, like the tip of an
iceberg, is exposed in the clear moonlight. The streams which
start as little trickles in the moonlight are pouring down in
ever-increasing spate through the clouds into the darkness
beneath, and only the noise of falling waters rises through the
mist to reveal their presence. As a psychological 'model' of the
conscious and unconscious mind, this picture was to haunt the
nineteenth century. The deep dark thoroughfare from whence
rises the roar of hidden waters still falling beneath the mist is one
of the most seminal Romantic visions of the unconscious. Here,
then, the 'Soul, the Imagination of the whole', is an obvious
counterpart, and even in some sense an explanation of the
Spirit 'nine fathom deep' beneath the Ancient Mariner's keel.
Coleridge had stressed the Imagination as linking man to the
inanimate external world through perception. What Wordsworth
here calls 'the Imagination' is the actual gap in the clouds: the
point where the curtain is parted between the conscious and

unconscious. At first sight this would appear to be a different model of the Imagination from that of Coleridge, or his own of the rainbow, but in fact the two models are complementary. Corresponding to the relationship between man and nature that is sense-perception, there is created an equivalent relationship between conscious and unconscious. The perception of a symbol opens up corresponding layers in our own awareness. Wordsworth's sense of 'something far more deeply interfused' in *Tintern Abbey*, is mirrored 'in the mind of man' by a 'motion and a spirit'. It would, I think, however, be over-simplifying to describe the first example of 'external' perception as corresponding to Coleridge's 'Primary Imagination' and the second, 'internal', 'opening-up' to his creative 'Secondary Imagination'. In such models as these, the two are always seen as parts of the same process. To create a symbol of the mind in nature was, for both Wordsworth and Coleridge, to produce a symbol of the relationship between the mind and nature. As with the Brocken-spectre, this is a symbol of a symbol—an illustrative image of the mind being opened to new levels of relationships, even while it is in the act of being so. This passage is one of the 'spots of time' in *The Prelude* when a striking effect in nature is completed by the beholding poet. Such moments, meditated upon afterwards, constitute nodal points in the growth and development of the mind: points at which the mind perceives more clearly its own processes, and in this understanding perceives again, in a new light, its own relationship to nature. Wordsworth is always aware of himself as the active contemplator. It is the 'spectacle', and not some 'objective' world of rock and water, unconnected and 'out there', which is 'grand in itself alone'. The constituent elements of moonlight and mist and the roar of unseen 'streams innumerable' were 'shaped for admiration and delight'—the emotion is an integral part of the perception.

But it is the 'meditation' that arose in Wordsworth afterwards—the emotion recollected in tranquillity—when the scene had passed away, that transforms it into a point of growth. There is a clear separation made between the primary and secondary stages: perception and meditation. The two stages in time are parts of a single whole. Wordsworth has laid stress on his own participation for a good reason. It is only possible to see the meditation as a part of the symbol (and not an ingeniously extended analogy from it) if one has already made the basic assumption that perception is a creative act of the mind, and not the passive product of 'sensations' in the Lockeian sense. Wordsworth argues this point in the meditation:

> A meditation rose in me that night
> Upon the lonely Mountain when the scene
> Had pass'd away, and it appear'd to me
> The perfect image of a mighty Mind,
> Of one that feeds upon infinity,
> That is exalted by an underpresence,
> The sense of God, or whatsoever is dim
> Or vast in its own being, above all
> One function of such mind had Nature there
> Exhibited by putting forth, and that
> With circumstance most awful and sublime,
> That domination which she oftentimes
> Exerts upon the outward face of things,
> So moulds them, and endues, abstracts, combines,
> Or by abrupt and unhabitual influence
> Doth make one object so impress itself
> Upon all others, and pervades them so
> That even the grossest minds must see and hear
> And cannot chuse but feel...

(66–86)

Thus the whole symbol is now revealed as of a great poetic mind (as it were, Wordsworth himself) in the act of creation. The way that genius compels even the least sensitive minds to share in its own refined experience is to present an image of *itself* in nature. The parallel with Coleridge's Brocken-spectre is now striking. What makes this mind great, however, is that it is (we are told) exalted 'by an underpresence': the 'blue chasm' in the clouds—the one object that impresses itself upon all others. This abnormal sense of illimitable depth and power underlying the illuminated upper level of consciousness is felt to be an essential part of genius. It is the vehicle of 'the sense of God', or, more puzzlingly, 'whatsoe'er is dim/Or vast in its own being'. This is a crucial experience for Wordsworth, and we shall be returning to it in Chapter 5. This chasm, it seems, is the home of the

> huge and mighty Forms that do not live
> Like living men…

that troubled his dreams when as a boy he stole the boat (1805: Book I, lines 372–427). There is in the Imagination for Wordsworth, like Coleridge, an essentially numinous quality that cannot be reached or explained away by the conscious mind. In spite of a superficial similarity, Wordsworth's symbol, with its 'domination…upon the outward face of things' is utterly different from Hartley's 'one visible idea, more glaring and distinct than the rest.'

The 'grosser minds', in sharing the poet's feeling, are not feebly reflecting an emotion at second-hand, but, since a symbol only operates through an active response in the receiving mind, they share in the original emotion. Though it may be a common quality, 'value' in an experience has to be felt as original and personal. We remember Mill's description of Wordsworth's poetry as 'a source of inward joy, of sympathetic and imaginative pleasure, which could be shared by all human beings'. Mill had good cause to be grateful to Wordsworth's affirmation that 'even the grossest minds…cannot chuse but feel'.

> The Power which these
> Acknowledge when thus moved, which Nature thus
> Thrusts forth upon the senses, is the express
> Resemblance, in the fullness of its strength
> Made visible, a genuine Counterpart
> And brother of the glorious faculty
> Which higher minds bear with them as their own.
>
> (84–90)

This is linked with an account of the nature of poetic creation itself. The twin process of projection and receptivity that underlies perception is shown as a fluid interplay:

> That is the very spirit in which they deal
> With all the objects in the universe;
> They from their native selves can send abroad
> Like transformations, and for themselves create
> A like existence, and, whene'er it is
> Created for them, catch it by an instinct;
> Them the enduring and the transient both
> Serve to exalt; they build up the greatest things

41

From least suggestions, ever on the watch,
Willing to work and to be wrought upon,
They need not extraordinary calls
To rouze them, in a world of life they live,
By sensible impressions not enthrall'd,
But quicken'd, rouz'd, and thereby made more apt
To hold communion with the invisible world.

(91–105)

In the ultimate purpose to 'hold communion with the invisible world' we find completed a parallel structure to Coleridge's in *Constancy to an Ideal Object*. As we saw in the case of I. A. Richards, a failure to understand what Wordsworth and Coleridge meant by 'Imagination' has resulted in a process of progressive 'mystification' by which such phrases as 'the invisible world' are made to bear a variety of mystical interpretations—pantheist, Platonic, and Christian. Here that they are hardly necessary—and, indeed, hinder our understanding of the rest of the passage. Wordsworth has been discussing how Imagination so organizes our perception that it becomes not a matter of passively receiving 'sense-data', but, through creating or sharing in poetic creation through the assimilation of symbols, interpreting what we see as *values*. In other words, Wordsworth is not using 'communion' loosely to mean 'communication' but in its theological sense of a sacrament. The inanimate world is apprehended directly as a personal encounter.

Such an 'encounter' is not in any sense 'mystical'. Wordsworth, looking at Snowdon in the moonlight, is not reading into nature something which is not 'objectively' there. What, after all, *is* the relationship between 'the mountain' and our apprehension of it? It so happens that a considerable amount of research has been done on one particular example of this question—since Cézanne looked at his painting of Mont St Victoire and said defiantly 'This *is* the mountain.'[1] Photographs have been taken from the spot where Cézanne painted and earnestly compared with his canvases. Professor E. H. Gombrich, commenting on this painstaking search after the reality of 'the mountain' asks 'should we believe the photograph represents the 'objective truth' while the painting records the artist's

[1] See John Rewald, *Cézanne* (Spring Books, 1948).

subjective vision?'[1] His answer is to dismiss the question. There is no such thing, he argues, as this assumed image-on-the-retina from which the painter's verison is supposed to have deviated.

there never was *one* such image which we could single out for comparison with either photograph or painting. What there was was an endless succession of innumerable images as the painter scanned the landscape in front of him.

The fallacy is to assume that something 'out there' is compared with something else which is 'in' the mind.

In Wordsworth's view from Snowdon by moonlight the new model of perception is being the instrument of a change in consciousness so profound that poetry could never be the same again afterwards. It was Coleridge who saw more clearly than any (perhaps including Wordsworth himself) what had been achieved in this culminating passage of *The Prelude*. When Wordsworth had finished reciting the thirteen books of the poem to his friend on the night of 7 January 1807 at Coleorton, Coleridge's reply is full of a consciousness that a historic moment had arrived:

> Friend of the wise! and Teacher of the Good!
> Into my heart have I received that Lay
> More than historic, that prophetic Lay
> Wherein (high theme by thee first sung aright)
> Of the foundations and the building up
> Of a Human Spirit thou hast dared to tell
> What may be told, to the understanding mind
> Revealable...

Wordsworth himself has changed the way we feel, and this defines his greatness:

> The truly great
> Have all one age, and from one visible space
> Shed influence! They, both in power and act,
> Are permanent, and Time is not with them,
> Save as it worketh for them, they in it.

Ironically, this poem marks something more. Under the influence of his friend, Coleridge has written one of his last great poems.

[1] *Art and Illusion* (Phaidon, 1960), p. 57.

Their work together was almost finished. Henceforth Wordsworth was largely to repeat himself, and Coleridge, spurred on by his determination to understand Wordsworth's past achievements, was to extend and, in some senses, to complete what *The Prelude* had begun.

What had been created during these years of Wordsworth's and Coleridge's collaboration was not just a new model of perception, but, culminating in *The Prelude* at this point, a new model of the human mind as a thing whose characteristic activity was creation. Let us, for a moment, recapitulate some of the elements that went into this 'boiling-point' of consciousness.

In contrast to the 'mechanical' psychology of Hartley, which had seen the human mind as a thing, passive and cumulative in its organization, they felt their own mental processes, at a personal level, as organic, active, and unified. The image most frequently used to illustrate the 'organic' view of the mind is that of a growing plant, whose growth, though it could be helped or stunted by outside forces, was essentially inner-determined. In contrast with the Lockeian and Hartleian *tabula rasa* of the passive mind awaiting external stimulation, the mind was seen as active and originating. In place of the Hartleian idea of character as the cumulative legacy of past events, the personality was felt to be a 'unity' in the sense that the whole was so integrated that to select a part in isolation was to distort it, and the rest. In other words, poetry was the 'science' of the whole man. It was seen by Wordsworth and Coleridge not merely as a means of understanding their own growth, but as influencing and liberating the form of the growth itself.

But, in making this kind of assertion, we must recall the dangers. It is very easy to make the claim, from what we have seen, that since Wordsworth poetry and creative literature have taken over from philosophy the role of interpreting man's experience to himself. The claim is often made. We might, for inatance, twist T. S. Eliot's famous defence of obscurity, that 'nowadays poetry is *bound* to be difficult', in support of this. Yet the pitfalls are yawning. Was there no poetry asserting value (in this sense) before the Romantics? Obviously there was. T. S. Eliot discusses this point very cautiously in his essay 'The

Modern Mind'[1] and comes out against it. He quotes, with qualified approval, Jacques Rivière:

> If in the seventeenth century Molière or Racine had been asked why he wrote, no doubt he would have been able to find but one answer; that he wrote for the entertainment of decent people (pour distraire les honnêtes gens). It is only with the advent of Romanticism that the literary act came to be conceived as a sort of raid on the absolute and its result a revelation.

He goes on to quote Jacques Maritain in his criticism of I. A. Richards's statement that 'poetry is capable of saving us'. 'By showing us where moral truth and the genuine supernatural are situate, religion saves poetry from the absurdity of believing itself destined to transform ethics and life: saves it from overweening arrogance.' I. A. Richards's position is an extreme one. It is not, of course, a statement about poetry at all—and Eliot, it seems to me, is right in attacking him from both a linguistic and metaphysical standpoint. But it is typical of the kind of assertion that can be made if the relationship between poetry and philosophy is misunderstood. What we *can* say is that Coleridge's perception of the link between poetry and growth has been of enormous significance in transforming what has been called (in a slightly different context) our 'structure of feeling'.[2] The basic proposition of both Abrams and Gombrich (applied in vastly different ways to the history of our sensibility) is the Romantic one that 'any well-grounded critical theory in some degree alters the aesthetic perceptions it purports to discover.'[3] With this in mind, our purpose in the following chapters is to try and follow the mysterious Brocken-spectre that appears and vanishes so ambiguously in the mists of Coleridge's creative life.

1 In *The Use of Poetry and the Use of Criticism* (Faber, 1933).
2 Williams, *Long Revolution*, pp. 64–88.
3 Abrams, *Mirror and Lamp*, p. 5.

2
Mechanism versus Organism

Any discussion of Coleridge's ideas of creativity starts with Hartley. Until sometime about 1800 Coleridge was obsessed by Hartley's 'mechanical' psychology, and the philosophical system that went with it. A frequently-quoted passage in *Religious Musings*, written on Christmas Eve 1794, pays fulsome tribute to the author of the *Observer on Man*:

> and he of mortal kind
> Wisest, he first who marked the ideal tribes
> Up the fine fibres through the sentient brain.
>
> (368–70)

Since, about the time that he was first reading Kant, Coleridge came to repudiate Hartley with the same vehemence with which he had originally followed him, it has been widely assumed that Hartley represented a clearly-defined 'stage' in Coleridge's development. Much of his later growth has been seen as a reaction against his early Hartleianism. Yet, if the distinction between a personal-existential and a physico-mechanical way of viewing people was as important to Coleridge as was suggested in the last chapter, the repudiation of Hartley represented something much more complex in the growth of Coleridge's ideas. There is a great deal of evidence to suggest that Kant did not so much supersede Hartley in Coleridge's thought, as make him aware of what was a fundamental ambiguity in his own experience. The explanation of man as a physical machine, even if it were true, did not help Coleridge to account for poetry, or for the 'Imagination'—and it is worth noticing that when *Religious Musings* was first published in 1796 it was prefaced by a passage from Akenside's *Pleasures of the Imagination*. Coleridge's final concept of the Imagination was unique in the way that it was able to combine two apparently incompatible 'models': organism, and dialectic. By the time he wrote *The Friend* (1809–11) he had come to see the principle of organic growth as operating in conjunction with the principle of 'polarity'—progressing 'by contraries', and 'reconciling opposite or discordant qualities'. The way in which he reached this position is a very good example of his whole mode of thought. Though the complete formulation was almost his life's work, continuing its development until *Aids to Reflection* in 1825, and drawing its final terminology mostly from German philosophy, the conception was in fact implicit in his work from the very beginning. The rejection of Hartley's mechanistic theory of association does not, in any sense, indicate a change of direction in Coleridge's thought. He remained, as he was from the first, consistently concerned with apprehending, recording, defining, and accounting for certain intuitively perceived phenomena in himself. For example, in October 1803 we find him observing a similar experience to that recorded by Wordsworth in meditation on the mountain:

a thing at the moment is but a thing of the moment; it must be taken up into the mind, diffuse itself through the whole multitude of shapes and thoughts, not one of which it leaves untinged, between (not one of) which and it some new thought is not engendered. Now this is a work of time, but the body feels it quicker with me.[1]

Coleridge would by this time no longer have described himself as a follower of Hartley, but there is much in this 'physical' description of thought that is reminiscent of the *Observations on Man*. Much more revealing, however, is that five years before, while still a fanatical Hartleian, he had recorded a phenomenon of similar complexity in the form of one of his finest poems, *Frost at Midnight*.

> Sea, and hill, and wood,
> With all the numberless goings-on of life,
> Inaudible as dreams! the thin blue flame
> Lies on my low-burnt fire, and quivers not;
> Only that film, which fluttered on the grate,
> Still flutters there, the sole unquiet thing.
> Methinks, its motion in this hush of nature
> Gives it dim sympathies with me who live,

[1] *Anima Poetae*, ed. E. H. Coleridge (Heinemann, 1895), p. 31; *Notebooks*, Vol. I, 1597.

Making it a companionable form,
Whose puny flaps and freaks the idling spirit
By its own moods interprets, every where
Echo or mirror seeking of itself,
And makes a toy of thought.

(11–23)

Coleridge is examining (or rather, articulately 'feeling') the working of his own mind at a particular moment in time.[1] Past, present, and future are brought to bear on a single moment of consciousness. Typically, the poem is centred upon the mind's search for ways of seeing itself. Its movement is complex and inner-directed. Coleridge turns slowly inward from the frosty calm of 'Sea, and hill, and wood' to the fluttering 'stranger' on the grate, which becomes for him a symbol of his own mind. An ambiguity in the word 'toy' suggests the new ordering of his awareness. Are the associations of boyhood brought back by the 'stranger' merely the trivial ramblings of an 'idling Spirit'?— or do they form a coherent pattern at a deeper level than that of the rationalizing intellect, whose activity in comparison is only a game? When Coleridge observed later that 'the body feels it quicker with me' was he, perhaps, making more than a simple observation about his nervous system, and implying a similar contrast between rational thought and the more rapid unconscious associative organization of the body?[2] Here, he goes on:

But O! how oft,
How oft, at school, with most believing mind,
Presageful, have I gazed upon the bars,
To watch that fluttering *stranger*! and as oft
With unclosed lids, already had I dreamt
Of my sweet birth-place, and the old church-tower,
Whose bells, the poor man's only music, rang
From morn to evening, all the hot Fair-day,

---

[1] I am indebted here to William Walsh's discussion of *Frost at Midnight* in his *Coleridge* (Chatto, 1967), pp. 125–8.

[2] D. W. Harding in his essay 'The Hinterland of Thought', *Metaphor and Symbol*, ed. L. C. Knights and Basil Cottle (Butterworth, 1960), discusses such 'bodily thought', and argues that 'An emergent impulse can be brought into relation with value systems long before imaging or verbal thinking occurs.' There is, he argues, an infinite gradation between such levels and the fully conscious ratiocinative processes of the mind.

So sweetly, that they stirred and haunted me
With a wild pleasure, falling on mine ear
Most like articulate sounds of things to come!

(24-33)

The associative drift of his mind reveals itself in a series of contrasts. The cold calm of the present night is juxtaposed with the bells of Ottery St Mary on a hot summer fair-day in his childhood. His own childhood is seen, in turn, through the bored nostalgia of the schoolboy at Christ's Hospital. This childhood is then contrasted with the present moment as he sits beside his sleeping baby, and then with his son's childhood and growth that lies ahead. Spanning each of these contrasts is an intuitive and unstated sense of their organic continuity: father and son, winter and summer. Young Hartley's growth is felt as partaking directly in the life of nature with which he is surrounded.

Organism and polarity: the elements which later were to be gathered into a theory of creativity in *Biographia Literaria*, are already here in the syncretic organization of Coleridge's poetry. Basil Willey has described Coleridge's 'triumph over the tradition of Locke and Hartley' as 'the great struggle and victory of his life',[1] and if we follow the development of his 'philosophy' this is undoubtedly true. Yet if this is taken to mean a drastic re-orientation of Coleridge's poetic experience, it is very misleading. It seemed at first that Hartley's model of 'association' explained the workings of his own mind as he experienced it in poems like *Frost at Midnight*. This, as Coleridge's starting-point, has been insufficiently stressed by many commentators on his relationship to Hartley. Coleridge accepted Hartley *only* so long as he could believe that he offered an adequate scientific explanation not merely of his own creativity, but also of his consciousness of value. He rejected Hartley when he came to see that physical science was by its very nature unable to do this. An early note of Coleridge's reads:

Materialists unwilling to admit the mysterious element in our nature make it all mysterious—nothing mysterious in nerves, eyes, etc., but that nerves think etc.! Stir up the sediment into the transparent water and so make all opaque![2]

---

[1] *Nineteenth Century Studies* (Chatto, 1949), p. 14.
[2] *Anima Poetae*, p. 14; *Notebooks*, Vol. I, 920.

In Chapter vi of *Biographia Literaria* Coleridge observes that the nerves which receive and transmit the Hartleian 'vibrati-uncles' (or little vibrations) are 'but the flint which the wag placed in the pot as the first ingredient of his stoneborth, requiring only salt, turnips, and mutton for the remainder!' The dig is a wickedly unfair one, for it was precisely Hartley's ability to make a convincing 'broth' from a stone that primarily appealed to Coleridge. It was only *after* he had refused the broth that he turned his attention to the 'stone' itself—the passive mind that for Locke and Hartley composed the initial *tabula rasa*.

Coleridge's letter to Southey of 11 December 1794 is surprisingly consistent: 'I am a complete necessitarian, and understand the subject as well almost as Hartley himself, but I go further than Hartley, and believe the corporeality of all *thought*, namely, that it is motion.'[1] This may 'go further than Hartley' in the sense immediately referred to, but the leap from thought as 'motion'—even 'corporeal' motion—to Coleridge's later description of 'A Shakespeare, a Milton, a Bruno' who 'exist in the mind as pure *action*, defecated of all that is material and passive',[2] may not be as great as the apparent about-turn over the status of the corporeal and material might suggest. Alice Snyder has observed how much of Coleridge's educational work 'consisted in distinguishing, by one means or another, between thinking that was dynamic, imaginative, and fertile, and the relatively passive thing that often went by its name'.[3] It seemed at first that Hartley provided the key to this distinction.

David Hartley was as concerned with the growth of the mind as Coleridge himself. Starting from Locke, he took as his second source the Reverend John Gay's 'Dissertation Concerning the Fundamental Principles of Virtue and Morality', which was prefixed by Bishop Law to his translation of King's latin *Essay on the Origin of Evil*. Believing that God had arranged the universe

---

[1] *Letters*, ed. Griggs, Vol. i (Oxford, 1956). p. 74.

[2] *Notebooks*, Vol. ii, 2026.

[3] A. Snyder, *Coleridge on Logic and Learning* (Yale, 1929), p. 12. I. A. Richards enlarges on this point in *Coleridge on Imagination*, and argues that the reason for this is that he 'had to extricate himself from the Locke tradition, not because it was "false", but because for himself, at some hours, it was too painfully true' (p. 60). Dorothy Emmet in 'Coleridge on the Growth of the Mind', *Bulletin of the George Rylands Library*, Vol. 34, No. 2 (Manchester, March 1952), makes a similar point (p. 292).

so as to make virtue equal happiness, Gay concluded that happiness is the proper and ultimate end of all our actions.[1] By association we are willing to accept what he called 'Resting Places' as ends in themselves. The desire for money, for example, Gay argued, was *really* the desire for the happiness that money can bring—with the last link forgotten or left out. Unlike Hartley's, this is still a reversible process in which everything can be explained in terms of its origins—though not always in a manner that seems clear. For example, finding it necessary to suppose what he calls a 'Moral Sense', he hastily adds: '...but I deny that this Moral Sense, or these public Affections, are innate, or *implanted* in us; they are acquired either from our own *Observation* or from the Imitation of others.' Even if we assume that the others who are to be imitated originally acquired their Moral Sense by 'Observation', we still seem to be left with the problem of how observation, not of others, can provide us with it. It is precisely this gap that Hartley's vibrationary hypothesis sets out to fill.

For Hartley 'ideas' did not appear and vanish independently; they were the product of little vibrations—or rather, 'vibratiuncles'. These, since they are modified by the unique individual pattern of personal vibrations aleady present, will take a different particular form in each person. Each man has a particular and continuing personality because all his previous vibrations will modify the succeeding ones—just as the ground-swell of the ocean will affect the ripple-pattern caused by a single stone. Thus the way in which the individual perceives things will be conditioned by the previous history of his mind. This gives, incidentally, a continuing physical basis to personality that was denied, for instance, by Hume. The reason why Coleridge adopted Hartley, while never ceasing to vilify Hume, lies primarily in the fundamental difference of approach that this implies to the creative powers of the mind.

Hume flatly insists that since 'ideas' are but weak reflections of 'impressions', every act of the mind is absolutely explicable

---

[1] This apparently Utilitarian use of 'happiness' is a good example of the danger of reading later meanings into eighteenth-century words: the distinction between Bentham's 'Happiness' and Coleridge's 'Joy' did not exist, and it is as misleading to read one into it, as the other.

in terms of its origins. Hartley, at first sight, appears to agree: 'The intellectual Pleasures and Pains are as real as the sensible ones, being, as we have seen, nothing but the sensible ones variously mixed and compounded together...'[1] but this is, in fact, the complete opposite of Hume's relentless 'nothing-buttery' (or what Lovejoy grandly calls the 'retrotensive method'). Hartley is using the same suppositions to draw a diametrically opposed conclusion. He goes on almost at once:

This Proposition and its Corollaries, afford some pleasing Presumptions; such are...That our ultimate Happiness appears to be of a spiritual, not corporeal Nature; and therefore that Death, or the shaking off the gross Body, may notstop our Progress, but rather render us more expedite in the pursuit of our true End.[2]

In other words, Hartley insists that complex ideas—even the most sophisticated mental concepts—are just as *real* as the original crude sensations, and are in no sense weaker or inferior. Moreover, the process of association by which these complex ideas are built up, though reversible in theory (for the purposes of moral analysis), is actually irreversible. A complex idea cannot be reduced to the terms of its origins. On the contrary, matter leads inexorably on to spirituality.

Similarly, at the material level, the possibility of new ideas is recognized, and even considered likely:

And it happens in most Cases, that the decomplex [i.e. highly complex] Idea belonging to any sentence, is not compounded merely of the complex Ideas belonging to the Words of it; but that there are also many Variations, some Oppositions, and numberless Additions.[3]

The question of new ideas is noticeably shrouded in vaguer language than has hitherto been used. While it is clear that a concentration or cluster of 'ideas' generates more by a process of constant conjunction and interplay, it is not clear if the 'Variations', 'Oppositions', and 'Additions' are ideas already present that are drawn into the snowball, or in some sense new-created ideas from simpler components. The difficulty of thinking about

---

[1] *Observations on Man*, Vol. I, p. 83.
[2] *Ibid*. p. 84.
[3] *Ibid*. p. 79.

'ideas' in *physical* terms is apparent. Hartley clarifies the problem slightly when he considers the relation of words to ideas:

Since Words thus collect Ideas from various Quarters, unite them together, and transfer them both upon other Words, and upon foreign Objects, it is evident, that the Use of Words adds much to the number and Complexeness of our Ideas, and it is the principal means by which we make our intellectual and moral Improvements.[1]

It is easy to see how Coleridge could find in this, and similar passages, something that seemed at first to correspond to his own experience, and it is salutary to remember that Hartley's conception of the creative powers of the mind remained stubbornly mechanical. We are still at a different level from Coleridge's 'active and originating power', but it is also worth remembering that the word 'mechanical' for Hartley was a good deal wider in scope than it was for Coleridge. As we shall see, Hartley did not draw any distinction between an organism and a machine; a plant was a 'machine' like any other. In September 1800 it is interesting to find Coleridge writing to Godwin as follows:

Are not words, etc., parts and germinations of the plant? and what is the law of their growth? In something of this sort I would endeavour to destroy the old antithesis of *Words and Things*: elevating, as it were Words into Things and living things too. All the nonsense of vibrating, etc. you would of course dismiss.[2]

A second point arising from this mechanical scheme of mental growth is that Hartley never seems able to make up his mind in what sense a 'decomplex' (that is, very complex) idea, formed from other complex ideas, is an *original* idea. Though it is always formed, as we have seen, from others by association and contiguity, it may show a change that is of kind rather than degree— especially when it represents a step towards greater spirituality. It is precisely this ambiguity between the mechanism of growth on the one hand, and the evaluation of its content on the other, that was to lead Coleridge eventually to dismiss the 'nonsense' of vibrations. Priestley, whom Coleridge had hailed in *Religious Musings* in terms only slightly less ecstatic than those applied to

[1] *Ibid.* p. 297.
[2] *Letters*, Vol. I, pp. 625–6.

Hartley, published in 1775 an introductory essay to Hartley's theory of the human mind which avoided his moral and religious aims altogether, preferring to add separate explanatory essays on them, with the result that the doctrine of association was made to appear even more rigidly materialistic than it really was.

Hartley, in fact, saw the principle of mechanical association as a hypothesis to explain certain phenomena, and to demonstrate a felt truth about human development. Within this framework he remained quite humble, always willing to admit that his theories were a 'model', and might have to be modified or abandoned if they could be replaced by a better. He was arguing towards a purpose that he never lost sight of, and never confused the means with the end he wished to show: that things were so constituted that 'some degree of spirituality is the necessary consequence of passing through this world'. To this end Hartley saw nothing inconsistent in arguing that free will may co-exist with necessity. Indeed, he argued that free will in the normal sense is just this freedom to act according to character:

It may be said, That a Man may prove his own Free-will by internal Feelings. This is true, if by Free-will be meant the Power of doing what a Man wills or desires...To prove that a man has Free-will in the Sense opposite to Mechanism, he ought to feel, that he can do different Things, while the Motives remain precisely the same...[1]

This definition of free will is an extremely plausible one, and, as we shall see, there is reason to doubt if Coleridge ever seriously questioned it. Moreover, it accounts for Hartley's attachment to his vibrationary theory. In controlling 'necessity', and building from the Lockeian passivity of the nerves, the chief factor is the state of mind of the person concerned, and the hypothesis of a personal rhythm of vibrations in the brain conveniently allows it, while remaining theoretically passive, to behave as if it were in fact active—and so circumvent the necessity that Hartley had been reluctantly forced to concede.

Coleridge's disagreement with Hartley finally came to a head when he saw that he could no longer accept the possibility of this mechanical progression from a passive receptivity to a creative and originating power of the mind. It was, as he says in *Bio-*

---

[1] *Observations on Man*, Vol. i, p. 507.

graphia Literaria, 'the impossible creation of a *something-nothing* out of its very contrary.'[1] The criticism of Hartley in Chapters v to vii is extraordinarly perceptive and discriminating. The attack on associationism is nowhere on associationism *as such*. A theory of association was to prove enormously fruitful in his later thought, playing a major part in his distinction between Imagination and Fancy. To clear the ground for this new associationary structure, however, the old mechanical and vibrationary connections had to be disposed of. Coleridge makes his onslaught on the mechanical basis of association on two fronts: firstly, he denies the passivity of the nerves, and secondly, he disputes, on logical grounds, that the 'will' can be both the cause of associative selection, and its product.

To begin with, then, Coleridge is concerned to demolish the theory of a 'ground-swell' of previous vibrations as a physical basis of personality. He points out that such an individual rhythm must, in addition, constitute the entire memory—operating, as it were, only on the energy of the incoming vibrations.

It is a mere delusion of the fancy to conceive the pre-existence of the ideas, in any chain of association, as so many differently coloured billiard-balls in contact, so that when an object, the billiard-stick, strikes the first red or white ball, the same motion propagates itself through the red, green, blue and black, and sets the whole in motion. No! we must suppose the very same force, which *constitutes* the white ball, to *constitute* the red or black...which is impossible.[2] ..

He clinches his argument with two brilliantly memorable illustrations: that of the stone-broth, already mentioned, and that of the weather-cock: it 'seems scarcely less absurd than to say, that a weather-cock had acquired the habit of turning to the east from the wind having been so long in that quarter...'[3]

Coleridge bases his second criticism of the theory of mechanical association on the fact that there must be an extra selective principle (which he calls the 'will') to organize the associative process. But, according to Hartley, the will itself must be a product of previously selected associations. Thus Hartley's

[1] *Biographia Literaria*, Vol. I. p. 82.
[2] *Ibid.* p. 75.
[3] *Ibid.*

concept of the 'will' founders on the same unresolved problem of origins as Gay's 'Moral Sense'—the very difficulty he had hoped to circumvent by his theory of vibrations. His whole argument is, in effect, a hen-egg one, and circular:

the will, the reason, the judgement, and the understanding, instead of being the determining causes of association, must needs be represented as its creatures, and among its mechanical effects. Conceive, for instance, a broad stream, winding through a mountainous country with an indefinite number of currents, varying and running into each other according as the gusts change to blow from the opening of the mountains. The temporary union of several currents in one, so as to form the main current of the moment, would present an accurate image of Hartley's theory of the will.[1]

Coleridge's attack here appears both simple and conclusive. It does, however, contain certain dangers for the unwary. It has been pointed out that Coleridge's use of terms like 'reason', 'understanding', or, in this case, 'will', implies an acceptance of a 'faculty psychology' that 'actually belied his own conception of the organic unity of living processes'.[2] This is, of course, very just—but the criticism would be even more telling if we could be certain exactly what Coleridge meant here by the 'will'. A. O. Lovejoy in his very salutary article 'Coleridge and Kant's Two Worlds'[3] attacks the notion that Coleridge's conversion from Hartley was due to Kant. He starts with Coleridge's determination to show that man is *morally* free, and therefore capable of genuine good and evil. But, Lovejoy points out, Kant's freedom of the will applies only to the higher 'moral consciousness' (which Coleridge called 'reason') and not to the 'empirical will' (Coleridge's 'understanding') which has to conform to the laws of our material nature, and which therefore excludes freedom. He concludes:

Coleridge cannot ever be said to have abandoned the form of necessitarianism which he held in his Hartleian period; for that related solely

---

[1] *Ibid.* p. 76. Coleridge would appear to be taking up Priestley's defence of Hartley's argument for the continuity of personality: that a river is still the same river, even though no part of it is ever the same (*Disquisitions on Matter and Spirit*, 'Theological and Misc. Works', ed. Rutt (1818), pp. 329–30).

[2] Snyder, *Coleridge on Logic*, p. 15.

[3] In *Essays in History of Ideas*.

to nature and to man's temporal existence. Coleridge merely supplemented this determinism with respect to the 'homo phenomenon' by finding (as he thought) another kind of freedom in another kind of world.

Following on from this, he adds that the 'freedom' and the 'will' defended against Hartley's associationism in *Biographia Literaria* have nothing to do with the Kantian 'will', but are a part of an *empirical* attack on a theory that was both circular and untrue to his own experience.

Within his own terms, the strength of Lovejoy's argument is overwhelming. Like Hartley, though for very different reasons, Kant saw nothing inconsistent in arguing that free will may coexist with necessity. But to pursue Coleridge in terms of ideas is to pursue a very slippery eel indeed. It is true, for instance, that what Coleridge calls the 'will' in *Aids to Reflection* is an essential attribute to 'Reason' (which clearly corresponds to the higher of Kant's two worlds, where the power of origination was found). Kant, however, was not interested in creativity in the sense that Coleridge was. Coleridge writes:

Nature is a Line in constant and continuous evolution...But where there is no discontinuity there can be no origination, and every appearance of origination in *Nature* is but a shadow of our own casting. It is a reflection from our own *Will* or Spirit. Herein, indeed, the Will consists. This is the essential character by which WILL is *opposed* to Nature, as Spirit, and raised *above* Nature, as self-determining Spirit—this namely, that it is a power of *originating* an act or state.[1]

Clearly Lovejoy is quite right. But if we confine our attention to seeing how this bears out Lovejoy's case, we are in danger of missing something even more important. Nor does it help us much to see this 'shadow of our own casting' in terms of Coleridge's Platonism. Coleridge is writing here about creativity in a form equally alien to Hartley, Kant, and the Platonists—even while owing something to all of them. He is trying to account for the 'power of originating' he had experienced existentially in himself, and in order to interpet this phenomenon he has brought into service his image of the Brocken-spectre as a symbol of the creative process. The 'shadow of our own casting'

---

[1] *Aids to Reflection*, p. 232.

is, however, here not a visual but an intellectual one. Coleridge is applying to rational thought the same ambiguous symbol that he applied to visual perception because he saw them both as a part of the same activity.

During, and increasingly after his rejection of Hartley he came to identify mechanism with clear, limited, and systematic thought, in contrast with the more intuitive poetic insights and value-judgements of personal development. It is this latter, 'self-consciousness' in its full meaning, that Coleridge sees as an essentially *organic* growth. Writing, for instance, to Wordsworth about the form he had hoped *The Recluse* would take, Coleridge, in May 1815, mentions:

the necessity of a general revolution in the modes of developing and disciplining the human mind by the substitution of Life, and Intelligence (considered in its different powers from the Plant up to that state in which the difference of Degree becomes a new kind (man, self-consciousness) but yet not by essential opposition) for the philosophy of mechanism which in everything that is most worthy of the human intellect strikes *Death*, and cheats itself by mistaking clear Images for distinct conceptions, and which idly demands Conceptions where Intuitions alone are possible or adequate to the majesty of the Truth.[1]

The superiority of intuitions over conceptions is a fundamental tenet of his final position. There are at least three very important reasons for this. The first is the realization that science—not only in its dubious Hartleian form—was not logically competent to investigate the powers of the mind that had, among other things, devised it. The second is Coleridge's quite empirical rejection of Hartley. The clarity and neatness of his psychology did not correspond, even at the most obvious level, with the actual complexity of Coleridge's personal awareness of himself. The third is that only an intuition could bridge the gulf that Coleridge increasingly felt between mechanism and consciousness, between science and value: a gap that *Frost at Midnight* had been able to span. We are brought up here against the fundamental religious cleavage between Hartley and Coleridge: the

---

[1] *Letters*, Vol. IV, p. 575.

former had never doubted that experimental science would one day give final proof to the truths of Christianity.

But there is a further point in Coleridge's reference to 'mistaking clear images for distinct conceptions'. As we saw in discussing the supposedly Hartleian *Frost at Midnight*, one of his most consistent preoccupations is the contrast between rational 'thought' and the irrational associative processes of the unconscious. It is this contrast between the two modes of apprehension that Coleridge is referring to here. Hartley had accounted for association in terms of 'trains of ideas'. Coleridge had *felt* it differently. Over and over again we find that Coleridge's insights are illustrated before they are formulated. For example, we find in a letter to Southey of 7 August 1803: 'Association depends in a much greater degree on the recurrence of resembling states of Feeling then on Trains of Ideas...And if this is so, Hartley's system totters.'[1] But for an illustration of this we need look no further than the 'Hartleian' *Frost at Midnight*, whose structure is almost entirely dependent on the mood. Yet, as we have seen so often, this new affirmation by Coleridge did not mean that one form of 'association' superseded the other. Only five months after his letter to Southey, in January 1804, Coleridge made a note complaining of his undisciplined will:

After I had got into bed last night I said to myself that I had been pompously enunciating as a difficulty, a problem of easy and common solution—viz., that it was the effect of association. From infancy up to manhood, under parents, schoolmasters, inspectors, etc., our pleasures and pleasant self-chosen pursuits (self-chosen because pleasant, and not originally pleasant because self-chosen) have been forcibly interrupted, and dull, unintelligible rudiments, or painful tasks imposed upon us instead. Now all duty is felt as a *command*, and every command is of the nature of an offence. Duty, therefore, by the law of association being felt as a command from without, would naturally call up the sensation of the pain roused from the commands of parents and schoolmasters. But I awoke this morning at half-past one, and...the shallowness and sohpistry of this solution flashed upon me at once. I saw that the phenomenon occurred far, far too early: I have observed it in infants of two or three months old...The fact is that interruption of itself is painful, because and as far as it acts as *disruption*. And thus without any reference to or distinct recollection of my former theory

[1] *Ibid.* Vol. ii, p. 961.

I saw great reason to attribute the effect, wholly, to the streamy nature of the associative faculty, and the more, as it is evident that they labour under this defect who are most reverie-ish and streamy...[1]

Here we find Coleridge balancing an orthodox 'linear' Hartleian associationism against the more subtle unconscious associative power of reverie. I think here, as so often, we miss the whole point of this painstaking analysis if we note merely the conclusion. What matters for Coleridge is how he reached it. His conclusion is in fact, a quite *empirical* one. What really concerns him is to find an explanation for the moods of dereliction and intellectual sterility when he found it impossible to apply himself even to tasks which he enjoyed:

I had begun and found it pleasant. Why did I neglect it? Because I ought not to have done this. The same applies to the reading and writing of letters, essays, etc. Surely this is well worth a serious analysis, that, by understanding, I may attempt to heal it. For it is a deep and wide disease in my moral nature, at once elm-and-oak-rooted.[1]

Coleridge is fascinated, for deeply personal reasons, with the mental conditions which make for creativity, and with those that prevent it. Each sheds light on the other. To this end he was fully prepared to accept whatever explanation best seemed to him to fit the 'fact of mind'. As we can see so clearly in his later philosophy, there was for Coleridge nothing inconsistent in using two basically incompatible systems if they seemed to him to explain his problem. Each new position he adopted comprehended and took over what was useful, or seemed true to experience in his previous position. He found himself aware, at different times, of both forms of association. As always, we find Coleridge's thought 'feeling' its way towards a whole that is organically more than the sum of its parts, rather than the mechanically greater unity that Hartley envisaged.

This highlights one of the fundamental differences between Hartley and Coleridge. It is partly concealed by an ambiguity in the Hartleian notion of progress and growth. It has been argued that while we can find no less than four different concepts of progress derived from Lockeian psychology current in the eighteenth century, only one, an 'individualistic and religious'

[1] *Anima Poetae*, p. 41; *Notebooks*, Vol. I, 1833.

ideal, is in fact applicable to Hartley.[1] Though Hartley saw the growth of the mind as a process of ascending from a passive *tabula rasa* to an active, and finally a spiritual power, he insisted, nevertheless, that 'the progress of the human mind...is a thing of determinate nature.' By this he meant that the development and perfection of man was ordained by God, and so built into the existing scheme of things that mankind could only develop on this pre-set pattern. Though this process is 'mechanical' and not 'organic' (in the sense that Coleridge was to borrow the word from A. W. Schlegel) it was determinate in the same sense as the growth of a plant is determinate. Hartley saw man as developing through seven stages of motivation: Sensation, Imagination, Ambition, Self-Interest, Sympathy, Theopathy, and Moral Sense. Thus when thinking of Coleridge's struggle against the 'mechanism' of the eighteenth-century empiricists, one has constantly to ask *which* doctrine of mechanism?—the one that saw the mind as the passive instrument of sensations? or the one that saw the seed developing into the flower? Both are to be found in Hartley. It is this fundamental confusion that prompted the most common complaint against the eighteenth-century necessitarian moralists:

The very people who as necessitarians (Holbach and Godwin, as well as Hartley), loudly proclaim that men's characters are the product of circumstances, are also the people who, as moralists and educators, are the most anxious to control and alter circumstances to produce the right kind of characters.[2]

But though this clearly has some justification—and Coleridge himself makes a similar charge—it ignores the possibilities inherent in Hartley's analogy. His religious and perfectionist views were, we must remember, the starting-point, and not the conclusion of his psychology. He argues not so much from cause to effect, as from effect to cause. His mechanism pre-supposes that the characteristics of a seed are acquired rather than innate, but from the moment that the seed is planted its growth is determined in the sense that it cannot be anything else than what it is. A daisy will never become a rose. On the other hand, its growth

---

[1] M. E. Leslie, 'The Political Thought of Joseph Priestley' (unpublished Ph.D. Thesis, Cambridge University Library), Appendix on Hartley.
[2] Basil Willey, *Eighteenth Century Background* (Chatto, 1940), p. 152.

may well be helped or hindered by its environment; a rose may be stunted, warped, or even nipped in the bud. Obviously it is the job of the gardener to nurture the predetermined growth of the shrub to the best of his ability.

Thus we can trace in Hartley's system not one, but *two* 'models' of growth, both built up from the same basic 'trains of association'. Both involve a progression from the simple to the complex, and involve a whole that is, by virtue of its organisation, greater than the sum of its constituent parts. For the first, Hartley draws on Newton's discoveries about light: 'Thus, also, White is vulgarly thought to be the simplest and most uncompounded of all Colours, while yet it really arises from a certain Proportion of the Seven primary Colours, with their several Shades, or Degrees.'[1] In his *Introductory Essays to Hartley*, Priestley takes up this idea of an inorganic and mechanical complexity that is different in kind from its parts:

What resemblence is there between *white*, and the mixture of the seven primary colours, of which it consists, all of which are so different from it, and from one another? In like manner, from the combination of ideas, and especially very dissimilar ones, there may result ideas, which, to appearence shall be so different from the parts of which they really consist, that they shall be no more capable of being analysed by *mental reflection* than the idea of white.[2]

In contrast to this stands the analogy of the plant. It cannot be truly described as 'organic' since Hartley had no conception of the organic in the sense that Schlegel and Coleridge were to use it. A plant is a mechanism to Hartley, just as much as a man was—which is one good reason for being wary of applying the modern meaning of 'mechanism' to his system. Each individual, though bound by the mechanism of necessity to grow from the material to the spiritual, was still held to be a unique growth. Hence the importance of education.

This ambiguity in Hartley's idea of mechanical growth contains, in embryo, much of Coleridge's later concept of the 'organic'. But, as so often when discussing Coleridge's ideas, this kind of analysis demands extreme caution. Generations of

---

[1] *Observations on Man*, Vol. I, p. 75.
[2] In 'Theological and Misc. Works', ed. Rutt, p. 189.

commentators have come to grief by attempting to tie Coleridge down to one or more of his sources—often irritably concluding that his thought is 'hopelessly inconsistent'. There were, for example, by the latter part of the eighteenth century two organic analogies for growth in common circulation. The first is the embryological theory of 'preformation', or *emboîtement*, which held that not only all species, but every organism had existed right from the beginning. It has been described in these terms:

The individuals, no doubt, unlike the species, seem to increase in numbers and undergo change, but in reality this is a mere expansion or 'unfolding' (evolutio) of structures and characters that were already pre-delineated, on a minute scale of magnitude, in the primeval germs which lay encased one within another like a nest of boxes.[1]

The second is the organic 'vitalist' theory advanced as an analogy for poetic creation in England as early as 1759 by Edward Young in his *Conjectures on Original Composition*, but taken up and refined in German *Natur-Philosophie* by such figures as Schelling and the Schlegels. We may take an illustration straight from A. W. Schlegel's *Lectures* of 1808:

Form is mechanical when, through external influence, it is communicated to any material merely as an accidental addition without reference to its quality...Organical form, again, is innate; it unfolds itself from within, and acquires its determination along with the complete development of the germ. We everywhere discover such forms in nature throughout the whole range of living powers, from the crystallisation of salts and minerals to plants and flowers, and from them to the human figure.[2]

Coleridge's apparent paraphrase of this in his own lectures on Shakespeare is almost identical, and in any case too well known to need quoting here;[3] there is, however, a revealing difference between Coleridge and Schlegel which is brought out even more clearly in his distinction between an organ and a machine in *Aids to Reflection*:

not only the characteristic Shape is evolved from the invisible central power, but the material Mass itself is acquired by assimilation. The

[1] Lovejoy, *The Great Chain of Being* (Harvard, 1936), p. 243.
[2] A. W. Schlegel, *Lectures on Dramatic Art and Literature,* trans. Black (1815), Vol. ii, p. 95.
[3] *Shakespearean Criticism,* ed. Raysor (Everyman, 1960), Vol. i, p. 198.

germinal power of the Plant transmutes the fixed air and the elementary Base of Water into Grass or Leaves; and on these the Organific Principle in the Ox and the Elephant exercises an Alchemy still more stupendous.[1]

Schlegel sees no difference in kind between mineral and animal forms, Coleridge, by introducing the idea of assimilation, specifically excludes the inanimate. He repeats the vitalist position he had taken up in his *Theory of Life* in support of Abernethy against Lawrence.[2]

It is important to remember, of course, that while Hartley's vegetable determinism is not that of Young, Schlegel, or Coleridge, it cannot, equally, be that of preformation, since for Hartley the mind begins as a *tabula rasa*. The preformation theory, however, has a long history, and in the course of the nineteenth century it becomes inextricably entangled with the other theories. Symonds, for example, applied an organic analogy to the history of the Elizabethan Theatre in *Shakespear's Predecessors in the English Drama* (1884) to produce a doctrine of literary evolution which has been described as 'an unfolding of embryonic elements to which nothing can be added and which run their course with iron necessity to their predestined exhaustion'.

But even if the vestigial confusions of preformation are rigorously excluded, there still remains an ambiguity in the organic theory of growth that Coleridge never satisfactorily resolved in its own terms. In excluding Hartleian mechanism and substituting (or rather, selecting) the analogy of organism to explain growth, Coleridge found himself in danger of replacing one mechanism by another. The added concept of 'assimilation' does not alter the fact that the predetermined growth of a plant from its seed fails to allow for an active and originating power in the mind any more than vibratory mechanism. The preliminary problem, that if we live in a world of complete necessity it is impossible to alter the environment in a way not pre-ordained, had already been overcome (as well as it was ever to be overcome) by Hartley's latent vegetable analogy, with the educator as gardiner. But if one followed Young and made

[1] P. 357.
[2] Snyder, *Coleridge on Logic*, pp. 16–23.

the growth *internally* determinate, the rôle of the educator became correspondingly less important. This Coleridge could not accept on empirical grounds; it did not accord with his own experience. Its effect on his creative theory was no less alarming. At the turn of this century Walter Pater put his finger right on the problem with his classic criticism of Coleridge:

What makes his view a one-sided one is, that in it the artist has become almost a mechanical agent: instead of the most luminous and self-possessed phase of consciousness, the associative act in art or poetry is made to look like some blindly organic process of assimilation.[1]

But Coleridge's position in his lectures on Shakespeare is, I think, neither as coherent nor as final as Pater would seem to suggest. Like Hartley, Coleridge's problem of creativity is simultaneously psychological *and* religious, and from this point of view the theory of organic growth was not merely of no help, since it retained the very ambiguity it had been employed to solve, but actually aggravated the very real problem, for Coleridge, of the origin of evil. Hartley differed little from Locke in seeing this world as a ruined one where one could not expect much good. Nevertheless, he still believed that from our final spiritual heights of 'Theopathy' sufferings and evil will seem both as necessary, and as painless as shadows in a picture. In such a closed and 'Optimistic' system as his it is interesting to see how the importance of morality is reduced. Since, in the long run, Evil is so much a part of things, and since he held that 'some degree of spirituality is the necessary consequence of passing through life', moral choice could only be between limited alternatives, and the results of a wrong choice were unlikely seriously to impede the inexorable benevolence of the wheels of God This was not the Ancient Mariner's experience:

> Since then, at an uncertain hour,
> That agony returns;
> And till my ghastly tale is told,
> This heart within me burns.

[1] Pater, 'Coleridge', *Appreciations* (Macmillan, 1928); and see Abrams, *Mirror and Lamp*, p. 224.

With the rejection of Hartley's mechanism had gone too a rejection of Unitarianism, and Coleridge had returned to a doctrine of a 'Fall'—partly for reasons of orthodoxy, but primarily on intuitional grounds. In his Appendix to *The Friend* he wrote:

This one conviction, determined, as in a mould, the form and feature of my whole system in religion and morals, and even in literature. These arguments were not suggested to me by books, but forced on me by reflection on my own being, and observations on the ways of those about me...From Pascal in his closet...to the poor pensive Indian that seeks the missionary in the American wilderness, the humiliated self-examinant feels that there is evil in our nature as well as good;—an evil and a good, for a just analogy to which he questions all other natures in vain.[1]

Organic growth, as a closed system, was incapable of dealing with a personal experience of evil any more than could mechanism. While he was considering Shakespeare this problem could, to some extent, be shelved, but in his later works a theological awareness of evil—and its corollary of Grace—is central to Coleridge's thought. A truly originating power in the mind is only possible in a system that allows for genuine moral evil. It is here that we are faced with the ambiguity in Coleridge's own experience that we mentioned at the beginning of this chapter. At one level his theory of 'organic' creation (however eclectically made up from elements of Hartley, Schelling, or Schlegel) seemed to offer an account of Shakespeare's creative genius that not merely illuminated Shakespeare himself, but gave Coleridge an insight into experiences of his own that seemed analogous. At another level, however, it seemed to deny the *personal* validity of the very experiences it so satisfactorily explained, and, in addition, the reality of the religious life which in later years of opium-addiction and a sense of failure became increasingly important to him as the touchstone from which the rest of his existence acquired meaning and relevance.

In the concept of the Imagination we find developing, almost from the very beginning, an ambiguity that reflected Coleridge's own experience at this point. It was never as purely and blindly 'organic' as Pater, and many modern critics have appeared to

---

[1] *The Friend* (1844), Vol. III, Appendix 'B', pp. 312–14 (not in Bohn ed.).

suggest. If it was seen as organic in its power of 'shaping into one', it was essentially *dialectical* in its 'reconciling of opposite or discordant qualities'. Time and time again we find in his references to the Imagination that he is speaking of it at two separate levels—as if they were the same thing. In Chapter XIII of *Biographia Literaria*, for example, while ostensibly making the famous distinction between the inanimate mechanism of 'Fancy' and the vital organic action of the 'Imagination', he refers to artistic creation (the Secondary Imagination) in these terms: 'It dissolves, diffuses, dissipates, in order to recreate; or where this process is rendered impossible, yet still at all events it struggles to idealize and to unify.' To 'idealize' (even if not intended in a Platonic sense) is still an aesthetic and evaluative activity; to 'unify', on the other hand, is essentially structural. For Coleridge, the imagination was a way of bringing simultaneously into focus two otherwise unrelatable areas of experience in the act of artistic creation.

Coleridge's thought always produces its most illuminating insights when it is turning around this problem of his own creativity and mental growth. The distinction between the poet and the philosopher is, as we have seen, at best an artificial one; at worst, it can be dangerously misleading. In December 1804 we find him noting:

How far one might imagine all the association System out of a system of growth/thinking of the Brain & Soul, what we know of an embryo— one tiny particle combines with another, its like. & so lengthens & thickens.[1]

Here we see yet another example of how an organic theory of growth has been merged with that of Hartley. Though this particular application is not followed up, the concept of association continued to occupy a key place in his own peculiar mixture of speculative and empirical thought throughout his life. The mechanism of association, as he observed and defined it intuitively in himself, never ceased to fascinate him. Moreover, it was this meticulous interest in his own creative processes, rather than any philosophical reading, that turned him more and more towards a theory of the unconscious as an essential part of

[1] *Anima Poetae*, p. 104; *Notebooks*, Vol. II, 2373.

association. Less than a month after the previous note we find this comment:

learnt not always, at all, & seldom *harshly* to chide, those conceits of words which are analogous to sudden fleeting affinities of mind/even as in a dance touch & join & off again, & rejoin your partner that leads down with you the whole dance spite of these occasional off-starts, all still not merely conform to, but (of, and) in, & forming, the delicious harmony—Shakespeare is not a 1000th part so faulty as the 000 believe him/[1]

The idea of musical harmony had been used by Priestley to express the continuity of the mind's processes,[2] but Coleridge seems to have taken it up here (as he does elsewhere) in its more specialized musical sense of the structure of the chords, as distinct from the melody—and only from there to its more general implication of the total unity of the dance and the music. In its strict musical sense the word came increasingly to offer Coleridge an analogy for the apparently endless possibilities of association. Yet, just as we found with the Imagination, Coleridge seems to be thinking at two levels simultaneously. Structurally, the idea of association as a harmony on, or below the fringes of consciousness is an important insight into the 'mechanism' of human thought; simultaneously, however, he is asserting harmony as a *value*. Music's double appeal to intellect and emotions offered a dim analogy for the unity which Coleridge felt, but found such difficulty in formulating satisfactorily. In his *Philosophical Lectures* he affirms again that music evokes and creates 'JOY...It is in all its forms still Joy.'[3] Here, in this passage from his notebooks, however, it is merged into the traditional Christian symbol of the great dance of creation— applied now not to the external world, but in the typically Romantic process of 'internalization', to the 'still more wonderful world within'—the working of the mind itself. That he saw in this a connection with the way Shakespeare's mind works only serves to stress the creative importance of these 'sudden fleeting analogies of mind'. In a letter to Southey already quoted, that of 7 August 1803, Coleridge goes on from his assertion that

[1] *Ibid.* p. 108; *ibid.* 2396.
[2] *Disquisitions on Matter and Spirit*, 'Works', ed. Rutt, p. 284.
[3] *Philosophical Lectures*, ed. Coburn (Routledge, 1949), p. 168.

'association depends in a much greater degree on the recurrence of resembling states of Feeling...' 'Believe me, Southey! a metaphysical solution, that does not tell you something in the heart is grievously to be suspected as apocryphal...' It is man himself who is a harmony.

During that same year, if we are to accept Alice Snyder's tentative dating, Coleridge was at work on his unpublished 'Outlines of the History of Logic'. Here he approached the process of association from another angle:

> tho' in every Syllogism I do in reality repeat the same thing in other words, yet at the same time I do something more; I recall to my memory a multitude of other facts and with them the important remembrance that they all have some one or more property in common. The phrase Identical Proposition should be applied exclusively to those propositions which occasion in the mind no recapitulation and as it were no refreshment of its knowledge and of the operations by which it both acquires and retains it. If you could take away from the human mind the power and habit of classing its experiences according to its perceptions of likeness you would sink it below the level of brutes.[1]

Here his insight into the nature of association is carried a step further. No two formulations of the same thing in different words can be exactly alike simply because of the associative overtones of the words themselves. We are familiar with William Empson on this point in *Seven Types of Ambiguity*. Coleridge described it as the power to classify experiences, but what he is actually arguing for is the uniqueness of every statement. He sees what Hartley never dreamed of: that there is no 'normal' associative train of ideas; every experience can be classified in an endless variety of ways according to how we have come to it. The process by which the mind acquires and retains knowledge is an integral part of that knowledge itself. Nor, it is worth noticing, is this entirely due to the ambiguity and associative undertones of words themselves. Precisely the same thing occurs in music; as we have seen, one cannot separate the individual notes from the 'meaning' of the whole. Association is thus seen here as one of the most important—and distinctively human—attributes of our thinking. The mind does not work by 'barren propositions'. Coleridge's dissatisfaction with formal

[1] Snyder, *Coleridge on Logic*, p. 54.

logic was that it was not exact enough: it failed to harness the full richness of human reason.

This may help us to see why his 'Logic' was to prove so abortive. As we have suggested, it was only by his concept of the Imagination that he seems able really to come to grips with his own deeply ambiguous experience, and to retain within a single formulation two apparently mutually exclusive levels of awareness. The advantage of his twofold concept of the Imagination is that he was able to envisage opposite and dialectical energies within a total organic structure. It is of course typical that having arrived at this insight by a kind of 'empirical intuition', Coleridge should then insist that it was not merely a 'fact of mind', but also a law of the physical universe. This, I suspect, is the reason for the kind of obscure utterance, like this, that we find not merely in *The Friend*, but throughout his later work: 'Every power in nature and spirit must evolve an opposite, as the sole means and condition of its manifestation: and all opposition is a tendency to reunion. This is the universal law of polarity...[1]

In the development of Coleridge's thought we find that the centre of his attention gradually moves from trying to account for the full complexity of association as he encountered it in himself, to viewing it as the *means* by which his mind apprehended symbols. We tend, as I have done with *Frost at Midnight* here in this chapter, to trace the interaction of organic growth and dialectical development in terms of the symbols through which Coleridge experienced them, without remembering that his concept of symbolism was itself based on this same unresolved tension. A symbol, in the sense in which Coleridge used the word, was the means by which we create and experience 'reality'. In it we find the same ambiguity between the actual method of growth, and the development of personal consciousness that accompanies it. The final and satisfactory outworking of the principle of the Imagination was in the vision of the human mind as an essentially symbolic, and symbolizing instrument—in an ever-unfolding growth of consciousness. In this, as we shall see, Coleridge was at last able to find an acceptable account of what he had perceived so clearly in *Frost at Midnight*.

[1] *The Friend*, p. 55.

3

Imagination: the Active Mind

We have already seen something of the sheer complexity of the concept of 'Imagination' for Coleridge. Complexity, however, is not vagueness. His idea of the Imagination was both brilliant and subtle—much more so than many of his critics, then or now, were prepared to concede. A good deal of confusion and misunderstanding has arisen simply because Coleridge's thought is rooted consistently in his own personal development, and not in the philosophy of Kant, Schelling, and Fichte—to whose vocabulary he was always so freely willing to help himself. As we have seen, Mill misunderstood Coleridge—and I believe he did so not primarily from any 'philosophic' weakness, but from his failure to understand the subtlety of Coleridge's response to a crisis fundamentally similar to his own. Mill's failure, in the last resort, was an empirical and intuitional one. Both he and Coleridge came to use the word 'Imagination' when they wished to describe the joy they felt in seeing beauty in the world around them, but each clearly means to say by this something quite different. Before we go any farther, therefore, we shall have to consider in some detail what Coleridge, and Wordsworth, came to understand by the word, and how this differentiates them from its other users.

Coleridge's concept of the Imagination was fundamentally a psychological theory. But, as we saw in the last chapter, what he meant by 'psychology' was different not in degree, but in kind from Hartley or Locke. He could only account satisfactorily for his own psychological processes by focusing simultaneously on two separate levels of his experience. The 'mind' was to him both organism *and* consciousness. Thus in *Biographia Literaria* we find him apparently trying to define the mechanism of sense-perception in terms of 'creation'. Imagination is, for Coleridge, the activity by which the mind achieves all outward contact—and is therefore, of course, also the activity by which the mind

71

sees itself. It is thus, by inference, the basis of all self-conscious reflection. The Primary Imagination he calls the 'agent of all human perception'—which is seen in the human mind as a repetition, or parallel, of the activity of God himself in Creation. The Secondary Imagination is unifying and consciously creative (in the artistic sense), and differs 'only in *degree* and in the *mode* of its operation' from the Primary. Coleridge is at pains to be explicit here. He defines both perception *and* artistic organization in terms of God's original act of Creation: 'Let there be...and it was so.'

Now at least three different ways of relating perception and creative Imagination have been attributed to Wordsworth and Coleridge. The first is also, perhaps, the oldest: that Wordsworth was fundamentally at odds with Coleridge by remaining throughout his career a thorough-going Hartleian. This view was very convincingly re-argued in 1922 by Professor Arthur Beatty in his book *William Wordsworth—his Doctrine and Art in their Historical Relations*. Beatty traces in Wordsworth's poetry a consistently Hartleian framework of thought: sensations are first received by the senses, and then interpreted by the 'mind', an organ conceived as neutral and mechanical like the senses, but separate from them in function, whose job is to interpret or ruminate on the information so provided. 'Imagination' in this scheme of things, if not purely the second of the seven stages leading man by slow degrees from the mechanical passivity of the senses to the spiritual heights of Moral Sense, still consists of little more than the capacity to reproduce, by combination and association, unseen images in the 'mind's eye'. This, broadly, assumes what E. H. Gombrich calls the idea of 'the image on the retina'—that like a mirror or a photographic plate the eye is neutral territory between the object perceived on the one hand, and the mind perceiving on the other.[1] Hardly surprisingly, Beatty's case is as difficult to prove as it is to disprove from the evidence of Wordsworth's poetry. The famous passage in Book II of *The Prelude* (1805), for example, describes the awakening and growth of the child's mind (lines 240–60), and was omitted in the 1850 version because of its supposedly 'Hartleian' tone. It is actually a close piece of empirical

[1] *Art and Illusion*, p. 252.

observation—and shows Wordsworth's powers of interpretative description at their very best. As such it can, of course, be read equally well as Coleridgean or Kantian. All it is possible for Beatty to show in fact is that the influence of certain Hartleian ways of thinking lingered in Wordsworth (as we have seen they did in Coleridge) long after the vibratory and associative mechanisms had been thrown overboard. It is also, moreover, worth observing the obvious: that if Wordsworth had really remained so consistent a Hartleian during his great decade up until 1810, Coleridge would hardly have been likely to have missed the fact. In his poem *To William Wordsworth*, 'composed on the night after his recitation of a poem on the growth of the individual mind' in January 1807, Coleridge in fact, as we shall see in a later chapter, gives an analysis of *The Prelude* that assumes a very close complementarity between Wordsworth's idea of the Imagination and his own. Nor does his carefully selective criticism of Wordsworth in *Biographia Literaria* substantially alter this position.

A second view finds its typical expression in Sir Maurice Bowra's *The Romantic Imagination*. He assumed that all the principal English Romantics—including Blake and Coleridge—saw the 'Imagination' as the means by which they perceived a private and visionary world which had no necessary connection with their material surroundings. Such an 'Imagination', clearly, might take a wide variety of forms. In Shelley, for example, one might interpret it as a political vision. Keats, on the other hand, could write to Bailey in November 1817:

I am certain of nothing but of the holiness of the Heart's affections and the truth of Imagination. What the Imagination seizes as Beauty must be truth—whether it existed before or not—for I have the same idea of all our passions as of Love; they are all, in their sublime, creative of essential Beauty.

Undoubtedly this would also be 'creative' in John Stuart Mill's sense—and, seemingly, in I. A. Richards's—but *not* in the sense of either Coleridge or Wordsworth.[1] Their problems were

---

[1] Abrams (*Mirror and Lamp*, p. 313) makes a similar distinction between the two different theories of the Imagination on the slightly different grounds that, in contrast to Blake and Shelley, who 'make poetic imagination the organ of intuition beyond experience', Wordsworth and Coleridge remain in the English

different. Such a view of creativity, if pressed home, relegates ordinary sense-perception to the 'image on the retina' no less firmly than dogmatic Hartleianism, and supports the very dualism between the mind and the external world that Coleridge was so explicitly at pains to avoid.

Coleridge insists in *Biographia Literaria* that artistic creativity is fundamentally the same as everyday sense-perception, differing from it only in degree. It is because of this that he lays such stress on the Imagination as being 'creative'. In this he seems to be following in outline Kant and Schelling. This is the third view—argued perhaps most fully by D. G. James in *Scepticism and Poetry*.[1] The Imagination is 'creative' because sense-perception and its interpretation were felt as a single and indivisible act in which the mind works from prehended wholes, or 'schemata', and, as it were, 'reads' external stimuli in terms of these pre-existing schemata, modifying the schema as necessary until it can be correlated with the object 'read'. Similarly, as in reading, the mind does not perceive the individual letters— for instance, patches of colour, gradiations of tone, etc.—but perceives the external world in wholes, which (to continue the reading analogy) are like 'words' or 'sentences'. Thus in encountering, for example, an unfamiliar word, or scene, the mind will read it as the nearest known one—or modify it until the known approximates more nearly to the unknown. This view, of course, was to become the foundation of our modern science of perception. For Coleridge, following this model, all contact between the external world and the sense pre-supposed an imaginative 'leap' by the mind, which remained at the same time always open to modification, and therefore renewal, from nature. He applied the word 'creative' to perception in this context to emphasize it as a process of active mental organization: neither simple projection on the one hand, nor passive sense-reception on the other, but always a razor-edge balance

---

empirical tradition, making 'no special cognitive claims for poetry'. While agreeing with this, I feel that by ignoring this change in the meaning of 'creativity', and by describing the Imagination as merely *one* of the 'powers of the mind' for creating poetry, Abrams suggests that he himself does not fully appreciate Coleridge's concept of the Imagination as the total unified activity of the mind.

[1] Pp. 18–24.

between the two. It was by means of this model that Coleridge and Wordsworth were able to feel their own perceptions as an organic and living co-operation between man and nature—as in the case of the rainbow, not a mystical affirmation, but a scientific fact.

The vexed question of Coleridge's exact debt to German philosophy in formulating this concept of the Imagination is almost impossible to assess, since there is a change not so much of ideas, as of criteria. Underneath the unsystematic and eclectic borrowings from Kant and Schelling the attitude to the mind remains fundamentally different from that of either. To explore this change, and to see it in perspective, we need to remember what Coleridge was trying to do. When, for instance, in *Biographia Literaria* Coleridge stresses that artistic creation and sense-perception are both aspects of the Imagination, he is rejecting Schelling's idea that the 'philosophic' (that is, the creative, or Secondary) Imagination is a gift of the favoured few. Again we are confronted by his attempt to focus on two simultaneous and ambiguous levels of experience. For Coleridge, the Secondary Imagination was the essential human power by which man perceived God—by a process parallel to that by which he perceived nature.[1]

The concept of the Imagination as a primary factor in all human knowledge is, of course, derived from Kant's *Critique of Pure Reason*. The mind, according to Kant, takes the 'manifold of sensation'—a mass of unrelated sounds, colours, etc.—and synthesizes them as an ordered world of objects. Of this world we can know nothing directly, and the sensations are only sketchy clues to whatever it may be like. Our minds transcend this impressionistic evidence to *create* a unified whole from it that is greater than the mere sum of its parts. In this creative synthesis of appearances, Kant divided human perception into three elements: 'sensibility', 'imagination', and 'understanding'. Sensibility is our intuitive and *a priori* awareness of time and space—so that colours, sounds, and the whole random range of sense-impressions are perceived as part of a spatio-temporal order (in a way that mechanical-associationist psychology had

---

[1] See Shawcross, Introduction to *Biographia Literaria*, pp. lxix–lxxiv; and Mackenzie, *Organic Unity in Coleridge*.

never been able satisfactorily to demonstrate). Both the 'Imagination' and the 'understanding', however, were also necessary parts of our perception of things. By 'understanding' Kant means the discursive or empirical intelligence (concerned with the everyday mechanical necessity of our material lives), which is distinguished from the abstract and spiritual insight of 'reason' (the area of our moral freedom and awareness of God). The 'Imagination' was the source of the 'schemata' which were applied to perception by both the understanding and the sensibility. Their precise relationship, however, remains a matter of dispute. To explain, for example, how we arrive from an unrelated mass of sense-data at a direct awareness of a world of individual things, Kant seems to have come to think of the Imagination as the common root from which his sensibility and understanding both sprang—though he continued to insist that no knowledge is possible without the two latter powers.[1]

One might be forgiven for expecting that the question of what Coleridge actually did borrow from all this would be considerably easier to settle than the question of how he used his borrowings. Yet on the former there is singularly little agreement. D. G. James has attributed Coleridge's doctrine of Imagination largely to Kant; René Wellek, however, finds little connection between it and Kant, and agrees with Shawcross in attributing most of it to Schelling: 'Of all the major writings of Coleridge least of Kant's immediate influence can be found in the *Biographia Literaria*, though there Coleridge gave an elaborate account of his relations to German philosophy.'[2] In his subsequent discussion of the ideas of *Biographia Literaria* he proceeds to omit all reference to the Imagination at all. There is something very ironic in the unanimity with which philosophical critics have pronounced Coleridge's thought to be plagiarized from the German, and their total inability to agree on what was plagiarized, or from whom. Wellek's answer to this is revealing in more ways than one. Complaining of the lack of any personal *style* in Coleridge's philosophical thought, he writes:

Whenever he makes a sustained effort to think abstractly his fundamental weakness is coming out...Coleridge has little insight into the

[1] *Critique*, p. 146; *Commentary* (Kemp Smith), p. 225.
[2] *Immanuel Kant in England*, p. 114.

incompatibility of different trends of thought...It is not the fact that several central passages in Coleridge are borrowed or influenced by other thinkers; it is rather the circumstance that these adaptations of others are so heterogeneous, incoherent and even contradictory which makes the study of Coleridge's philosophy ultimately so futile.[1]

We may well take this as a warning (if one were needed) to draw as careful a distinction as possible in such doubtful terrain between Coleridge's powers as a systematic philosopher, and his unsystematic psychological insights. Yet there remains something very crude and over-simplified in such a division. We can sympathize with the exasperation of the rigorous thinker, but the inescapable fact remains that the study of Coleridge's thought is very far from futile. His concept of the Imagination is in no sense an unsystematic insight; it is, as we have seen, a very sensitive and systematized codification of his own experience of creativity. The question of how he used his borrowings, difficult as it is, is very much easier to answer than the question of what he borrowed. His plagiarisms do not remain the fixed and fundamentally incompatible units of thought that Wellek seems to assume. There is, instead, an almost irresistible internal pressure in Coleridge's ideas so to shift and change their meaning in response to certain 'organizing insights' that the scholarly process of identifying and labelling them becomes transparently useless.

To take another example: of Kant's three functions of the 'Imagination', the 'reproductive', the 'productive', and the 'aesthetic', the first is *nearly* the same as Coleridge's 'fancy', in that it remains a mechanism; the second, the 'productive', is a spontaneous and active power, and *might* be said to correspond to the Primary Imagination of Coleridge; while the last, the 'aesthetic', which transforms the objects into material for a possible act of cognition, *may* be said to correspond to the Secondary Imagination.[2] Like the other two, the correspondence is not exact: Coleridge's Secondary Imagination has, for instance, a much greater influence than Kant could have allowed. What we are left with is an apparently baffling amalgam of con-

---

[1] *Ibid.* p. 67.
[2] Mackenzie, *Organic Unity*, pp. 16–20; see also Shawcross, Introduction to *Biographia Literaria*, for a very similar argument.

cepts and theories that are neither original, nor a clear and useful application of Kantian philosophy—yet which, nevertheless, represent one of the greatest critical insights of the Romantic movement.

The answer, of course, is that Coleridge was never really concerned with the same problems as Kant or Schelling at all. In this sense he was not talking about the same thing. Like Wordsworth, he was constantly struggling to articulate what he already knew, existentially, in his own experience. Other people's systems were useful to him in so far as they served to illuminate his feelings of joy and dereliction—and if they did offer an insight into these conditions of his own creativity, then their compatibility was irrelevant. In December 1804 he made the famous note:

In the Preface of my Metaphys. Works I should say—Once & all read Tetens, Kant, Fichte, &—& there you will trace or if you are on the hunt, track me. Why then not acknowledge your obligations step by step? Because I could not do in a multitude of glaring resemblances without a lie/for they had been mine, formed, & full formed in my own mind, before I had ever heard of these Writers, because to have fixed on the partic. instances in which I have really been indebted to these Writers would have been very hard, if possible, to me who read for truth & self-satisfaction, not to make a book, & who always rejoiced & was jubilant when I found my own ideas well expressed already by others (& would have looked like a *trick*, to skulk there not quoted) & lastly, let me say, because (I am proud perhaps but) I seem to know, that much of the matter remains my own, and that the Soul is *mine*. I fear not him for a Critic who can confound a Fellow-thinker with a Compiler.[1]

The trouble is that Coleridge's thinking ws frequently *not* fellow to the philosophy from which he borrowed, and in Welleck's sense it sometimes *was* mere compiling. Yet I think this same note goes a very long way to explain why. Here, as so often elsewhere, there seems to be a semi-Platonic 'recognition' theory underlying his method of reading and acquiring knowledge. He does not seem to be reading Kant and Fichte to understand what *they* have to say, but to understand what he already (in some sense) *knows*. He scythes through abstruse

[1] *Anima Poetae*, p. 106; *Notebooks*, Vol. ii, 2375.

German philosophy in search of himself. If we want, for example, to understand the distinction between Fancy, and the two modes of Imagination, we must turn to *Dejection* rather than to the Germans. Over and over again we find that it is only in his poems that he can adequately relate the central ideas with which he so vainly seems to be struggling in his prose. What he really wanted to say was simply not capable of expression in the form of limited and defined reasoning that Kant laid down. Even in his unpublished 'Logic' Coleridge is struggling to produce a formulation that will do justice to the richness of association and development in every concept, without sacrificing rigour or precision. Almost inevitably we find him turning from such concepts towards symbols to convey what he felt—and as we look back on this movement we can recognize that he had always tended to use his concepts as if they had been symbols. If, for example, we look back at the way he attempts to define the Imagination in *Biographia Literaria*, in terms both of organic unity and creation, it is astonishing to notice how closely the two levels of this method of 'definition' correspond with his definition of a symbol in *The Statesman's Manual*, which, we recall, involves bringing into simultaneous focus the material and temporal, and the spiritual and eternal. It is also typical of Coleridge that *The Statesman's Manual*—written at almost exactly the same time as *Biographia Literaria*—should, in fact, be about the Bible. If we call him unsystematic, we must also come to terms with the fact that in him, more than any other thinker of his day, there is to be found a central consistency and unity between his ideas on literature, politics, education, and religion. As always, the nexus seems to be his own creativity. The need to explain this very phenomenon of his own inner intuitive unity explains why for him 'reason' is dependent on his psychological insight—and not vice versa, as in Kant.

Hartley's theories failed to dominate Coleridge's thinking at any one time. His concentration moved from necessity to association, and at one time we find him apparently supporting Hartley and Berkeley simultaneously.[1] Similarly, Coleridge used Kant primarily to suit his personal needs of the moment: helping

[1] Lawrence Hanson, *The Life of Samuel Taylor Coleridge* (Allen and Unwin, 1938), p. 296.

him, for example, in 1800 to see where he parted company from Hartley. To try and establish in terms of Kant's or Schelling's 'Imagination' what Coleridge is saying in *Dejection*, when he laments the suspension of his 'shaping spirit of imagination', would be, I think, (even supposing it possible) a quite meaningless exercise. Even to try and put it in his own terms, and say, for instance, that he feels his Secondary Imagination is in abeyance, leaving his mind incapable of a creative response, does *not* adequately interpret:

> I see, not feel, how beautiful they are...

—the complaint that perception no longer gives any confirmation of *value*, as J. S. Mill was to discover in his breakdown. Coleridge's problem is that here he is no longer able to fuse the two levels of his experience.

It is interesting to see how little Wordsworth's account of the Imagination, as the prime instrument of perception, differs from that of his friend during these years. In Book II of the 1805 *Prelude* he describes, in almost an exact parallel to Coleridge, the growth of the boy's Imagination:

> such a Being lives,
> An inmate of this *active* universe;
> From nature largely he receives; nor so
> Is satisfied, but largely gives again,
> For feeling has to him imparted strength,
> And powerful in all sentiments of grief,
> Of exultation, fear, and joy, his mind,
> Even as an agent of the one great mind,
> Creates, creator and receiver both,
> Working in alliance with the works
> Which it beholds.—Such, verily, is the first
> Poetic spirit of our human life...
>
> (265–76)

The 'creative' power of the mind in perception is an echo of God's in Creation (like 'an agent of the one great mind Creates...'). Whether such a 'God' more resembles that of Berkeley or Kant would, I think, have troubled Wordsworth even less than Coleridge; like him, he is concerned with explaining two levels in his own poetic experience. The alliance between man and nature, where he 'receives' and 'gives again', is the same razor-edge balance that we have found already in Wordsworth when he sees the rainbow—as well as in both Coleridge and his German reading. Significantly, however, whereas Coleridge describes the process as one of giving and receiving, for Wordsworth it is receiving and giving. We shall have more to say about this inversion later. Here, what is important is the creative power that Wordsworth draws from 'exultation', 'fear', and 'joy'; this 'poetic spirit', he stresses, is the same as that by which all human perception is made.

As with Coleridge's formulations, this statement of Wordsworth's reveals a view of the Imagination that in its mature form is fundamentally different in kind both from that of contemporary German philosophy, *and* from that of the eighteenth-century English thinkers. This is a point, however, on which we must be careful. Just as Coleridge was liable to use the terminology of German writers in exploring his own creativity, so he and Wordsworth continued to use not only the Hartleian language of association but also words and ideas taken from a minority tradition of British writers who stood outside the massive orthodoxy of Locke. There were, for instance, a variety of concepts of the 'Imagination' current in the latter half of the eighteenth century in Britain, besides that of Hartley. Edward Search's *The Light of Nature Pursued*, published in 1768, was well known to Coleridge—who had even proposed to write a Preface to Hazlitt's projected reprint of it.[1] Edward Search was the pen-name of a Surrey magistrate named Abraham Tucker. Though he is prepared to claim the authority of Locke, he advances in fact the most un-Lockeian argument that we do in effect experience two opposing qualities in the mind, one active, the other passive:

Thus it appears evidently that we are passive in sensation of every kind: but the matter is not quite so plain in the business of reflexion, which the mind seems to carry on entirely upon its own fund without aid of the body, without intervention of the senses or impression of anything external, acting solely and immediately in and upon itself. (p. 7)

[1] See J. A. Appleyard, *Coleridge's Philosophy of Literature* (Harvard, 1965), pp. 103–4.

By itself, and if we skate over the implications of the last clause, this might still be a re-statement of Hartleianism. But if we combine this with Search's description of the 'Imagination', which, for him, was a part of the active faculty, its appeal to Coleridge is clear. Search compares the Imagination with a rushing river which cannot be dammed: 'For imagination will always be at work, and if restrained from roving in all that variety of sallies it would make of its own accord, it will strike into any passages remaining open...' (p. 12). The use of such images for intuitive experience are clear symptoms of a total change in philosophic outlook in which Coleridge was to be a key figure, but Search's 'active' quality of mind is still a very long way from Coleridge's creative Imagination.

Alexander Gerard, a Scot, in his *Essay on Genius* in 1774 approached the 'Imagination' from a different angle, declaring that the hypothesizing power of Imagination was an essential part of all scientific discovery. He even went on to suggest a rudimentary distinction between imagination and fancy. 'Indigested notions, contradictory positions, trite and vulgar sentiments', and even 'association', are all, according to him, the products of fancy. In contrast, 'genius' is closely (if vaguely) linked with the imagination, but its associative power is not different in kind, but merely efficient to a much greater degree. Fancy assembles diverse materials; imagination uses them at the right moment. But this power of genius *is* essentially organic— and all but 'esemplastic', or 'shaping into one' in Coleridge's sense:

When a vegetable draws in moisture from the earth, nature, by the same action by which it draws it in, and at the same time, converts it into the nourishment of the plant... In like manner, genius arranges its ideas by the same operation, and almost at the same time, that it collects them. (pp. 63–4)

Nevertheless, the 'activity' of the mind—even in genius—is confined firmly to the arrangement and association of sensations. We are still left with a theory of the image-on-the-retina that separates the mind of the perceiver from the external world perceived.

The psychological revolution of Coleridge and Wordsworth

is actually far greater than its terminology would immediately suggest. We have noticed how the 'happiness' which motivated John Gay's 'associationism' is neither the 'happiness' of Bentham, nor the 'joy' of Coleridge—nor, indeed, is his 'associationism' the same as Hartley's. But shifts of sense like these are small compared with the complete transformation of meaning that we find in the words used to describe the new concept of the creative mind. When Hartley, for example, writes of 'the springs of action' in man, he is describing a mechanism: the hairspring of the clockwork man, built to seek the happiness preset by the spiritual engineering of the Great Clockmaker.[1] When Coleridge uses a similar phrase, he is using it not merely at a different level, but with a totally different image in mind: the spontaneous welling-up of emotion, like a spring of water from the unconscious—'the *Joy*...of which the Heart is full as of a deep and quiet fountain overflowing insensibly, or the gladness of Joy, when the fountain overflows ebullient',[2] a direct contrast with his overtly mechanistic 'mainspring of the feelings'.[3] Such a revolution of meaning within a stock metaphor is partly symptomatic, and partly itself creative of the new attitude to the mind.[4] The kind of *pressure* suggested by a spring of water is utterly different from that suggested by the tension of a mainspring. For Coleridge wells and springs irresistably suggested depth. The mind of man is essentially solitary and hidden: 'Man exists herein to himself & to God alone/—Yea, in how much only to God—how much lies *below* his own consciousness.'[5] In *Aids to Reflection* Coleridge elaborates this point: 'The lowest depth that the light of our Consciousness can visit even with a doubtful glimmering, is still at an unknown distance from the ground.'[6] The spontaneous overflow of powerful feelings is the result not of a tightly wound watch-spring, but of pressures so

---

[1] *Observations on Man*, Vol. I, p. 506.
[2] *Anima Poetae*, p. 84; *Notebooks*, Vol. II, 2279.
[3] For example, *Notes on Shakespeare* (Raysor), Vol. I, p. 56.
[4] See Owen Barfield, *History in English Words* (Faber, 1962). pp. 182–3 on the widespread use of this image in the eighteenth century.
[5] *Anima Poetae*, p. 31; *Notebooks*, Vol. I, 1554.
[6] P. 60. 'Ground' may be used here in its original sense of 'the lowest part or downward limit of anything' (*O.E.D.*) or alternatively, as sea or water image (i.e. peering down into the depths), in which case: 'the solid bottom or earth underlying the sea' (*O.E.D.*).

profound and unknowable that we can only guess at them by the force with which they break surface. The change in the meaning of the word 'spring' in Coleridge's psychological vocabulary represents a movement from mechanism, to a theory of the unconscious. With this, 'creativity', and its typical expression, 'genius', take on a new meaning. We can see at last the real gulf that lies between Alexander Gerard, and Wordsworth or Coleridge. In his essay 'On Poesy or Art' Coleridge writes:

In every work of art there is a reconcilement of the external with the internal; the conscious is so impressed on the unconscious as to appear in it; as compare mere letters inscribed on a tomb with figures themselves constituting the tomb. He who combines the two is the man of genius; and for that reason he must partake of both. Hence there is in genius itself an unconscious activity; nay, that is the genius of the man of genius.[1]

It was Wordsworth, in his description of the chasm in the moonlit clouds on Snowdon in Book XIII of *The Prelude*, who had symbolized what Coleridge is here struggling to conceptualize.

But the new 'well' or 'spring' image of the creative mind brings with it more than a theory of the unconscious—revolutionary as that was to prove. If we conceive the Imagination as *creating* perception by means of 'schemata', and applying them to the external world, we must expect a similar process when it intuitively perceives the internal activity of the mind itself. Hence the new poetic symbols of the mind—the spring, the cloud-covered mountain, and finally, the Brocken-spectre—became vitally important, since they offered Coleridge and Wordsworth the schemata by which they were to observe the workings of their own creative processes. They became the means of self-consciousness. A long and bitterly self-analytical note of Coleridge's in April 1805 concludes with this remarkable image:

Thought and Reality two distinct corresponding Sounds, of which no man can say positively which is the Voice and which the Echo. O the beautiful Fountain or natural Well at Upper Stowey...The images of the weeds which hung down from its sides, appeared as plants growing

[1] *Biographia Literaria*, Vol. II, p. 258.

up, straight and upright, among the water weeds that really grew from
the bottom/& so vivid was the Image, that for some moments & not
until after I had disturbed the water, did I perceive that their roots
were not neighbours, & they side-by-side companions. So—even then
I said—so are the happy man's *Thoughts* and *Things*—[1]

The fact that this was written while he was in Malta is important—it is an image recollected in tranquility. It is chosen and
used as carefully as any of the retrospective images of boyhood in
The Prelude. What is so interesting here, of course, is that
Coleridge has brought his developing theory of the Imagination
(voice and echo/thoughts and things/schema and reality) together with the symbol of the spring, to illustrate the ambiguity
of his own attempts at self-analysis. It illustrates as well as anything we have seen the unbridgeable gap between the old
psychology and the new. While the 'mind' was thought of as
passive and mechanical, in the Lock–Hartley tradition, with no
discontinuity between its mechanism and consciousness, it
could be studied as one might study any other external phenomenon. As a mechanism, it was possible to create a science of its
study—and to consider Hartley in the light of his own dream as
'the Newton of the mind'. But the psychological revolution of
Coleridge's active, creative mind, by the same stroke with
which it had solved his first problem, suggesting a new unity
between the different levels of his experience, had opened up a
second, and rendered the old methodology totally useless. The
mind becomes a mirror. The hypothesis or method used will
determine the result. In looking down into the deep well of the
mind we darken and change what we are looking at, even as we
try to distinguish between the 'reality' and the 'reflection'—
indeed, in these circumstances, can there be said to be a 'reality'
independent of what we see? 'The chameleon darkens in the
shade of him who bends over it to ascertain its colours.'[2] It is
here, it seems to me, precisely at this threat of a complete stale-
mate at the methodological level, that the concept of the
Imagination ceases to be a revolutionary psychological theory,
and becomes, for Coleridge, an aesthetic one. There is a very

[1] *Anima Poetae*, p. 143; *Notebooks*, Vol. ii, 2557.
[2] *Aids to Reflection*, p. 70.

strong tendency in Romantic criticism—and not only that of
Coleridge and Wordsworth—to shift attention from the work of
art itself, to the mind of the artist who produced it. In his Preface to the *Lyrical Ballads* Wordsworth explains what he intends in his poetry by answering the question 'What is a poet?'
Behind the apparently haphazard arrangement of *Biographia
Literaria*, with all its philosophic and psychological trappings,
lies Coleridge's determination to try and work out why his
friend Wordsworth, despite so much in him that was seemingly
'unpoetic', was unquestionably a great poet.[1] Such a shift in
critical attention is what one would expect if one believed in the
primacy of the mind over the material world. What is less
obvious is the corollary—that if one believes that the mind is
'creative' in this sense, the actual growth of the mind is of
central importance to poetic theory. For example, *Dejection* is
both a deliberately constructed 'work of art', and, at the same
time, an organic process of mind, recapitulating and showing us
the whole mode of Coleridge's poetic development. Wordsworth, of course, is doing the same thing in his epigramatic 'My
heart leaps up when I behold/A rainbow in the sky'. More
obviously, *The Prelude* is also an extended version of the same.
In Book IV, for example, Wordsworth uses the symbol of a
lake for the depths of his own mind:

> As one who hangs down-bending from the side
> Of a slow-moving Boat, upon the breast
> Of a still water, solacing himself
> With such discoveries as his eye can make,
> Beneath him, in the bottom of the deeps,
> Sees many beauteous sights, weeds, fishes, flowers,
> Grots, pebbles, roots of trees, and fancies more;
> Yet often is perplex'd, and cannot part
> The shadow from the substance, rocks and sky
> Mountains and clouds, from that which is indeed
> The region, and the things which there abide
> In their true dwelling; now is crossed by gleam
> Of his own image, by a sunbeam now,
> And motions that are sent he knows not whence,

[1] See both George Whalley's 'The Integrity of "Biographia Literaria"', *Essays
And Studies* (1953), and Hort, 'Coleridge', *Cambridge Essays*, Vol. II.

Impediments that make his task more sweet;
—Such pleasant office have we long pursued
Incumbent o'er the surface of past time
With like success...

(247–64)

Written probably in 1804—just the year before Coleridge's example of the well at Upper Stowey—the obvious parallels with it are striking: looking down into the weeds and reflections of the still water he is 'perplex'd', and 'cannot part/The shadow from the substance'. But the symbol is not identical to that of Coleridge's well. This is specifically an image of time as well as depth. The 'bottom of the deeps' does indeed represent the depth that Wordsworth feels in his own mind, but here it is explicitly the *memory* of his past life. The beauty and fear that fostered Wordsworth, as he tells us, in his boyhood, are now the schemata by which he reads his memory and so feels its renovating power. His memory is shaped and ordered even by the very act of remembering.

We have already noted the curious aspect of the attitude to growth shown by Wordsworth in *The Daffodils*, where the memory of past insight, and consciousness, is essential to the continuation of it in the future. In Book VII of *The Prelude* Wordsworth gives an even more remarkable image of how he sees this, as it were, dialectical function of the poem in the poet's growth:

Amid the moving pageant, 'twas my chance
Abruptly to be smitten with the view
Of a blind beggar, who, with upright face,
Stood propp'd against a Wall, upon his Chest
Wearing a written paper, to explain
The story of the Man, and who he was.
My mind did at this spectacle turn round
As with the might of waters, and it seem'd
To me that in this Label was a type
Or emblem, of the utmost that we know,
Both of ourselves and of the universe...

(609–19)

Man is blind: bound to the present so that he can see directly neither past nor future; locked in himself so that he can know nothing of 'things in themselves', but only as they may seem to him through his senses. As we shall see, Coleridge was to use a very similar image of the human situation in his late poem *Limbo*. Here man's overwhelming need is to find an image, or schema, of himself ('the story of the Man, and who he was') and to discover himself by the act of hanging a label on his chest. The perception of self is as much a creative act of the Imagination as the perception of others, or the world at large. Now, as Wordsworth himself realized here, this is exactly what he was doing by writing his autobiographical poem *The Prelude*. The poem was an essential part of Wordsworth's own mental growth, since it was the act by which he defined himself as a poet and so established his relationship with the rest of the world— reading back into his past to *create* the present. *The Prelude* is an attempt to see—and Wordsworth accepts the startling paradox that in this sense all sight is like a blind man hanging a label around his own neck for others to read. In the shock of self-conscious recognition, when Wordsworth suddenly sees this ('My mind did at this spectacle turn round/As with the might of waters,') his symbol is of the irresistible movement of a river. The labelling of the poet, as he recognizes it here, is the definitive act of the Imagination. Created by the active mind from past experiences, it opens up for him, by a constant process of modification and renewal from nature, the possibility of new growth, so that for Wordsworth and Coleridge alike poetic creation becomes an essential part of mental development. In particular, dereliction and dejection become the springhead of joy and new growth.

D. G. James in his Warton Lecture, 'Wordsworth and Tennyson', has shown us how Wordsworth between 1796 and 1798 overcame his despair at the moral débâcle of the French Revolution, and his failure to find either in Godwin, or conventional philosophy, the assurance of value in human life he so desperately wanted.[1] As we have seen, this was, in essence, Mill's problem—as well as Tennyson's. What divides Wordsworth from Tennyson, James argues, was 'the visionaries of dereliction'. For Wordsworth, when he lacked his sister's influence,

---

[1] *Proceedings of the British Academy*, Vol. xxxvi (1950), pp. 113–29.

the education of nature was one of *fear*. As he himself admits in Book XIII of *The Prelude*, he

> too exclusively esteemed *that* love
> And sought *that* beauty, which, as Milton sings,
> Hath terror in it.
>
> (224–6)

James's comment on this is extremely important: 'There was now for Wordsworth, a was always to be, in *dereliction*, in extreme dreariness, in foresakenness, in lostness, a visionary quality; dereliction was always to light up his imagination.'[1] This is a quality in Wordsworth that is far too often ignored. It is one thing to observe, as many critics have done, that much of Wordsworth's best work is concerned with the loss of his imaginative power; it is another to assert that his best poetry is often the *result* of contemplating dereliction and loss. Yet this is one meaning of the incident of the blind beggar; he can, by assimilating the memory of dereliction, so redefine himself, and who he is, that new strength comes from this feeling of past history in the present. At the end of Book I Wordsworth shows himself consciously aware that in describing his boyhood moments of joy and terror he is affecting his own creativity:

> One end hereby at least hath been attain'd,
> My mind hath been revived...
>
> (664–5)

The aesthetic importance of Coleridge's well at Upper Stowey, or Wordsworth gazing down into the mingled weeds and reflections from the boat is now clear. The very chameleon receptivity of the mind that had defeated the empirical philosophers is exploited as a source of poetry and growth. The new, surprising, superb self-confidence of the Romantics can articulate mental dereliction and the memory of childhood fear into joy and renewal. In so doing, they elevated growth into a conscious preoccupation.

William Empson, in *Seven Types of Ambiguity*, goes out of his way to taunt Wordsworth for having frankly admitted 'no inspiration other than his use, when a boy, of the mountains as a totem or father-substitute.'[2] In fact, however, Wordsworth goes

---

[1] *Ibid*. p. 119.   [2] P. 20.

much further than this, and even claims, in Book II of *The Prelude*, a further corollary: that joy, and a love of nature are a direct extension of the child's 'intercourse of touch' by which he 'held mute dialogues' with his mother's heart. Coleridge notes a similar progression in the child's development:

The first education which we receive, that from our mothers, is given to us by touch; the whole of its progress is nothing more than, to express myself boldly, an extended touch by promise. The sense itself, the sense of vision itself is only acquired by a continued recollection of touch...[1]

For Wordsworth this 'infant sensibility' is the 'Great birth-right of our Being'—the source of that total contact with the external world which is the Imagination. He describes how, weaned at last from his mother, and no longer sustained by intimate physical contact, he found himself capable of standing alone, and—much more—that his love for his mother was now extended to his perception of the natural world:

> I was left alone,
> Seeking the visible world, nor knowing why,
> The props of my affections were remov'd,
> And yet the building stood, as if sustain'd
> By its own spirit! All that I beheld
> Was dear to me, and from this cause it came,
> That now to Nature's finer influxes
> My mind lay open...
>
> (Book II, lines 292–9)

In the child's physical love for his mother Wordsworth could already distinguish the two levels of experience which, for him, characterized the Imagination: the sense of touch, and love. Sensation and emotion—two discontinuous levels—are naturally experienced by the child as a unity. By slow degrees this first infant unity of sense and 'feeling' is extended simultaneously on the one hand into a wider physical perception, and on

---

[1] *Philosophical Lectures*, p. 115. In this connection it is interesting to note Constable's remark: 'painting is with me but another word for feeling'. In what sense is the word 'feeling' being used here—consciously or unconsciously? Gombrich, who quotes the letter (*Art and Illusion*, p. 324), goes on to suggest that Constable's link with Wordsworth through their common patron, Sir George Beaumont, was more than coincidence.

the other into a growing consciousness. Now it is perfectly possible to interpret this, and the accompanying passages of *The Prelude*, as Beatty interpreted the closely parallel 'Letter to Mathetes' which Wordsworth wrote for Coleridge as a contribution to *The Friend*—that is, as pure Hartley. The stages of growth, from the baby's first contact with its mother's breast, to the appreciation of abstract thought, could all be held up as illustrations of the inexorable growth of spirituality from simple sensations which was, for Hartley, 'the necessary consequence of passing through this world.' The overtly associationist description of growth from lines 244 to 257 in the 1805 version was omitted altogether when Wordsworth came to revise *The Prelude* near the end of his life. But the simple conclusion that in 1805 Wordsworth was a declared Hartleian, and that by 1850 he had repudiated this position, is, I think, untenable. The mistake is to see Wordsworth as a philosopher at all. Like Coleridge, he was looking for an intellectual framework that would formalize his vivid intuitive and observational grasp of mental development. I think it would be possible to show, for example, that the whole of the omitted passage is perfectly consonant with *Kantian* principles—an illustration of 'epigenesis'.[1] I do not believe for one moment that it is: merely that Wordsworth's account of childhood development was based not on any philosophical theory, but only common-sense observation of babies. I think we must be very wary of suggesting even that such passages as these *illustrate* Wordsworth's theory of the Imagination. What we can say is that here we can see Wordsworth's idea of the Imagination in the actual process of being formulated—as a direct response to what he saw and knew. As so often, Wordsworth is far more detailed and explicit than he is

[1] See Kant, *Critique*, p. 104, and Ewing, *Short Commentary*, p. 130.
  'Epigenesis' is a biological theory that maintained there was a genuine development of new organs not contained in the original embryo in diminutive form (and thus the opposite of the theory of 'Preformation'). Kant applies the term to his own philosophy either 'because we are not given innate ideas from the start, but merely possess faculties which develop themselves under the influence of the environment and only relatively late in life attain full consciousness, or that catagories are a new contribution to nature by our mind, not there from the beginning in something existing before we experience it.' (Ewing) Clearly the Wordsworth passages in question *could* be interpreted in the light of this theory.

often given credit for being. The explicitness, however, is in the observation, not in the philosophy. For example, Hartley, like Wordsworth, insisted that a growing knowledge of the 'external' world went hand-in-hand with the growth of 'internal' consciousness. The difference between them is that Hartley saw the former as *causing* the latter, at a simple physical and mechanical level, while Wordsworth always treats it as an interdependent relationship—two parts of the same thing, which is neither 'internal' nor 'external' in Hartley's sense. Moreover, Wordsworth only seems to be concerned with the two levels of mechanism and consciousness in so far as they coincide in 'spots of time' which are recalled as moments of 'disclosure':

> The seasons came,
> And every season to my notice brought
> A store of transitory qualities
> Which, but for this most watchful power of love
> Had been neglected, left a register
> Of permanent relations, else unknown,
> Hence life, and change, and beauty, solitude
> More active, even, than 'best society',
> Society made sweet as solitude
> By silent inobtrusive sympathies,
> And gentle agitations of the mind
> From manifold distinctions, difference
> Perceived in things, where to the common eye,
> No difference is...
>
> (Book ii, lines 307–20)

The creative power of the Imagination is a universal human experience: one and the same with the first dim feelings of the baby in its mother's arms. Above all, the Imagination is founded upon 'love'. Without this, the original relationship of mother and child, our whole perception of the universe can have neither meaning nor growth. The difference between the poetically creative and the 'common eye' lies in this 'most watchful power of love' by which the 'transitory qualities' of childhood, by most people passed over and forgotten are transformed into a 'register/Of permanent relations'. Nor are these fleeting minutiae referred to as if they were unclassified experiences: they are 'qualities'. It is, Wordsworth stresses, not these qualities themselves, but, as it were, a kind of abstract pattern of their relationships that is essential in putting growth into words. By this means, new and ever finer distinctions are constantly being drawn from past experience as a basis for future perception. It is a kind of poetic dialectic in which the organization itself—or, as Wordsworth elsewhere calls it, the 'harmony'—has become more important than the original event. Hence he goes one:

> I would stand,
> Beneath some rock, listening to the sounds that are
> The ghostly language of the ancient earth,
> Or make their dim abode in distant winds.
> Thence did I drink the visionary power.
> I deem not profitless those fleeting moods
> Of shadowy exultation: not for this,
> That they are kindred to our purer mind
> And intellectual life; but that the soul,
> Remembering how she felt, but what she felt
> Remembering not, retains an obscure sense
> Of possible sublimity.
>
> (326–37)

The key process Wordsworth is describing here is one of *abstraction*: the 'soul/Remembering how she felt, but what she felt/Remembering not.' What matters is always the pattern—and it is the pattern, we notice, that is for him the 'visionary power'. We have passed from a discursive to a presentational mode of consciousness, where such symbols are a shorthand of all the emotional and intellectual growth which has built up to the 'moment of disclosure'. Such experiences are of universal reference because they offer the symbols by which growth ceases to follow the instinctive unity of childhood perception and becomes instead a self-conscious activity. It follows that only by the liberating effect of symbols is the mind truly 'active' and creative. Hence the use of symbols is a distinctively human attribute: the Imagination involves us all in a symbolic universe.

'What the plant is by an act not its own and unconsciously—that thou must make thyself become,' wrote Coleridge in

Church and State.[1] In *Aids to Reflection* he goes on to argue that there is a gradual transformation from mechanism to free will as one ascends in consciousness up the Great Chain of Being.[2] The growth of the mind, the refinement of perception, and the unfolding sensibility of the poet are, for Wordsworth and Coleridge, inseparable aspects of that personal and organic unity which is the Imagination. Poetry, for them, was the Imagination in words: it was that 'sublime faculty by which a great mind becomes that which it meditates on.'[3]

[1] *Church and State*, ed. H. N. Coleridge (1839), p. 268.
[2] P. 80.
[3] *Notes on Shakespeare*, Vol. I, p. 188.

4

Unity and Creativity

When Wordsworth or Coleridge tried to describe what they meant by 'unity of the mind' in connection with the Imagination, one frequently finds that they were using the same phrase to cover two distinct and different experiences. On the one hand they seem to have used the words to convey an over-riding sense of inner unity and integrity that they felt transcended all hesitations, doubts, and conflicts within themselves in their day-to-day lives; on the other, they also used same words directly to describe that unity between the mind and nature that they believed was the essence of all sense-perception. It seems that for them, these two ideas of unity were inseparably linked. Indeed, the completeness of the psychological revolution they achieved is here illustrated at its most dramatic. We may, perhaps, formulate what happened like this: whereas for the empirical psychologists and the more 'mystical' Romantics alike, a feeling of unity with the external world was the concomitant, or more often the product, of an inner psychological unity, for Wordsworth and Coleridge, any inner unity seemed to depend on first being able to perceive beauty and harmony in nature. We can see, in fact, how this followed from their theory of the Imagination. The mind is seen through symbols taken from nature because, in its own way, the inner unity of the mind—and even 'consciousness' itself—is as much a creation of the Imagination as external perception. The symbol of water, or a mirror, is frequently used (as we have seen) to suggest how the outward reach of the Imagination is always balanced by a corresponding inward reach of 'reflection'.

There is a good example of this in Wordsworth's *Tintern Abbey*. We are familiar with Empson's attack on this poem, where he critizes the 'non-denominational uplift' of the famous lines:

And I have felt
A presence that disturbs me with the joy
Of elevated thoughts; a sense sublime
Of something far more deeply interfused,
Whose dwelling is the light of setting suns,
And the round ocean and the living air,
And the blue sky, and in the mind of man:
A motion and a spirit, that impels
All thinking things, all objects of all thought,
And rolls through all things.

In common with quite a number of critics, Empson assumes that Wordsworth's vagueness is the cloak for some sort of woolly pantheism.[1] Such an approach, however, is more hallowed by custom than by reference to the text.[2] If, for example, we ignore the attributed 'pantheism' and concentrate instead on the interpenetration of man and nature in perception that Wordsworth describes to us elsewhere, much of the vagueness vanishes at once. As even J. S. Mill was quick to point out in his argument over the imagination with his friend Roebuck, the 'light of setting suns' holds for us great natural beauty—which we value for its own sake. But for Wordsworth this is only part of the experience. The parallels with *This Lime-Tree Bower* would suggest that he is being, to some extent, 'Berkeleian' here, though whether, as in the case of the pre-existence of the soul in the *Immortality Ode*, he is using Berkeley as more than a 'convenient fiction' must remain open. What is more important is to see how, as we noted in the Introduction, the effect of Berkeley on both Wordsworth and Coleridge is to affirm the 'reality' of subjective sense-perception: the round ocean, and the living air, and the blue sky. Perception is itself a 'deeply interfused' relationship between man and his surroundings. The 'motion and a spirit' that '...rolls through all things' is, by a deliberate ambiguity of phrasing, made to belong both to the external world and to 'the mind of man'. The poem takes the two worlds, inner and outer, at their point of intersection. For Wordsworth, the central problem of *Tintern Abbey* is that these moments of

---

[1] *Seven Types of Ambiguity*, 2nd ed. (Peregrine, Penguin Books, 1961), pp. 151–4.
[2] See Leavis's refutation of Empson on this point in *Revaluation* (Chatto, 1936), p. 164.

inter-penetration with nature, and the corresponding sense of inner unity, are never more than intermittent phenomena. For them to become a nodal point of growth they must undergo that process of 'recollection in tranquillity' that feeds and nourishes the poet's mind.

We can see this even more clearly in an example from *The Prelude* where the moment of harmony and insight is not so generalized but experienced as the dramatic turning-point of a journey. The description of the Simplon Pass was thought by Wordsworth to be sufficiently important, and self-explanatory, to stand alone as a separate poem, and he finally published it in 1845. With significant deliberation he put it among the 'Poems of the Imagination'. In its proper setting, however, in Book vi of the 1805 *Prelude* its intentions are even more clear. Words-worth loses his way before he reaches the Pass, and then, to his astonishment, finds out from a peasant that in his wanderings he has already, and without knowing it, '*crossed the Alps*'—the italics are his. There follows immediately a great apostrophe to the Imagination, which, 'like an unfather'd vapour':

> In all the might of its endowments, came
> Athwart me; I was lost as in a cloud,
> Halted, without a struggle to break through.
> And now recovering, to my Soul I say
> I recognise thy glory...
>
> (528–32)

The crossing of the Alps was the fulcrum, the turning-point of the whole journey for Wordsworth, yet (like the Ancient Mariner's blessing the water-snakes) it comes quite *uncon-sciously*—at a moment when he felt himself to be lost and on the wrong path. The long description of the Imagination, imme-diately juxtaposed with this moment of discovery, suggests that the mist-shrouded Alps are mountains of the mind. The ambi-guity of 'Athwart' is given stress by its position in the line; in addition to 'across', it carries (typically for Wordsworth) its northern dialect suggestion of 'in various directions'—imply-ing perversity and even opposition. Imagination is a swirling, blinding mist. Again and again we find in Wordsworth this association between the Imagination and the unconscious—the overflow of whose turbulent, creative energy can be blinding and bewildering. We are reminded of Book I:

> For I, methought, while the sweet breath of Heaven
> Was blowing on my body, felt within
> A corresponding mild creative breeze,
> A vital breeze which travell'd gently on
> O'er things which it had made, and is become
> A tempest, a redundant energy
> Vexing its own creation.
>
> (41–7)

The Imagination matches internal and external experience, but in this moment of creativity the 'vital breeze' blowing over its own artifacts—the 'schemata' of normal sense-perception—becomes a tempest (Wordsworth's change of tense at this moment is important). What happens is violent and disruptive. The energy which now vexes 'its own creation' is described as 'redundant', and again the word is important, suggesting an untapped excess, or an overflowing wave, so intense or powerful as to imply a boiling-point: a total change of state. This is the creative energy which Wordsworth feels underlying the whole *Prelude*—the whole attempt to recapitulate the growth and development of his mind. The moment of transformation and of discovery as they enter the Simplon Pass typifies what, for Wordsworth, is the continuing creative activity of the entire poem:

> The immeasurable height
> Of woods decaying, never to be decay'd,
> The stationary blasts of water-falls,
> And every where along the hollow rent
> Winds thwarting winds, bewilder'd and forlorn,
> The torrents shooting from the clear blue sky,
> The rocks that mutter'd close upon our ears,
> Black drizzling crags that spake by the way-side
> As if a voice were in them, the sick sight
> And giddy prospect of the raving stream,
> The unfetter'd clouds, and region of the Heavens,
> Tumult and peace, the darkness and the light
> Were all like workings of one mind, the features
> Of the same face, blossoms upon one tree,

Characters of the great Apocalypse,
The types and symbols of Eternity,
Of first and last, and midst, and without end.

(556–72)

The downward-flowing brook and the travellers' road lead together into the narrow chasm. We have just been told, in the preceding passage on the Imagination, how the creative 'access of joy' covers the mind 'like the overflowing Nile'; now Wordsworth leads us into the turbulence of 'stationary' waterfalls. The scene echoes Milton's description of Chaos: constant movement without time or form—and it is from this that the landscape of the mind is created as a universal polarity:

> Tumult and peace, the darkness and the light,
> Were all like workings of one mind...

The contrast is continually made between the wildness and darkness below, and the calm and light above; the clouds are 'unfetter'd' and the stream 'raving', while above is the clear blue sky of consciousness and reason. It is the sense of unity overriding these contrasts that suggests to Wordsworth the mind. Decay and eternity, order and confusion, are together blossoms on one tree. Order includes chaos as one of its constituents; eternity is not separate from decay, it *contains* it. The mind of man is seen as a unity of order and ungovernable conflict. This canyon, or 'hollow rent' in which the travellers find themselves is our first introduction to that 'deep dark thoroughfare' which Wordsworth saw in the clouds on Snowdon, and which symbolized for him the Imagination.

There is a description in one of Coleridge's notebooks that provides an interesting parallel to this experience. Like the Simplon Pass, it is a record of an actual event, but as raw material, without the second recollective stage of poetic creation, it shows the amazing way in which Coleridge saw nature directly as symbols of his own mind. On 2 March 1805 Coleridge made the note:

Friday—Saturday 12–1 o'clock/What a sky, the not yet orbed moon, the spotted oval, blue at one edge from the deep utter Blue of the Sky, a *mass* of *pearl*-white Cloud below, distant, and travelling to the Horizon, but all the upper part of the Ascent, and all the Height, such *profound* Blue, *deep* as a deep river, and deep in colour, & those two (depths) so entirely *one*, as to give the meaning and explanation of the two different significations of the epithet (here so far divided they were scarcely *distinct*) scattered over with thin pearl-white Cloudlets, hands, & fingers, the largest not larger than a floating Veil/Unconsciously I stretched forth my arms as to embrace the sky, and in a trance I had worshipped God in the Moon/the Spirit not the Form/I felt in how innocent a feeling Sabeism might have begun/O not only the Moon, but the depth of Sky!—the Moon was the *Idea*; but deep Sky is of all visual impressions the nearest akin to a Feeling/it is more union of Feeling & Sight...[1]

Coleridge's feeling of the 'interpenetration of man and nature' reveals itself here in a typical, but very curious complexity of perception. He contemplates nature in a state of intense emotion, and reads it simultaneously (not by any recollection in tranquility) as a symbol of his own mind. The link between these inner and outer worlds is, he stresses, the *feeling*. For Coleridge, it seems that the experience of an emotion is identical with an act of introspection. Here, in 'the melting away and entire union of Feeling and Sight', his Imagination has created a symbol of the correspondence between the mind and the nature it perceives.

In looking out into the illuminated profundity of the night sky, '*deep* as a deep river, and deep in colour, & those two (depths) so entirely *one*...', he is simultaneously looking into the unfathomable depth of the mind itself—'The Moon was the *Idea*; but deep Sky is of all visual impressions the nearest akin to a Feeling.' The sudden disclosure of likeness in unlikeness comes in his sense of the sky and the mind alike *not* as objects, but as *depths*: being space and colour, but without form. The ambiguity of the word 'deep' (used in both its sense of 'intense' for colour, and 'profound' for space) provides two separate adjectives to qualify the prevailing metaphor of a river; since emotions can also be described in terms of intensity and depth, we are led straight from the sky to the mind perceiving it. Each meaning, in turn, appears to qualify the other: is the sky deep like the mind, or the mind deep like the sky?[2] The word 'deep'

1 *Anima Poetae*, p. 125; *Notebooks*, Vol. II, 2453.
2 See Empson on this point (*Seven Types*, p. 40): 'For a Pathetic Fallacy to cause much emotional reverberation it must be imposed upon the reader by an ambi-

seems to pinpoint the imaginative dialectic of reconciling or discordant qualities.

To the mind liberated by the Imagination from the 'tyranny of the eye', all things, including both nature and art, can be read as hieroglyphics.[1] The depth of the sky is as significant as the art of Raphael and Michelangelo, Coleridge argues:

> we look at the forms after we have long satisfied all curiosity concerning the mere outline; yet still we look and feel that these are but symbols... Why, having seen their outlines, why, having determined what they appeared to the eye, do we still continue to muse on them, but that there is a divine something corresponding to something within, which no image can exhaust but which we are reminded of when in the South of Europe we look at the deep blue sky? The same unwearied form presents itself, yet still we look on, sinking deeper and deeper, and therein offering homage to the infinity of our souls which no mere form can satisfy.[2]

It is here that Coleridge's underlying Platonism seems to be absorbed into a scientific and psychological theory of perception. At the back of his mind is a clear system of symbolic correspondences by which Man, the microcosm, contains within himself 'A syllepsis, a compendium of Nature.'[3] A 'syllepsis' is defined by the *O.E.D.* as 'a word made to refer to two other words in the same sentence, while properly agreeing with only one, or both in different senses'. From recognizing the fundamental ambiguity in man between consciousness and organism, Coleridge quickly passed to the parallel ambiguity between his 'inner' and 'outer' experience; here, in the *Theory of Life*, he is now proceeding to *define* man as possessing this ambiguity. Mental unity was, for him, the creation of the Imagination in perceiving simultaneously the 'inner' and 'outer' worlds. He continues:

---

guity.' The complete interpenetrative correspondence of man and nature in this instance, however, is not strictly Pathetic Fallacy: it may perhaps fall within Empson's 'fourth' kind of ambiguity—indicating an extreme complication in Coleridge's own mind.

[1] For the use of this image in connection with Hamlet, see *Shakespearean Criticism* (Raysor), Vol. II, p. 224, and below, p. 115, n. 1.

[2] *Philosophical Lectures*, p. 193.

[3] *The Theory of Life*, 'Misc. Aesthetic and Literary' (Bohn/Bell, 1892), p. 423.

Nor does the form of polarity, which has accompanied the law of individuation up its whole ascent, desert it here. As in the height, so in the depth...As the ideal genius and the originality, in the same proportion must be the resignation to the real world, the sympathy and the intercommunion with Nature.[1]

The height at once suggests the depth. Creative consciousness does not withdraw man into an 'ideal' world (in a Platonic sense) but plunges him back into further and deeper preception of the world around him. Thus when Coleridge is contemplating the night sky, the sky is both the actual sky, and the unconscious —with all its associations of a river, where antithetic qualities are reconciled, unified, and retained in tension. It is this unity-with-tension that Coleridge finds he can only describe as 'feeling'. Yet even this word itself is, of course, used ambiguously: a sense of texture has pervaded the whole description, and he records the 'pearl white cloudlets' as 'hands and fingers', and then as 'a floating veil'. In the next sentence the sense of touch is actually put into words as he ('unconsciously'!) tries to *embrace* the sky in a moment of trance and joy.

Joy is, as it were, the catalyst of these intermittent moments of unity between man and nature. Between the dramatic crossing of the Alps, and Wordsworth's entry into the Simplon Pass comes the swirling mist of the Imagination, with its 'access of joy', swamping and nourishing the mind like the 'overflowing Nile'. Joy is Wordsworth's experience when he 'beholds the rainbow in the sky'. In *Tintern Abbey* he claims that:

> with an eye made quiet by the power
> Of harmony, and the deep power of joy,
> We see into the life of things.

For Coleridge, in *Dejection*, joy is itself the harmony, the 'strong music of the soul':

> This light, this glory, this fair luminous mist,
> This beautiful and beauty-making power.

The way in which he juxtaposes joy and 'glory' in *Dejection* is not accidental. The *O.E.D.* shows that as late as the time of Chaucer there was no direct translation into English of the

---

[1] *Ibid.*

Church Latin 'gloria'—the prime meaning of 'glory' being still
'boastfulness'. As a result 'bliss' and 'joy' were used for a long
time to describe the spiritual glory of Heaven. Later, the two
words 'glory' and 'joy' became almost interchangeable in this
context, while 'glory' also came to include the aureole or
nimbus which was used to halo the heads of saints in pictures,
or appeared in such natural phenomena of light as the Brocken-
spectre. The association in Coleridge's own mind is clear.

But there was an even more important association between
joy and the act of creation itself. There are strong roots in Greek
and Hebrew thought, but the immediate source of this association for Coleridge was, I think, the Methodist revival—and in
particular the hymnology of the Wesleys. Joy had no central
place in the Augustan theories of poetic creation, nor in the
Calvinist theology of Whitfield or the Countess of Huntingdon.
It comes, if it is to be traced at all, through Herbert and Traherne
to the High-Church Arminianism of the Wesleys—in whom a
submerged current of religious fervour can be seen breaking
surface. We find in them a tradition utterly opposed to that
'happiness' of Gay's on which Hartley based his mechanism of
associative psychology. 'Joy', for the Wesleys, was not
primarily an attribute of man's at all, but of God's—and in
particular, of God in Creation. Joy was thought of as the divine
concomitant of creativity. Man's joy came from sharing in the
joy of his Master. In this, man was only echoing the entire
cosmos. At the Creation 'the morning stars sang together, and
all the sons of God shouted for joy.'[1] John Wesley, in one of the
few hymns he wrote himself, praises the:

> Father of all! whose powerful voice
> Called forth this universal frame;
> Whose mercies over all rejoice,
> Through endless ages still the same.[2]

Charles Wesley takes a passage from Zephaniah, 'He will save,
he will rejoice over thee with joy, he will joy over thee with
singing' (iii. 17), and transforms it into this:

> Thy gracious Lord shall soon for thee
> His whole omnipotence employ,

[1] Job xxxviii. 7.   [2] *Methodist Hymn Book* (London, 1933). No. 47.

Delight in thy prosperity,
And condescend to sing for joy;
Thy God well pleas'd and satisfied
Shall view his image in thy breast,
Shall glory o'er his spotless bride,
And in his love for ever rest.[1]

God's relationship with his Church—his 'New Creation'—is exemplified by his joyful perception in it of his own image. Secularized, this is essentially the creative relationship that we find in both Coleridge's and Wordsworth's perception of nature.

Theologically, the connection between Coleridge and the Wesleys is not hard to find. Orthodox, non-Calvinistic theology held that the primal unity between Man and God had been disrupted by the Fall. Though man's whole relationship with nature was thus dislocated, in Christ, God's new creation and restoration was immanent in this world. The new relationship between man and nature figures prominently in the Wesleys' poetry as a part and symbol of the new unity to be found in Christ. Even more important, by turning their attention from natural 'evidences' of Christianity to the 'inward witness' of its truth, the Wesleys came to see nature not as a vast mechanistic analogue, but in symbols of human religious experience. Addison's hymn gives us the classic statement of nature as an analogue:

The spacious firmament on high,
With all the blue ethereal sky,
And spangled heavens, a shining frame,
Their great Original proclaim...

What though in solemn silence all
Move round this dark terrestrial ball;
What though no real voice nor sound
Amidst their radiant orbs be found:
In reason's ear they all rejoice,
And utter forth a glorious voice,
For ever singing as they shine:
The hand that made us is divine![2]

[1] Charles Wesley, *Short Hymns on Select Passages of the Holy Scriptures* (1796), Vol. II, p. 82.
[2] *Methodist Hymn Book*, No. 44.

This is still the view of Archdeacon Paley in his hugely popular *View of the Evidences of Christianity* which was published at the end of the century, in 1794, and against which Coleridge reacted so fiercely in *Aids to Reflection*. Partly through his contact with the Moravians, John Wesley was influenced by a different strand that had appeared in German theology, and which seemed to speak straight to his own conversion experience. How different his attitude to nature is from Addison's can be seen in his translation of Ernst Lange:

> O God, Thou bottomless abyss!
> Thee to perfection who can know?
> O height immense! What words suffice
> Thy countless attributes to show?...
>
> Eternity Thy fountain was,
> Which, like Thee, no beginning knew;
> Thou wast ere time began his race,
> Ere glowed with stars the ethereal blue.[1]

He seeks to read nature in terms of his own inner experience. The divine organization of the universe is not 'out there' but in the mind of man—'a motion and a spirit'—a *quality* of experience, not only at a rational level, but in the depth and mystery of the unconscious. Such a new attitude to man's relationship with nature is supported by a renewed stress on the Incarnation— where God's immanence in nature is revealed simultaneously as a physical and as a moral event. The close parallels of thought between the Methodist revival and the English Romantic movement at this point can be seen, for instance, in Southey's discussion of Wesley's theology in his *Life of Wesley* which appeared in 1820. Southey here quotes Wesley directly:

It is the internal evidence of Christianity, a perpetual revelation, equally strong, equally new, through all the centuries which have elapsed since the incarnation, and, passing now, even as it has done from the beginning, directly from God into the believing soul...It requires no less power thus to quicken a dead soul, than to raise a body that lies in the grave. It is a new creation; and none can create a soul anew, but He who at first created the heavens and the earth. 'May not your own experience teach you this?' said Wesley. Can you

[1] *Ibid.* No. 42.

give yourself this faith? Is it in your power to see, or hear, or taste, or feel God?—to raise in yourself any perception of God, or of an invisible world? to open an intercourse between yourself and the world of spirits?—to discern either them or Him that created them?—to burst the veil that is on your heart, and let in the light of eternity? You know it is not. You not only do not, but cannot (by your own strength) thus believe...[1]

To this passage Coleridge, in his own edition, added the enthusiastic footnote (dated 1 May 1820):

I venture to avow it as my conviction, that either Christian faith is what Wesley here describes, or there is no proper meaning in the word. It is either the identity of the reason and the will (the proper spiritual part of man), in the full energy of each, consequent on a divine rekindling, or not at all.[2]

For the Wesleys, the divine rekindling incorporated redeemed man into the extended family of Christ, able at last to share in God's eternal creative joy. From the text: 'The Word was made flesh, and dwelt among us...' (John i. 14), Charles Wesley produces this:

> Transform'd by the extatic sight,
> Our souls o'erflow with pure delight,
>   And every moment own
> The Lord our whole perfection is,
> The Lord is our immortal bliss,
> And Christ and heaven are one.[3]

The perception of God changes man's total organization, and consequently all future perception. By experiencing joy, 'transform'd' man was partaking in an essentially divine activity, and touching the very mystery of creation. There is here an embryo theory of *poetic* creation that bears a surprising resemblance to the 'spontaneous overflow of powerful feelings' —however alien its other-worldly application would have been to Wordsworth in 1800. Similarly, there are detectable verbal

---

[1] *Life of Wesley*, ed. C. C. Southey, with notes by S.T.C. (1858), Vol. II, pp. 57–8.
[2] *Ibid.* p. 58. F. C. Gill, in *The Romantic Movement and Methodism* (Epworth, 1937) misquotes this footnote (p. 169), substituting 'text' for 'word'. Unfortunately he does not relate it to the passage in Southey, or point the parallels in thought between the Wesleys and Southey and Coleridge.
[3] *Hymns on Select Passages*, p. 202.

echoes in the ending of the published version of *Dejection* to indicate how much Coleridge's complex and still-evolving theory of creativity owed to its Wesleyan origins:

> Joy lift her spirit, joy attune her voice;
> To her may all things live, from pole to pole,
> Their life the eddying of her living soul!
>   O simple spirit, guided from above,
> Dear Lady! friend devoutest of my choice,
> Thus mayest thou ever, evermore rejoice.

This association of glory and joy with the act of creation is, however, neither simple nor automatic. After his rejection of Hartley, Coleridge was constantly on his guard against creeping mechanism. Joy accompanied creation; it does not seem to have been thought of directly as either its cause or result. Creator and creation were, rather, felt to be unified by it. In the hands of John Stuart Mill this could lead to the simple equation of poetry and feeling, but for Coleridge and Wordsworth this is a way of saying that unity (in the sense we have been describing it) is not just a quantitative all-inclusiveness but a *value*. It emphasized for them too that this 'unity' was essentially intermittent: the mind finding a resonance in nature only when the poet was in a suitable emotional state:

> I may not hope from outward forms to win
> The passion and the life, whose fountains are within.

What is not always clear is the link between this *felt* unity, and that other unity of personality which was a part of their theory of organic growth, and which remains a quantitative unity. Clearly this could not disappear when it was not felt. Coleridge, even while at one level he blames himself for indolence and divided purpose, never seems to deny this other unity. The active and passive moods of the mind are two sides of the same coin, each necessary for the other. On the one hand he writes bitterly of the 'two contrary yet co-existing propensities of human nature, namely, indulgence of sloth, and hatred of vacancy':

this genus comprises as its species, gaming, swinging or swaying on a chair or gate; spitting over a bridge; smoking; snuff taking; tête-à-tête quarrels after dinner between husband and wife; conning word by word all the advertisements of a daily newspaper in a public house on a rainy day, &c. &c. &c.[1]

on the other hand, in his seventh lecture on 'A New System of Education', while endorsing the current horror of 'idleness' in children, he adds: 'Never, however, imagine that a child is idle who is gazing on the stream, or laying upon the earth...all the healthy processes of nature may then be forming.'[2] His distinction is always between a healthy lying-fallow of the mind, and that debilitating 'idleness' whose symptoms were mechanical association and creeping mental atrophy—what is significant is that this latter state is not acquired by bad habits, but is an innate mental tendency. This is perhaps Coleridge's central problem. Dorothy Emmet has commented:

I believe that Coleridge was concerned to explore not only a source of the creative power of the imagination shown in genius but also more generally the liberation of the mind from deadness and dereliction, a liberation on which growth depends...Coleridge's 'empirico-religious' philosophy was concerned with exploring the conditions which made possible, and the conditions which frustrate this joy which underlies the creative growth of the mind.[3]

This seems to me one of the most illuminating insights ever offered into the structure of Coleridge's thought. It helps to explain, for a start, why so much of his energy was devoted to the apparently barren philosophical game of trying to say exactly what he meant by this 'unity of the mind'. For him, growth and unity were inseparable. If, on the one hand, the mind ceased to grow when it lacked unity, on the other, it could only be unified when it was growing. Both of these activities (for 'unity', in this sense, was thought of as active) were in some way felt to depend on joy—one of the 'springs of action' in the mind.

Yet if this were the whole truth, one would expect Coleridge's philosophical speculations to develop out of his loss of joy—and this, of course, is not what happened. Much of his best philosophical thinking (such as his turning from Hartley to Kant

[1] *Biographia Literaria*, Vol. I, p. 34.
[2] Lecture given at the White Lion Inn, Bristol, 18 November 1813. Reprinted (from the *Bristol Gazette*) in the *Athenaeum*, 13 March 1909.
[3] 'Coleridge on the Growth of the Mind', *Bulletin*.

around the year 1800) coincides with his most poetically creative period. In the first chapter of *Biographia Literaria* he describes how his interest in metaphysical speculation was highly developed by the time he was fourteen. But Coleridge's own accounts are not always to be trusted. He writes:

Well were it for me, perhaps, had I never relapsed into the same mental disease; if I had continued to pluck the flower and reap the harvest from the cultivated surface, instead of delving in the unwholesome quicksilver mines of metaphysic depths.[1]

The mock-humility of the philosopher here is not altogether comfortable. The contrast between surface and depth is enough to give away Coleridge's rather heavy-handed irony, as it was clearly meant to—but at another level this contrast between disease and health reveals Coleridge's real preoccupation. In the next sentence he says:

And if in after time I have sought refuge from bodily pain and mismanaged sensibility in abstruse researches, which exercised the strength and subtility of the understanding without awakening the feelings of the heart; still there was a long and blessed interval, during which my natural faculties were allowed to expand, and my original tendencies to develop themselves: my fancy, and the love of nature, and the sense of beauty in forms and sounds.

The problem is to differentiate between balanced and unbalanced development. There is no suggestions here that to cultivate 'the strength and subtility of the understanding' is to inhibit the 'feelings of the heart'—and, indeed, one of the great achievements of *Biographia Literaira* is to show how the two are complementary. Dorothy Emmet is surely right in refusing to accept that these are in any way conflicting preoccupations. What does preoccupy him is the evaluation of his own mental growth. The real difficulty seems to me to be here: Coleridge's own attitude towards his 'abstruse researches' is profoundly ambivalent. It is as if he is quite unable to make up his mind whether this endless process of philosophical self-analysis actually fostered or inhibited the growth of his creativity. Only a page after the disclaimers quoted above he can write: ' ... actuated too by my former passion for metaphysical investiga-

[1] *Biographia Literaria*, Vol. i, p. 10.

tions; I laboured at a solid foundation, on which permanently to ground my opinions, in the component faculties of the human mind itself . . .'[1] Such an ambivalence had been with Coleridge for a long time before he wrote *Biographia Literaria*. In 1802, for instance, it is exactly the same problem that lurks behind the sixth stanza of *Dejection*. Are we to conclude that abstruse researches are the cause or the result of his loss of unity and joy when he determines:

> not to think of what I needs must feel,
> But to be still and patient all I can;
> And haply by abstruse research to steal
> From my own nature all the natural man—
> This was my sole resource, my only plan:
> Till that which suits a part infects the whole,
> And now is almost grown the habit of my soul.

Is the state being described one of sickness, or maturity? Coleridge is ostensibly describing a disaster—but out of that disaster, the suspension of his creative powers, he is in the very act of creating one of the great poems of the English language. This passage is the emotional turning-point of the poem. A momenent later he turns his attention to the wind outside, and the process of catharsis and purgation which is to lead him on to his hymn to joy—which we have already quoted—is begun. The whole poem is, in a very real sense, an investigation into the suspension of his creative power that, by investigating it, releases it. This crucial passage is peculiarly ambivalent in its attitude to the abstruse research. For example, was his 'plan' 'not to think of what I needs must feel' the stoic acceptance of a change in his mental condition—a kind of poetic menopause? Or a comment on the damaging power of thought on feeling ('we murder to dissect')? or a dislocation of the whole mind? Similarly, is there—perhaps unconsciously—a suggestion of a *verb* in 'patient': to imply the cultivation of something akin to negative capability?[2] The crux is surely the words 'natural man'. Is this implying man as 'naturally' good (as, for instance Rousseau might have used the phrase)?—in which case the

[1] *Ibid.* p. 14.
[2] The *O.E.D.* cites Digby (1644): 'An overflowing reward for thy enduring and patienting in this darksome prison.'

result of stealing it is a real disaster; or does it imply that man is 'naturally' corrupt (in, for instance, St Paul's sense)?—in which case Coleridge is hinting at a process of spiritual refinement by philosophy. Coleridge certainly had a higher opinion of Paul than Rousseau (for whom he reserves some choice abuse) but *both* ideas are present elsewhere in his writings. 'Haply' can take its cue from this, meaning either 'perhaps' or even 'by accident', *or* 'fortunately' and 'happily'. Nor does even an apparently obvious word like 'infect' settle the question. The Latin root, *infecere*, is an image from dying cloth, and its earliest English uses follow this, meaning merely to 'die', 'dip in', or 'stain'.[1] It is conceivable that such a meaning is present in Coleridge's mind as a submerged clothing image, since 'suits'[2] is followed on the next line by 'habit'. Is there just a suggestion here of a monkish philosopher? Such interpretations must remain open speculation: what we can say, I believe, is that there is a feeling of qualitative mental change in Coleridge following on his 'loss' of the creative (Secondary) Imagination that he certainly regrets, but is not quite sure whether to regard as a disaster or a development. If, on the one hand, he talks of it as if it is an unmitigated disaster, on the other, *Dejection* itself is one of his greatest insights into the workings of his own creativity— and he is always aware of this. We have seen a similar ambivalence of attitude at the end of *The Ancient Mariner* that has led some critics to see the Mariner's final state as one of irreparable damage, and others as a new depth of understanding that leaves him 'no longer at ease in the old dispensation'. Certainly it is the latter that seems to aflict the Wedding Guest. Yet, if the Mariner's experience can be given any articulable meaning, it is surely the discovery of the dual meaning of 'unity' which we have been examining. The shooting of the Albatross is 'a crime against nature'; the blessing of the water-snakes is a re-affirmation of unity between the Mariner and the natural world—an insight perceived in a moment of beauty and joy. It is his sense of unity with nature which restores him to wholeness.

---

[1] This meaning remains current until almost 1700. The *O.E.D.* also gives 'to take hold of feelings', and, from *King John*, to 'infect with delight'.

[2] In addition to the obvious, 'to court', or 'seize by law', the *O.E.D.* also offers the rarer meaning of 'to harmonize'.

But the result is again this ambivalent change. As we have seen, for Coleridge and for Wordsworth perception involved a razor-edged balance of projection and receptivity—an interplay that worked always in wholes. The importance of our being aware of the unifying activity of the imagination is so that we may learn consciously to explore and interpret the entire cosmos of our experience by the perception of ever more inclusive wholes. Wordsworth felt the 'spots of time' to be vital and 'renovating' because they constituted moments when the mind perceived the object and its own response as a single entity—and through such moments, recollected afterwards, he could learn to re-order and define the disorganized mass of the rest of his experience. He felt his powers of perception to be shaped and refined by them as Coleridge felt his to be before great works of art. What Coleridge is lamenting in *Dejection*, then, is his loss of the power to develop and shape his perception from these experiences, as well as the loss of the experiences themselves. His turning to the 'abstruse researches' of philosophy was now, for him, the only way of retaining that qualitative sense of unity. It still offered him a possibility of new growth, and, as we see in the seventh stanza, rapport with nature. Simultaneously, there is a shift of interest from the growth itself, to the process by which it is achieved. Coleridge's attention turns more and more to analyzing the success and failure of his own creativity. The Ancient Mariner does not complete his regeneration on his return, but suffers instead from a compulsion to tell others what had happened.

A similar ambivalence to that of the final state of the Mariner can be found in the construction of *The Prelude*. In the 1800 Preface to the *Lyrical Ballads* Wordsworth claims that poetry and prose share the same language—and then, faced with the problem of differentiating between them, he does so not by defining poetry, but a poet. The whole structure of *The Prelude* seems to imply that the creation of poetry involves telling us about it: the actual describing of the growth of a poet's mind is an essential part of that growth. When Wordsworth, in the Simplon Pass, says that 'tumult and peace' are 'blossoms upon one tree' he presumably intends it as a permanent affirmation, but, coming where it does as the climax of Wordsworth's crossing of the Alps, we cannot escape the alternative suggestion that such contradictions are only meaningfully reconciled in moments of crisis. Nor can we escape this same feeling in the view of the clouds by moonlight from the top of Snowdon. The scene symbolizes for him the act of poetic creation, even as he creates poetry about it. Are we to assume that this 'dark deep thoroughfare' of the imagination is a permanent phenomenon, or one that occurs only in the act of poetic perception? Wordsworth's whole preoccupation in the last books of *The Prelude* with 'Imagination, how repaired and how restored' is, of course, essentially the same as that of Coleridge in *Dejection*. Articulation is an essential part of regeneration and growth. In other words we can go farther than Professor Emmet, and say that the philosophy of Coleridge (and Wordsworth) is concerned not merely with the conditions which inhibit and those which release the joy underlying the creative growth of the mind, but also, that in so doing, the philosophy itself becomes an integral part of that creative growth.

Nevertheless a problem remains, and it seems to me the central problem of this particular romantic theory of growth. That 'unity' of the mind which we have described as a *quantitative* wholeness is dependent on the *qualitative* wholeness that comes from the inter-penetration of man and nature in a state of joy—that razor-edged balance between projection and resonance that we see, for example, in Wordsworth's rainbow. Thus, in the 'creative menopause' of both Wordsworth and Coleridge we find a stage when the internal unity is threatened by a sense of external dislocation that seems, extraordinarly enough, to provide a further impetus towards further integration. At the centre of this apparent paradox is the old ambivalence we noted in *The Ancient Mariner*: is there, or is there not a sense in which growth comes through assimilating loss? Is *all* growth beyond a certain point achieved only through coming to terms with defeat and loss?

There is here, of course, an unresolved tension in the theory of organic growth itself. The word 'growth', as Wordsworth uses it in calling *The Prelude* 'the growth of a poet's mind', is quite ambiguous. Is he thinking of 'growth' as a purposive process, ending when its object ('Maturity'?) is reached? or is it a continuous and active process synonymous with life itself? We have already looked at John Stuart Mill's discovery that 'growth' implies a purpose, yet needs at every stage a value apart from the possibility of further growth. The idea of 'growth' as organic implies that it is an inevitable cycle coming to maturity and then decay. Wordsworth, by his very title 'The Prelude', as well as in his later description of the poem as an 'ante-chapel' to the main body of his work,[1] seems to be thinking of 'maturity' as a stage that is reached, rather than as a process. Coleridge, similarly, writing on the growth of a child into a poet, recalls his own 'delightful intoxication' on reading Young and Gray as 'as necessary to a future poet, as the bud to the flower or the flower to the seed'—visibly led by the organic image he has chosen to think of a final state of being 'A Poet', which is as static and complete as a flower. On the other hand, the second alternative of growth as something continuous and not implying a corresponding decay is a traditional Christian one, and is found, for instance, in the idea behind *The Pilgrim's Progress*, or even, as in Dante, an unfolding development never to be completed even after death.

> Oh! who is he that hath his whole life long
> Preserved, enlarged, this freedom in himself?
>
> (120–1)

writes Wordsworth in his concluding book of the 1805 *Prelude*. Coleridge, similarly, in an undated note in *Anima Poetae* (somewhere about 1820?) constructs a long and rigorous intellectual discipline 'for a man who would wish to keep his mind growing.'[2]

When the mind ceases to grow, it ceases to be unified. Neither Wordsworth nor Coleridge, one feels, was fully conscious of the dangers of an introspective poetic theory depending on continual mental growth, while at the same time seeking fruition and completeness. Wordsworth's difficulties were not,

---

[1] Wordsworth's actual words are, with hindsight, ominous. *The Prelude*, he claims in the Preface to *The Excursion*, 'conducts the history of the author's mind to the point when he was emboldened to hope that his faculties were sufficiently matured for entering upon the arduous labour which he had proposed to himself...'

[2] *Anima Poetae*, p. 298.

in the long run, made any easier by his choice of himself as his great exemplum of development. Coleridge, in contrast, turned to the one place where he could find exhibited at every stage simultaneous growth and completeness: Shakespeare.

Just as Shakespeare was to Coleridge the *type* of genius, so Hamlet is the fullest self-revelation, and therefore the fullest mirror to man of his own nature. In a sense, we can see Coleridge comments on Hamlet's mind as a parallel to those of Wordsworth on himself in *The Prelude*:

Hence it is, that the sense of sublimity arises, not from the sight of an outward object, but from the beholder's reflection upon it; not from the sensuous impression, but from the imaginative reflex. Few have seen a celebrated waterfall without feeling something akin to disappointment: it is only subsequently, that the image comes back into the mind, and brings with it a train of grand or beautiful associations. Hamlet feels this; his senses are in a state of trance, and he looks upon external things as hieroglyphics.[1]

For Coleridge, Shakespeare was the supreme example of the primacy of the mind over its material environment. In him was an internal dynamism and a balanced completeness that Wordsworth's 'egotistical sublime' could only achieve at rare moments. In outlining Shakespeare's development from the mechanical constructions of Fancy to the unity of Imagination, Coleridge is simultaneously giving in detail what he wanted his friend to achieve in *The Prelude*:

And still mounting the intellectual ladder, he had as unequivocally proved the indwelling in his mind of imagination, or the power by which one image or feeling is made to modify many others, and by a sort of

---

[1] Both this quotation, and that referred to in the following note, are taken from the text edited by H. N. Coleridge for *Literary Remains* (1836–9)—which, in both cases, I prefer to that of Raysor. For comparison, however, I append the corresponding versions from Raysor below. The page references are to the 'old' and 'new' Everyman editions—H.N.C. text, ed. Rhys (1907), and Raysor (1960). Thus this quotation from H.N.C.'s 'Notes on Hamlet' (0. 136) appears in Raysor (Vol. II, p. 224) as:

'The sense of sublimity arises, not from the sight of an outward object, but from the reflection upon it; not from the impression, but from the idea. Few have seen a celebrated waterfall without feeling something of a disappointment: it is only subsequently, by reflection, that the idea of the waterfall comes into the mind and brings with it a train of sublime associations. Hamlet felt this: in him we see a mind that keeps itself in a state of abstraction, and beholds external objects as hieroglyphics.'

fusion to force many into one...which, combining many circumstances into one moment of consciousness, tends to produce that ultimate end of human thought and human feeling, unity, and thereby the reduction of the spirit to its principle and fountain, who is alone truly one.[1]

Shakespeare and Wordsworth are in many ways opposites for Coleridge. Yet they are both creative writers, and, as such, models to which he could turn. As so often, it is dangerous to quote Coleridge in fragments when he is writing about creativity. Here, he is not just seeing 'unity' as a 'moment of consciousness' when things are perceived in an order and relationship; he is also suggesting that such a moment of consciousness is an inseparable part of the method that led up to it—the 'intellectual ladder' of the Imagination. It is method that lies at the heart of Coleridge's final concept of creativity. The ordering of experience as an organic and artistic unity is not something haphazard, or even God-given, if by this we mean beyond human organization. Coleridge seems in fact to be taking up a position very similar to that apparently re-discovered by certain twentieth-century religious thinkers. One might quote, for example here, Simone Weil:

Actually, from remote antiquity, long before Christianity, right up to the latter half of the Renaissance, it was always universally recognised that there is a method to be followed in spiritual matters and in everything connected with the soul's welfare. The ever greater and greater methodical control which men have exercised over matter since the 16th. Century has led them to believe, by way of contrast, that the things of the soul are either arbitrary or else bound up with some sort of magic, with the immediate efficacy of intentions and words... everything in creation is dependent on method, including the points of intersection between this world and the next.[2]

For Coleridge, creativity was dynamic, organized, and unified, in that it affected every level of our awareness. What was, at one extreme, a law of sense-perception, was, at the other,

---

[1] H.N.C. 'Shakespeare a Poet Generally' (p. 39); Raysor, Vol. II, p. 188:
  'Still mounting, we find undoubted proof in his mind of imagination, or the power by which one image or feeling is made to modify many others and by a sort of *fusion to force many into one*...'
  The rest of the H.N.C. quotation is missing.
[2] *The Need for Roots* (Routledge, 1952), p. 180.

an insight into man's spiritual existence. 'Method,' he wrote, 'implies a progressive transition, and it is the meaning of the word in the original language.' He continues:

But as, without continuous transition, there can be no method, so without a pre-conception there can be no transition with continuity. The term, method, cannot therefore, otherwise than by abuse, be applied to a mere dead arrangement, containing in itself no principle of progression.[1]

In yet another parallelism in Coleridge's thought, 'method' turns out to be a description of the way in which the Imagination works. It is a mode of growth. The term, he argues, can only apply to a continuous transitional process by which an initial pre-conception (or mental 'schema') is modified according to its own dynamic self-generating principle of further progression. For Coleridge, the movement and development of Shakespeare's thought, as a totality, is the supreme example of 'method' in this sense.

Method, therefore, becomes natural to the mind which has become accustomed to contemplate not things only, or for their own sake alone, but likewise and chiefly the relations of things, either their relations to each other, or to the observer, or to the state and apprehension of the hearers. To enumerate and analyse these relations, with the conditions under which alone they are discoverable, is to teach the science of method.[2]

The development of the concept of mental growth may, therefore, itself be expected to obey the laws of method. That is, it can neither be an outwardly similar succession of utterances by a series of poets, nor can it be an accidental succession of isolated insights. Creativity is not just a phenomenon that occurs in an individual as an isolated unit; it occurs because that individual stands in a certain relationship with other individuals, living or dead. The artist least of all is an island. In his *Lectures on Shakespeare* Coleridge re-applies the concept of method that he sees as characteristic of Shakespeare's internal development to the external development of literary tradition. This act of cross-reference between inner and outer development is of tremendous

---

[1] *The Friend*, Vol. ii, Essay 4, p. 304.
[2] *Ibid.* p. 300.

significance. Coleridge's formulation of creativity as an *external* tradition is a turning-point in the history of English criticism:

few there have been among critics, who have followed with the eye of the imagination the imperishable, yet ever-wandering, spirit of poetry through its various metempsychoses, and consequent metamorphoses; —or who have rejoiced in the light of clear perception at beholding with each new birth, with each rare *ovatar*, the human race frame to itself a new body, by assimilating materials of nourishment out of its new circumstances, and work for itself new organs of power appropriate to the new sphere of its motion and activity![1]

The powers needed to see the development of literary tradition (not, we notice, '*a* tradition', but the main stream of developing human consciousness, 'the spirit of poetry') are the same powers by which the individual mind grows. The true critic sees 'with the eye of the imagination' and 'in the light of clear perception' a process of organic growth, in which each new 'avatar' involves a re-creation of all that has gone before in a form appropriate for its time and purpose. The word 'avatar' is an Indian one describing the descent of a Hindu deity to the earth in a particular incarnation. For Coleridge, it suggests very nicely the idealist, almost Platonic, form of this tradition. 'The relation of the parts to each other and to the whole,' he wrote, in *The Friend*, 'is predetermined by a truth originating in the mind, and not abstracted or generalised from observation of the parts.'[2]

This whole concept of tradition, even to the description of it as an ideal order, is of course a familiar one. It is the origin of T. S. Eliot's far more famous account of 'tradition'. Ninety-one years later, in 'Tradition and the Individual Talent', we find this:

No poet, no artist of any sort, has his complete meaning alone. His significance, his appreciation is the appreciation of his relation to the dead poets and artists... The necessity that he shall conform, that he shall cohere, is not onesided; what happens when a new work of art is created is something that happens simultaneously to all the works of art which preceded it. The existing monuments form an ideal order among themselves, which is modified by the introduction of the new (the really

---

[1] Raysor, Vol. I, p. 174.
[2] *The Friend*, Vol. II, Essay 5, p. 305.

new) work of art among them...To conform merely would be for the new work not really to conform at all; it would not be new, and would therefore not be a work of art.[1]

Eliot's theory of tradition is an organic development of Coleridge's. Like Coleridge, he needed a way of seeing creativity as at once an intensely individual, *and* a total cultural phenomenon. Tradition is an order existing in the mind. But it is not an order that can be defined from an external observation of its links; tradition in Eliot's sense, like 'method' in Coleridge's, can only be understood by participation. For Eliot, like Coleridge, it is the few who can recognize a significant new work and see it in its context of the whole history of poetry, who can share in the re-ordering of the past by the creative writer—who, in changing the tradition, himself joins it. Our entire twentieth-century idea of tradition turns out to be an extension of the Romantic idea of organic development, with its fundamental paradox that the only true continuity is in change. The peculiar genius of Shakespeare, for Coleridge, is his ability through his symbols to elicit from his audience a participation in the 'method' of his own myriad-mindedness. For him, Shakespeare modifies our entire awareness of the rest of literature.

[1] *Selected Essays* (Faber, 1951). p. 12.

5

Memory and Perception

We have already noticed that in Book ɪᴠ of *The Prelude* Wordsworth can describe himself in relation to his memory

> As one who hangs down-bending from the side
> Of a slow-moving boat...
>
> (247–8)

He is in the poem, he says, 'incumbent o'er the surface of past
time', reading his memory like the ambiguous appearance of the
murky lake-bottom, unable to tell 'the shadow from the substance'. This is one of a number of images where he deliberately
calls attention to the ambiguity of his own memory. Just as the
way he sees the present is partly dependent on his experience of
the past, so (less obviously) his view of the past is coloured by
the present. Memory is, in fact, treated as a form of perception
that operates in the same way as the senses. We find in memory
the same dialectic between projection and receptivity. For him,
sense-perception and artistic creation are both alike part of the
Imagination, which

> Creates, creator and receiver both,
> Working in alliance with the works
> Which it beholds...

In the *Immortality Ode* there is a similar passage which again
raises the ambiguous relationship of memory to our interpretation of the present. In lines 152–5 he writes of

> Those shadowy recollections,
> Which, be they what they may,
> Are yet the fountain light of all our day,
> Are yet the master-light of all our seeing...

The recollection of certain 'shadowy' childhood experiences,
which, in themselves he finds difficult to interpret ('be they what
they may'), provide the schemata for all his interpretation of the

present. It is looking back in this 'master light' that orders his present experience in a particular way. Wordsworth here, as so often, is being much more explicit than he is often given credit for being. What he is doing, quite carefully, is trying to define the way in which the child can be seen as the 'best philosopher'. What is the particular quality of childhood experience that we value most when we come to look back on it afterwards? And—even more specifically—how does this quality organize the whole of our perception of the past?

> The thought of our past years in me doth breed
> Perpetual benediction: not indeed
> For that which is most worthy to be blessed;
> Delight and liberty, the simple creed
> Of Childhood, whether fluttering or at rest,
> With new-born hope for ever in his breast:
> Not for these I raise
> The song of thanks and praise;
> But for those obstinate questionings
> Of sense and outward things,
> Fallings from us, vanishings...
>
> (136–46)

I think we may see more clearly what Wordsworth is doing here if we turn for a moment to a visual analogy from elsewhere. Professor E. H. Gombrich, in his book *Art and Illusion*, investigates the method by which visual schemata are progressively modified until they are felt to correspond with the information offered by the eye. He takes as an example how the lithographer, Garland, was so dominated by his 'gothic' schema of Chartres Cathedral in 1836 that he made the windows of the west front pointed, whereas a modern photograph shows us that they are (contrary to all expectation) romanesque and rounded. Gombrich's point, of course, is not that Garland did not draw what he 'saw', but that his schemata at this point were so rigid that he failed to 'see' romanesque arches at all because he was expecting to see pointed gothic ones.[1] Going on from here to look at schematic figure construction, Gombrich comments that 'we hear a lot about training the eye, or learning to see, but that this phraseology can be misleading if it hides the fact that what

[1] *Art and Illusion*, p. 63.

we can learn is not to see but to discriminate.'[1] We need, he argues, a wrong schema to arrive at a correct portrait.

If we look again at the *Immortality Ode* we can, I think, see the point of the comparison. Wordsworth seems to be seeking an exact definition of his mental state by a very similar process of first stating his feeling as he expects it to be, and then progressively modifying his statement, point by point, until it corresponds more nearly with the as yet inarticulate feeling that he is struggling to put into words. In the first stanzas, for example, he is contrasting with his so far ill-defined sense of loss a 'simple creed of childhood'—a view of childhood that is idyllic, pastoral, and conventional in a particular late eighteenth-century sentimental tradition:

> the Earth herself is adorning,
> This sweet May-morning,
> And the Children are pulling
> On every side,
> In a thousand valleys far and wide,
> Fresh flowers; while the sun shines warm,
> And the babe leaps up in his mother's arm...
>
> (43–9)

But as the poem continues he proceeds to define much more narrowly both the sense of loss, and the childhood experiences that he now feels to have been truly nourishing. Yet in this process a certain ambivalence becomes apparent. The innocent joy of childhood that he celebrates at the beginning of the poem is modified, and finally cast off as being irrelevant. Not this joy, it seems, but rather the 'obstinate questionings/Of sense and outward things' are in the last analysis the true 'master light of all our seeing'. What exactly these obstinate questionings and misgivings are is left unexplained. From the first book of *The Prelude*, however, we can recognize here without much difficulty the 'spots of time' when, for instance, he stole the boat, and felt the terrifying presence of the mountain rearing up behind him, or the moment of fear on the crag above the ravens' nest. Something of what we might call the moral ambivalence of these moments is carried over into the *Immortality Ode*. In both

[1] *Ibid.* p. 147.

examples we have mentioned from *The Prelude* we can find the
same ecstatic animal vitality of childhood which colours the
Immortality Ode's stylized pastoral opening (so different, say,
from *Tintern Abbey*). Co-extensive with this, however, is a feeling of terror and guilt—ostensibly for stealing the boat, or the
ravens' eggs. But as with the 'low breathings' that Wordsworth
felt following him, the terror and guilt is out of all proportion to
the nature of the deed. In the case of the boat and the mountain
William Empson links Wordsworth's fear directly with his
feelings for his father—as we shall see, a highly significant
suggestion. What I think it is important that we notice here,
however, is that these moments are the very opposite of
innocent. What makes the child in Wordsworth's eyes the 'best
philosopher' is, on the contrary, his capacity to be 'haunted for
ever by the eternal mind': the openness to irrational fear in the
face of a felt moral (or rather, numinous) judgement of a 'living
universe'. They are the moments when the child encounters
inarticulately *values* outside himself:

> Blank misgivings of a Creature
> Moving about in worlds not realis'd,
> High instincts before which our mortal Nature
> Did tremble like a guilty thing surpris'd...
>
> (147–50)

The use of a capital letter for 'Creature' seems to stress both its
meanings: not just as a 'created being', but also the older more
specific meaning of 'one who owes his position to another'. This
suggestion appears to be reinforced by the next line. If we may
take 'not realiz'd' as meaning 'not yet made real', as Lionel
Trilling argues,[1] we are confronted with the implication that
'reality' is somehow dependent upon a loss of innocence and an
acceptance of guilt. The terrifying moment of insight with which
Wordsworth is struggling is of man's *moral* interdependence
with nature—an insight the more important for being irrational
and hidden, as Coleridge felt so agonizingly in *The Ancient
Mariner*. Wordsworth's description of these feelings in the
Immortality Ode corresponds very closely with, for instance, such
passages as this in *The Prelude*:

[1] Lionel Trilling, 'The Immortality Ode' (from *The Liberal Imagination* (Secker
and Warburg, 1951)), reprinted in *English Romantic Poets* (Galaxy, 1960).

> for many days, my brain
> Work'd with a dim and undetermin'd sense
> Of unknown modes of being; in my thoughts
> There was a darkness, call it solitude,
> Or blank desertion, no familiar shapes
> Of hourly objects, images of trees,
> Of sea or sky, no colours of green fields;
> But huge and mighty Forms that do not live
> Like living men mov'd slowly through the mind
> By day and were the trouble of my dreams.[1]

The impact of these 'unknown modes of being' on Wordsworth's growth is, he discovers on looking back, much more significant than the 'simple creed of childhood'—the original schema which he applied to his memory. His first naive and conventional impression is found wanting, and has to be modified on two levels. On the first, and simplest, he succeeds in isolating the actual ambivalent moments of 'renovating power' from the golden haze of nostalgia which surrounds them; simultaneously, the simple amoral idyllic picture of childhood bliss has been modified to a much more complex moral awareness. The result, we notice, is ambiguous, just as for Coleridge the final state of the Mariner, doomed at uncertain intervals to recount the guilt and terror of his own moral awakening, remains ambiguous. Just as all sense-perception is ambiguous, so too memory is capable of a variety of conflicting or equivocal interpretations.

This brings us to a fundamental point about ambiguity. Gombrich claims that 'ambiguity as such cannot be perceived'. To perceive, he argues, means to form a complete and reasonably probable image—even if it means being mistaken. Thus an ambiguity can never be 'seen': it can only be inferred by a process of making first one reading, then another, until all the possibilities are satisfied. Gombrich is specifically concerned with

---

1 *Prelude* (1805), Book I, lines 418–27. There is a curious ambiguity in lines 25–6. Are we to understand that the 'Forms' are alive, but alien and utterly unlike the human life we know, or that they are dead, but appear to move like 'Living men'? I suspect Wordsworth himself was not sure. D. W. Harding discusses this experience in 'The Hinterland of Thought' (*Metaphor and Symbol*, ed. Knights and Cottle) and suggests that at the level at which Wordsworth apprehends these 'infantile forms of awareness charged with intense emotional significance' he could not be more explicit.

visual perception, but the principle can equally well be applied verbally. Gombrich adduces the famous figure which can either be seen as a rabbit or a duck:[1]

His point is that however fast we switch from one reading to the other we can never *see* both creatures at the same time. The mind insists rigorously that it shall be 'either or'. Dealing with the problem of verbal ambiguity, Empson claims similarly that a word can never be read with two meanings at the same time. The words 'rose' and 'rows', for instance, Empson argues

never got in each other's way; it is hard to believe that they are pronounced the same. Homonyms with less powerful systems of association, like the verb 'rows' and the 'roes' of fishes, lend themselves easily to puns and seem in some degree attracted towards the two more powerful systems; but to insist that the first two are the same sound, to pass suddenly from one to the other, destroys both of them, and leaves a sort of bewilderment in the mind.[2]

In looking at a visual ambiguity, or in grasping a verbal pun there has to be a real effort of distinction which, even in unconsciously selecting one reading from two or more possible ones, increases what one might call the 'charge' of the passage—the sensation of multi-layered meaning that a prose account would almost certainly lack. Anton Ehrenzweig, in *The Hidden Order of Art*,[3] takes this point a stage further with his interesting hypothesis that while the mind will only accept one alternative at a time at the conscious level, unconsciously there also exists a syncretistic scanning mechanism which enables us to grasp opposites simultaneously. A great deal of our most sensitive response to a work of art, he argues, is unconscious, and cannot be made conscious in the contradictory forms in which it first comes. Though there is clearly some evidence to support this,

[1] *Art and Illusion*, p. 4.
[2] *Seven Types*, p. 64.
[3] Weidenfeld and Nicolson, 1967.

such a case is very difficult to establish in general terms. What is interesting to us here is the light this can throw on a very interesting analysis of Wordsworth's 'Lucy' poem, *A Slumber Did My Spirit Seal*, by A. P. Rossiter, who demonstrates how Wordsworth can draw a most disturbing tension between a terror of death and a joyful acceptance, even while each reading firmly excludes the possibility of the other.[1]

One could not hope to do justice to Rossiter's analysis in a brief summary like this, but since it provides a direct refutation of Empson's charge that Wordsworth (and, indeed, all the 'Romantics') were lacking in genuine ambiguity, it is worth recapitulating. The poem is a familiar one:

> A slumber did my spirit seal,
> I had no human fears:
> She seem'd a thing that could not feel
> The touch of earthly years.
>
> No motion has she now, no force;
> She neither hears nor sees;
> Roll'd round in earth's diurnal course,
> With rocks, and stones, and trees!

The ambiguity lies primarily in the change of tense between the two stanzas. Thus, if we assume that the first stanza describes a past situation, to be contrasted with the present, the poet was living in a trance-like state of bliss when his love seemed temporarily inviolate. Now, however, she is dead and gone, her vitality absorbed into the cold earth. Read in this way the poem suggests a physical horror of death. If, on the other hand, the first stanza can be taken as describing a particular visionary moment after the death of his love, then the second stanza can be interpreted as a comfort to his grief by the realization that in her union with nature she has acquired a kind of mute immortality. Clearly, read in this way the poem is resigned, or even hopeful. The point is that for all the apparent contradiction, neither meaning can fully obliterate the other in our assimilation of the poem, and we are left not with a resolution, but a very radical feeling of doubt about death.

[1] A. P. Rossiter, 'Ambivalence: The Dialectic of the Histories', from *Angel with Horns* (Longmans, 1961), p. 48.

It is, I would suggest, partly because of a similar radical doubt in Wordsworth's mind that the ambiguity we have noted in the *Immortality Ode* obtrudes in so complex a manner. In the last line, for example, it is clear that the 'thoughts that do often lie too deep for tears' may be either affirming a new philosophic certainty beyond grief, or admitting his overwhelming sense of loss. The key to this ambiguity is in the previous stanza:

> Though nothing can bring back the hour
> Of splendour in the grass, of glory in the flower;
> We will grieve not, rather find
> Strength in what remains behind,
> In the primal sympathy
> Which having been must ever be...
>
> (180–5)

'What remains behind' may *either* refer to what is left of a ravaged sensibility under the 'inevitable yoke' of advancing years, truncated now and maimed in its powers of response to nature, *or* it may mean the total residue of memory itself: not like a framed and fading photograph of childhood, but a dynamic presence, now so orientated and organized by the 'obstinate questionings' as to contain within it what he has come to reject— the 'simple creed of childhood' that he neither can, nor wishes to experience in the present. After all, what Wordsworth is doing in the poem is re-creating, brilliantly, that very childhood quality he claims to have lost.

If, then, we take the former interpretation, the whole poem is about his sense of loss. It is the long farewell to the greatness of his poetic powers that some critics have seen it as. Viewed like this, the *Immortality Ode* is a magnificent rearguard action of poetic nostalgia. 'The years that bring the philosophic mind' teach the poet to learn to live with the loss that he has analyzed in the poem. Though he has relinquished 'one delight', he can still press forward with Roman stoicism and learn to substitute experience for inspiration. On the second interpretation, however, the 'primal sympathy/Which having been must ever be' is neither a pius hope, nor a bold metaphysical defiance of time, but the direct outcome of the careful conscious process of analysis and modification of memory that has been going on throughout

127

the poem. The 'Beauty' and 'Fear' that fostered Wordsworth in *The Prelude* are felt here not as parallel influences, but as the two sides of a balance, a tension of opposites, that he is trying to assimilate in equilibrium, without trying to resolve. Thus, for example, he can in the next stanza 'Love the brooks...even more' without contradicting what he has previously said because this new 'Philosophic mind' is founded on the assimilation of both 'the innocent brightness of the new-born day' *and* 'the clouds that gather round the setting sun'. Such an assimilation of opposites: guilt and innocence; beauty and fear; sunrise and sunset; has sharpened his schematic powers of discrimination to the point where

> the meanest flower that blows can give
> Thoughts that do often lie too deep for tears.
>
> (205–6)

Clearly there is in the *Immortality Ode* a very radical ambiguity between loss and gain that reflects a similar ambiguity in Wordsworth's own experience. Yet even this does not fully account for the ambiguous complexity of thought we find in the poem. There is, it seems to me, a further ambiguity in Wordsworth's attitude to memory that has its counterpart both in language and in visual perception. He prefaces the poem with a quotation from one we have already discussed, *My Heart Leaps Up*... :

> The child is father to the man

The reason for Wordsworth using such a deliberate paradox we shall discuss in a moment. What concerns us here is the kind of logical paradox so created. It is worth cross-referencing again to Gombrich, who shows us a drawing by Saul Steinberg:

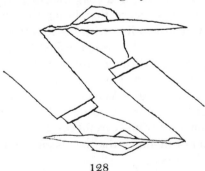

He writes:

We have no clue as to which is meant to be the real and which the image; each interpretation is equally probable, but neither, as such, is consistent. If proof were needed of the kinship between the language of art and the language of words, it could be found in this drawing. For the perplexing effect of this self-reference is very similar to the paradoxes beloved of philosophers: the Cretan who says that all Cretans lie, or the simple blackboard with only one statement on it which runs, 'The only statement on the blackboard is untrue.' If it is true it is untrue and if untrue true.[1]

The paradox about the lying Cretan has been squarely tackled (if not resolved) by Bertrand Russell in his doctrine of types.[2] It rests, of course, on the question of whether a definer of a class may be legitimately included in that class. In this case, can the Cretan defining the class be held to be a member of the class even to the point of ceasing to define it? Similarly, the paradox underlying Steinberg's joke depends on whether the definer (in this case, the hand and pen) can include itself...Now when Wordsworth writes 'The child is father to the man' he is (logically) only playing. He is using the shock-effect of the paradox to say something that is not really a paradox at all. But there is a very real Cretan paradox in the *Immortality Ode*. Wordsworth cannot be included in the specified class of 'six-years darlings of a pigmy size'. But what is predicated of this class is that they can see and understand truths which are beyond the reach of any adult. Wordsworth is an adult; yet he describes this vision to us. The child cannot. Wordsworth can only create the poem by including himself in a class from which his poem specifically excludes him. The resolution of this paradox—from the poet's point of view—is, of course, the memory. Steinberg's drawing, and the Cretan lies are both outside the dimension of time. Memory, however, permits Wordsworth to place side by side the vision that has been lost, and the present vision that, paradoxically, must in some sense contain the other in proclaiming its loss. As Coleridge could show in the dialogue between the

[1] *Art and Illusion*, pp. 200–1.
[2] Bertrand Russell, *The Principles of Mathematics* (Allen and Unwin, 1903), Ch. x, 'The Contradiction', and Appendix 'B'.

Wedding Guest and the Ancient Mariner, memory puts the past and present into an immediate relationship.

If all perception involves the modification of an existing schema to fit a new situation, then (as Gombrich among others has pointed out[1]) the amount conveyed is in inverse proportion to its expectedness. The more startling the modification or the more radical the discrimination the reader or listener is forced to make, the greater the actual information conveyed. What is most expected tells us least. Hence Wordsworth's attack in his Preface of 1802 on the old idea that 'by the act of writing in verse an author makes a formal engagement that he will gratify certain known habits of association'. The attack on 'known habits of association' is one of the fundamental premises of 'Romantic' poetry. As we have seen, the whole movement of the *Immortality Ode* is from simple cliché towards a growing discrimination of emotion. Similarly, of course, the statement 'the child is father to the man' conveys to us much more than any circumlocution about childhood experiences influencing adult development. When I said just now that Wordsworth was only 'playing' I was referring to his technique. He was completely in earnest about what he had to say—which was why he said it in the most effective way possible.

But there is a second way in which such an ambiguity may convey information. Coleridge has a note made in November 1801 querying:

Whether or no the too great definiteness of Terms in any language may not consume too much of the vital and idea-creating force in distinct, clear, full made images & so prevent originality—*original* thought as distinct from positive thought—Germans in general—[2]

It is not, I think, immediately clear what he is talking about. Perhaps, again, an analogy from the visual arts may come to our assistance. One of the most far-reaching discoveries of nine-teenth-century painting was that if the beholder could be persuaded to select the right schema, his eye would in fact 'see' far more than the most meticulous representation could show. Gombrich comments on how Manet paints galloping horses as a

[1] *Art and Illusion*, p. 148.
[2] *Anima Poetae*, p. 19; *Notebooks*, Vol. I, 1016.

vague blur: 'He uses the very ambiguity of his flickering forms to suggest a variety of readings and to compensate thereby for the absence of movement in the painting...'[1] The moving legs of racehorses are still some way from Coleridge's desire for blurred edges to his ideas, but if we take another example used by Ehrenzweig the connection becomes clearer. As we have mentioned, Anton Ehrenzweig argues that unconscious 'syncretistic' apprehension is much more inclusive than any conscious reasoning when we are faced by any very complex problem—such as that presented by a work of art. He takes another example: that of a good bridge-player:

His attention was blank and blurred while unconscious scanning went on in deeper levels of his mind. Any attempt at a more precise visualization would be as confusing for him as it is in a creative search. If at the crucial moment of choice we try to size up the situation too clearly we will automatically narrow the scope of our attention and so deprive ourselves of the faculty of low-level scanning on which the right move depends.[2]

It is one of the recurrent features of Coleridge's thinking that he treats ideas as if they were works of art; we shall be discussing some of the implications of this in a later chapter. Clearly, here he is thinking of ideas in terms that will allow for the 'variety of readings' that Gombrich finds in Manet, or the process of 'unconscious scanning' referred to by Ehrenzweig. All three writers seem to be describing a common phenomenon. It is, I think, this same phenomenon that William Empson is describing when he emphasizes that the process of 'getting to know' a new poet is primarily a matter of learning to control and discriminate between the range of 'less probable alternatives' ready in the mind to impose themselves if they are found to answer. Once again, at another level, we are reminded that preception—whether of objects or ideas—is a creative act of imagination depending on the interplay of perceiver and perceived:

as, to take another coefficient which the eye attaches to things, as you have an impression of a thing's distance away, which can hardly ever be detached from the pure visual sensation, and when it is so detached

---

[1] *Art and Illusion*, p. 181.
[2] *Hidden Order of Art*, p. 39.

leaves your eye disconcerted (if what you took for a wall turns out to be the sea, you at first see nothing, perhaps are for a short time puzzled with a blur, and then see differently), so the reading of a new poet, or any poetry at all, fills many readers with a sense of mere embarrassment and discomfort, like that of not knowing, and wanting to know, whether it is a wall or the sea.[1]

Now in the *Immortality Ode* we find Wordsworth similarly insisting that some communications actually have more meaning, and are more creative, if they are left vague and ambiguous than if they are made fully explicit. He describes, for instance, the moments of excitement and fear that constitute 'the master-light of all our seeing' as:

> Those shadowy recollections,
> Which, be they what they may...

He has no intention of trying to clarify or schematize these recollections beyond a certain point. Because the mind is no passive instrument, but a creative participator, such shadowy schemata will serve to interpret his memory far more truthfully than mere conscious clarity would permit; similarly, of course, at another level, such vagueness actually allows the reader to understand more than any fully articulate explanation would. Similarly, too, in the case of the epigram 'the child is father to the man' it is precisely the fundamental inconsistency of each possible interpretation of this kind of ambiguity—whether it be, as here, in a poem, or visually in Steinberg's hands—that forces us to refer to what Empson calls the range of 'less probable alternatives'. Significantly, this is not the case with ambiguities where the alternatives are fully self-sufficient and consistent—in, for instance, *A Slumber Did My Spirit Seal*, or the ambiguity we have noted in the idea of 'strength in what remains behind'. In such extreme cases the mind is trained to a very high degree of exclusion.

We are thus faced with what seem to be three different kinds of ambiguity in Wordsworth's *Immortality Ode*: a complete kind, where the contradiction between the various readings is absolute, and the consciousness demands a rigorous 'either, or...'; an inconsistent, or incomplete kind, where in the last resort the

---

[1] *Seven Types*, pp. 239–40.

consciousness can accept neither without its opposite; and a third, which while it may overlap with the others, remains largely unconscious, and is often characterized at a conscious level only by a certain deliberate vagueness and refusal to clarify. All three occur at points where memory and perception are interacting : where the present is shaping how he looks at the past, or the past shaping the present.

Coleridge's attitude to memory is, similarly, no less complex and equivocal. We have already noted in the last chapter the ambiguity of the ending of *The Ancient Mariner*, where the Mariner's final state can either be interpreted as irreparable damage, or as a depth of insight so profound as to leave him no longer at ease. As we saw, a similar, though less immediately obvious ambiguity is present in stanza VI of *Dejection*. The process of stealing by abstruse research from Coleridge's own nature all the natural man can be interpreted either as growth or decay. Neither interpretation, though, is completely self-consistent. We are forced to start searching among the 'less probable alternatives'. This, we may begin to suspect, can help to account for the curious way in which future growth and renovation seems to depend on articulating the poet's ambiguous sense of loss. This ambiguity between renovation and decay is neatly taken up in the next stanza of *Dejection*, stanza VII. The wind, 'which long has raved unnoticed', suddenly forces itself upon Coleridge's attention at this juncture, and he proceeds to read into the sound of the æolian harp a whole series of fantasies not immediately related to the main development of the poem, but which project schemata from the undercurrents of his mind. In the voice of this 'Actor, perfect in all tragic sounds', Coleridge hears two descriptions of himself. First, defeat —and dramatic sudden death:

> 'Tis of the rushing of an host in rout,
> With groans, of trampled men, with smarting wounds—
> At once they groan with pain, and shudder with the cold!
> But hush! there is a pause of deepest silence!
> And all that noise, as of a rushing crowd,
> With groans, and tremulous shudderings—all is over...

But following this dramatic downfall in battle is another image offering a cautious hope :

It tells another tale, with sounds less deep and loud!
A tale of less affright,
And tempered with delight,
As Otway's self had framed the tender lay,—
'Tis of a little child
Upon a lonesome wild,
Not far from home, but she hath lost her way:
And now moans low in bitter grief and fear,
And now screams loud, and hopes to make her mother hear.

The images of being defeated in the battle of life, or as a little child lost, but not in reality far from home are both peculiarly expressive of certain sides of Coleridge—as he was well aware—but it is not necessary to identify either image with him in any detail, any more than it is with the earlier version's 'Lucy Grey', to feel the impact of the two fantasies. It is sufficient for us to be aware of how these images were running just under the surface of his thoughts for us to feel how ambiguous was his attitude to his own predicament in *Dejection*.

For both Coleridge and Wordsworth mental growth was itself equivocal. It is no accident that Wordsworth, for example, was so carefully non-committal about the idea of the pre-existence of the soul on which he had based the central section of the *Immortality Ode*. To Miss Fenwick he wrote:

To that dream-like vividness and splendour which invest objects of sight in childhood, everyone, I believe, if he would look back, could bear testimony... I took hold of the notion of pre-existence as having sufficient foundation in humanity for authorizing me to make for my purpose the best use of it I could as a poet.[1]

Nor does the question of whether he believed it, or merely used it as a convenient extended metaphor, seriously affect our interpretation of the passage. In a sense, it is a schema that he is trying out to see if it matches with his own experience. Almost at once we realize that the two alternatives, true or false, are a part of the ambiguity he is trying to state. Mental growth, as he experienced it, was both ambiguous and inconsistent. To see it

[1] *Poetical Works*, ed. De Selincourt (5 vols. Oxford, 1940–9), Vol. IV (1947), pp. 463–4.

as a gain immediately involved him in an assertion of what he remembers he has lost; to see it as a loss cannot be done without recognizing his present ability to recall and evaluate what he has lost with far deeper understanding than a child. This ambiguity haunts the whole 'Romantic' attitude to childhood. Critics, from Coleridge onwards, have been right in stressing the central position of 'moral consciousness' in Wordsworth. Nevertheless, we begin to observe that in his attitude to childhood this 'moral consciousness' turns out to be an unexpectedly ambiguous quality—in all the three senses we have so far analysed. It is, for example, acquired more through memories of guilt than innocence. The moments in *The Prelude* that were to become what in the *Ode* he was to call 'the master light of all our seeing' were, we recall, moments of both intense physical awareness, and of an irrational moral guilt; moments, we suggested, when Wordsworth's hypersensitive consciousness was confronted, however arbitrarily, by an overwhelming sense of values beyond and outside himself. In some cases, indeed, what he describes is not 'moral' at all (in the normal sense), but a numinous primitive awe of taboos. Such moments seemed to be for him, as he remembered them, nodal points which expressed in a single incident the complex growth of his feeling for the 'permanent relations' between himself and nature. There is one image in particular in *The Prelude* which sums up the ambiguity that he came to see in all his childhood development. In Book XII (1805), immediately after the description of 'visionary dreariness', he goes on to add what he calls one more 'affecting incident':

> One Christmas-time,
> The day before the holidays began,
> Feverish and tired, and restless, I went forth
> Into the fields, impatient for the sight
> Of those two Horses which should bear us home;
> My brothers and myself. There was a crag,
> An Eminence, which from the meeting-point
> Of two highways ascending, overlook'd
> At least a long half-mile of those two roads,
> By which the expected Steeds might come,
> The choice uncertain. Thither I repair'd

Up to the highest summit; 'twas a day
Stormy, and rough, and wild, and on the grass
I sate, half-shelter'd by a naked wall;
Upon my right hand was a single sheep,
A whistling hawthorn on my left, and there,
With those companions at my side, I watch'd,
Straining my eyes intensely, as the mist
Gave intermitting prospect of the wood
And plain beneath.

(346–64)

It is another such moment of intense physical awareness, like
those we have been considering in the opening Books of *The
Prelude*. Wordsworth is acutely conscious both of his own position on the windy crag, 'half-shelter'd by a naked wall' with the
sheep and the hawthorn bush, and, simultaneously, the reason
that has brought him there. The two roads beneath him part in
the mist; it is not important, nor does he even bother to tell us,
down which road the horses did finally come. It is the two roads,
the visual image of ambiguity, that dominates his memory;
that—and a quite gratuitous feeling of guilt with which the
incident is afterwards associated. His sense of guilt over his
father's death is utterly irrational, yet it pervades the whole
scene in retrospect:

Ere I to School return'd
That dreary time, ere I had been ten days
A dweller in my Father's House, he died,
And I and my two Brothers, Orphans then,
Followed his Body to the Grave. The event
With all the sorrow which it brought appear'd
A Chastisement; and when I call'd to mind
That day so lately pass'd, when from the crag
I look'd in such anxiety of hope,
With trite reflections of morality,
Yet in the deepest passion, I bow'd low
To God, who thus corrected my desires...

(364–75)

What were these 'trite reflections of morality' that contrast so
sharply with the depth of his passion? Is it merely the gap
between feelings and understanding at this stage of the boy's

development? The relationship of this passage to the rest of the sentence is interesting. Syntactically it clearly describes his state of mind when afterwards he recalled the event and tried to make sense of it. Yet at a first reading it is very easy to transfer these 'trite reflections of morality' to his mood on the crag itself. Such an ambiguity, more apparent than real at a conscious level, may well be no more than the result of loose construction; but there are very few accidents in poetry if we look hard enough. The juxtaposition suggests, almost casually, how his thoughts about the event afterwards have come to colour his memory of the event itself. Such an ambiguity is not unlike his own image of peering into the lake of his memory, unable to part 'the shadow from the substance'. So here at one level there is a contradiction. At another, the schema by which he distinguishes has merged with what is distinguished. His irrational feeling that his father's death was a winnowing, or 'chastisement', is thus either an example of the 'trite reflections of morality', or, by implication, and in the strange Wordsworthian sense of 'morality' we have already seen, an expression of a *deeper* morality. Wordsworth, it seems to me, is poised between a conventional Christian resignation, and a much more profoundly disturbing memory of a numinous childhood awe, more akin to the 'low breathings' that chased him over the hills, or the

> Blank misgivings of a Creature
> Moving about in worlds not realised...

There is behind this 'morality' a very deeply-rooted tension.

It seems also that this 'corrected' morality was associated with the two roads. What had been in his mind originally an image of future hope had been suddenly transformed into an image of impending death. Looking back on the event in 1799 (if we are to accept De Selincourt's dating) as he wrote the first draft of *The Prelude*, Wordsworth balances the hope and the sense of death against each other as opposite interpretations of the scene for which the two roads has come to stand as a symbol. I think Empson's suggestion that Wordsworth's guilt when confronted by the mountain after he had stolen the boat was really a fear of his father is significant here. I doubt if one could show with any certainty that the feelings of guilt and awe on such occasions were always unconsciously associated with his father, whereas the intense sensual awareness was always connected with his mother, but the polarity of these two elements can nearly always be discerned at such moments. In this sense, too,

> Foster'd alike by Beauty and by Fear

has a surprisingly literal meaning. Nor, I think, would Wordsworth have shied away from the notion that beauty was associated with his feelings for his mother, or fear with his father. He uses such symbols—as here—too explicitly. Moreover they *are* symbols. The process of abstraction is, as we have seen, quite deliberate:

> Remembering how she felt, but what she felt
> Remembering not...

They are symbols of the *security* that his upbringing with nature had given him, so that he can turn afterwards to such moments of ambiguous emotion as when he looked down from the crag as a source of spiritual refreshment:

> And afterwards, the wind and sleety rain
> And all the business of the elements,
> The single sheep, and the one blasted tree,
> And the bleak music of that old stone wall,
> The noise of wood and water, and the mist
> Which on the line of each of those two roads
> Advanced in such indisputable shapes,
> All these were spectacles and sounds to which
> I often would repair and thence would drink,
> As at a fountain; and I do not doubt
> That in this later time, when storm and rain
> Beat on my roof at midnight, or by day
> When I am in the woods, unknown to me
> The workings of my spirit thence are brought.
>
> (376–89)

The image of a fountain for such an experience is extraordinary. Yet the recollection of this ambiguous emotion, poised between hope and despair, is plainly one of Wordsworth's 'springs of action'. The mist, whose shapes are 'indisputable' in the sense of being impenetrable and not to be questioned, is like a visual equivalent of the 'shadowy recollections' of the *Immortality Ode*. Even as it obscures the two roads before the young Wordsworth, it lends them too a kind of numinous or mysterious quality that a greater clarity would dispel. What is so interesting about Wordsworth's accounts of these 'spots of time' is that, in spite of the great deal he writes about them and their effects on his development, there remains something misty and vague about what actually happens to him in contemplating them. Such a reticence, when we contrast it with the explicitness of so much of his psychological thinking, is clearly deliberate.

As we shall see in the next chapter, there are significant differences between Wordsworth and Coleridge in their attitudes to mental growth. Here, however, we are stressing for the moment the wide measure of continuity in their ideas. The springs of action in Coleridge's experience were as ambiguous as Wordsworth's in their own way. For example, it seems to me that the long discussion about the 'meaning' of the albatross in *The Ancient Mariner* is beside the point unless we first of all admit that it remains fundamentally equivocal. Though the bird, and the shooting of it, can be given a wide variety of interpretation,[1] I think we miss the whole point of the shooting unless we see it as arbitrary and meaningless. Coleridge was taking his stand very close indeed to Wordsworth when he told Mrs Barbauld that *The Ancient Mariner*

ought to have no more moral than the *Arabian Nights* tale of the merchant's sitting down to eat dates by the side of a well, and throwing the shells aside, and lo! a genie starts up, and says he *must* kill the aforesaid merchant, *because* one of the date shells had, it seems, put out the eye of the genie's son.[2]

The 'morality' that Coleridge is claiming for his poem here has the same irrational compulsion that Wordsworth experienced in feeling that his father's death had come as a punishment to him. Like Wordsworth, Coleridge seems to feel a quality of vital importance in this irrational 'responsibility' for arbitrary

---

[1] See, for instance, Robert Penn Warren, 'A Poem of Pure Imagination', *Selected Essays* (Eyre and Spottiswoode, 1964).
[2] *Table Talk*, ed. H. N. Coleridge (Murray, 1852), 31 May 1830.

actions. The ambiguity of the albatross's death is stressed with
some care:

> And I had done a hellish thing,
> And it would work 'em woe:
> For all averred, I had killed the bird
> That made the breeze to blow.
> Ah wretch! said they, the bird to slay,
> That made the breeze to blow!
>
> Nor dim nor red, like God's own head,
> The glorious Sun uprist:
> Then all averred, I had killed the bird
> That brought the fog and mist.
> 'Twas right, said they, such birds to slay,
> That bring the fog and mist.

I am aware, obviously, that one cannot evaluate the 'meaning'
of these two opposite judgements without taking into account
the total context—such symbols as the breeze, and the sun, for
example. Yet even were we able to say categorically—which
we cannot—that the breeze is a 'benign' force and the sun
'malignant', it would still not exonerate the doubtful justice of
the marginal gloss at this point: that his shipmates 'make themselves accomplices in the crime'. Nor, I believe, are we meant to
accept it as 'justice'. The sailors' guilt, true to the entire pattern of the action, is as arbitrary as that of the poor merchant in
the *Arabian Nights*. Even the Mariner's own guilt is essentially
out of all proportion to the nature of his crime. To interpret
it—as indeed it must be interpreted—on a symbolic level, is to
admit its ambiguity as an event.

In the last chapter I argued that it is precisely because the
'Romantic' attempt to look back upon childhood experience was
so fundamentally ambiguous, that the possibility of future
growth existed. Coleridge's theory of the Imagination in perception was essentially dialectical: schema; adaptation to sense-
impression; new schema. Just as it was not possible for
Coleridge to 'conceive an act of seeing wholly separate from the
modification of the judgement and the analogies of previous
experience',[1] so, too, the development of perception was seen

[1] Snyder, *Coleridge on Logic*, pp. 116–18.

by him as a continuous reaction of new experiences on what had gone before:

there is a previous discipline of the senses, that even in the general functions of touch, and taste, and smell, and sight and hearing we pass from our birth into a school beginning at the lowest forms and at our death we have not yet attained the highest.[1]

Two opposite streams of thought are meeting here: one the one hand the 'previous discipline' of the senses echoes something like a Platonic recognition theory in our growth of perception; on the other, Hartley's rigidly schematized seven stages of growth have been modified into a much more flexible intuitive observation. The process of mental growth, organic, active, and unified, came to be seen by Coleridge as a dialectic in which the mind develops not as an even progression, but by a series of leaps, in which moments of doubt and ambivalent feelings are assimilated into a new synthesis. What Empson calls the 'tap-root' which, he says, was kept by the romantic artist as a way back to his childhood for reference, was seen by Wordsworth and Coleridge quite seriously as an essential pre-requisite for all integrated growth. In *The Friend* Coleridge writes, for example:

Men are ungrateful to others only when they have ceased to look back upon their former selves with joy and tenderness. They exist in fragments. Annihilated as to the past, they are dead to the future, or seek for the proofs of it everywhere, only not (where alone they can be found) in themselves.[2]

He then quotes 'The child is father to the man'. It is this continual internalization of development, by which, at every stage, the mind is referred back to its own roots in childhood memory that is so characteristic of this 'Romantic' attitude to mental growth. More surprising, but, as we have seen, equally distinctive, is the fact that these moments of insight, conceived retrospectively as memories, should be preserved as an ambiguous tension between intense physical self-awareness, on the one hand, and dereliction and irrational guilt on the other. We are forced back, time and time again, to the basic question why, for both Wordsworth and Coleridge, the most typical feature

[1] *Ibid.*
[2] Introduction, Essay v.

141

of these moments of insight is not the feeling of the Imagination at work in perception, but of its *suspension*.

I believe it may be helpful for us, here, to look again at John Stuart Mill's breakdown, and to try and see more closely what it was that he found so healing in the poetry of Wordsworth. It was, we suggested, primarily a sense of value in man and nature that existed for its own sake, and quite apart from any capacity for further growth. Value, as Mill discovered when he woke up one morning at the age of twenty to a meaningless universe, is a quality much more conspicuous by its absence than by its presence. What he was able to find in Wordsworth was a surer, more subtle and more precise expression of his own awakened feelings. In his *Autobiography* he wrote: 'What made Wordsworth's poems a medicine for my state of mind, was that they expressed, not mere outward beauty, but states of feeling, and of thought coloured by feeling, under the excitement of beauty.'[1] Nature invoked in Wordsworth a particular union of thought and feeling. Even more important, as an affirmation of this value his poetry was immediately relevant to Mill's situation:

I needed to be made to feel that there was a real permanent happiness in tranquil contemplation. Wordsworth taught me this, not only without turning away from, but with a greatly increased interest in the common feelings and common destiny of human beings.[1]

What appealed to him to Wordsworth was not the 'bad philosophy' of the *Immortality Ode*, but the sense of belonging to a community of feeling: a sureness of response to the interaction of man and nature where Mill could only find reflected his own emotional bankruptcy. Wordsworth could write with all the assurance of having known, and come through, the collapse of all the beliefs that had made his youth worth living.

For Wordsworth this was primarily a 'moral' event. I think we should be missing the point of his influence on Mill if we ignored this aspect of Wordsworth's relation to nature. This is the other side of Wordsworth's primitive awe. The assurance Mill needed was that his precocious Gradgrind education had not 'proved' by 'facts' the meaninglessness of all other aspects

---

[1] Ch. v.

142

of his experience—and, in particular, of his emotions. Words-worth's answer was consistent. Perhaps the most specific example is in his 'Letter to Mathetes' which appeared in *The Friend*. 'Mathetes' was the pen-name, according to De Quincey, of two Scots, John Wilson and Alexander Blair, who had written to Coleridge with some doubts about the powers of genius to survive the education system of the day. It is a good indication of how close their views of the growth of the mind were, that Coleridge gives the reply to Wordsworth.

Wordsworth's reply is to see 'education' as a direct call and challenge to youth:

We would tell him that there are paths which he has not trodden, recesses which he has not penetrated; that there is a beauty which he has not seen, a pathos which he has not felt, a sublimity to which he has not been raised.[1]

Mill's own dramatic despair—indeed, all excesses of youth, whether moral or intellectual—are not, as it might appear, the result of overdevelopment, but of its opposite: mental mal-nutrition:

but let him first be assured, before he looks about for the means of attaining the insight, the discriminating powers, and the confirmed wisdom of manhood, that his soul has more to demand of the appropriate excellencies of youth than youth has yet supplied to it; that the evil under which he labours is not a superabundance of the instincts and the animating spirit of that age, but a falling short, or a failure.[1]

The first stage in growth towards the 'insight' and 'dis-criminating powers' of manhood (the terms are significant in view of what we have been saying about perception), is, according to Wordsworth, to be found in a new attitude towards the memory of past failure. It must not be suppressed, because that would be to deracinate his whole character. The past must be accepted and interpreted.

But what can he gain from this admonition? He cannot recall past time; he cannot begin his journey afresh; he cannot untwist the links by which, in no undelightful harmony, images and sentiments are wedded in his mind. Granted that the sacred light of childhood is and

[1] *The Friend*, p. 265.

must be for him no more than a remembrance. He may, notwithstanding, be remanded to nature, and with trustworthy hopes, founded less upon his sentient than upon his intellectual being: to nature, as leading on insensibly to the society of reason...[1]

The argument that feeling grows out of an intellectual appreciation of nature, rather than vice versa, has a very eighteenth-century ring about it. Wordsworth's apparently eighteenth-century framework of thought has often been pointed out. We have seen, however, how the Romantics changed the meaning of terms already in circulation. The whole movement of the *Immortality Ode* can, for example, be interpreted as a redefinition of the sentimental pastoral convention that Wordsworth inherited from 'the age of sensibility'[2]—the post-Augustan eighteenth century. We have also seen how capable Wordsworth was of building a very complex emotional response to nature upon a scientific theory—as in the case of the rainbow. Wordsworth, in fact, transformed the concept of nature.[3] The example he gives here in the 'Letter to Mathetes' of nature's teaching makes it clear how he means nature to be consciously interpreted as symbols of our 'moral' life. A boy is lying in bed in the dark looking at the dying spark of the candle he has just snuffed. The spark

fades and revives—gathers to a point—seems as if it would go out in a moment—again recovers its strength, nay becomes brighter than before: it continues to shine with an endurance which, in its apparent weakness, is a mystery; it protracts its existence so long, clinging to the power which supports it, that the observer, who had lain down on his bed so easy-minded, becomes sad and melancholy; his sympathies are touched...[4]

Wordsworth, in relating this incident which had obviously happened to him as a boy, is making explicit the attitude to nature that runs right through his work. There is no importance intrinsic in the event itself—the dying spark on the wick.

[1] *Ibid.*
[2] Northrop Frye, 'Towards Defining an Age of Sensibility', from *Eighteenth Century English Literature*, ed. Clifford (Galaxy, 1959).
[3] See Basil Willey's discussion of this point in *Eighteenth Century Background*, Ch. 12.
[4] *The Friend*, p. 266.

Its significance is entirely in its symbolic value to the mind contemplating it. In looking back on the event afterwards, the associated emotions are re-organized with a new insight and discriminating power so that what was originally quite trivial has become a focal point in the growth of the mind:

and the image of the dying taper may be recalled and contemplated, though with no sadness in the nerves, no disposition to tears, no unconquerable sighs, yet with a melancholy in the soul, a sinking inward into ourselves from thought to thought, a steady remonstrance, and a high resolve.—Let the youth go back, as occasion will permit, to nature and solitude, thus admonished by reason, and relying upon this newly acquired support. A world of fresh sensations will gradually open upon him as the mind puts off its infirmities, and as instead of being propelled restlessly towards others in admiration, or too hasty love, he makes it his prime business to understand himself.[1]

'Contemplation' is clearly a key concept: the term is used by both Wordsworth and Mill. The question is, of course, *what* exactly does Wordsworth mean by it? He has stressed, we remember, that it is primarily an intellectual activity; but at this level distinctions between 'feelings' and 'intellect' are probably valueless—whatever Wordsworth means by 'reason' (and it is not what Coleridge came to mean by it), it seems to comprehend both. The boy recalls and reviews the dying taper-spark purely as a symbolic event: a way of recalling the emotions originally associated with it. But to remember an emotion is not the same as participating in it—as Wordsworth elsewhere points out. Here, the youth sees in the dying taper a symbol 'for the moral life of himself'. It provides him with what is initially a quite arbitrary schema for viewing the ambiguous evidence of his past in a process of matching and interpretation, 'sinking inwards' systematically, as Wordsworth says, 'from thought to thought'. The 'teaching of nature' is based on contemplating memory. In this sense, the recollection of emotion in tranquillity is an intellectual process—or rather, an activity of 'reason'. The result we are promised is the opening up of a world of 'fresh sensations' in the present—a deepening of his powers of moral discrimination. It is, however, possible to interpret this, as it is his much misunderstood 'sermons in stones'

[1] *Ibid.*

utterances, in the conventional terms of an 'age of sensibility'—or (which is not dissimilar) to draw from nature, as the 'Wordsworthian' Victorians did, a few simple morals. But this sounds suspiciously like the 'trite reflections of morality' that Wordsworth found so out of key with the depth of his feelings when he contemplated his vigil beside the hawthorn tree at the point where he could see the two misty roads before him. This notion of morality was swept aside by the death of his father. Like the author of the Book of Job, he is henceforth trying to come to terms with a nature that is neither rational nor just—and it is this struggle, he claims, that can be looked back on as a source of comfort, and 'newly acquired support'. In so contemplating the moral complexity of external nature he finds the clue to the ambiguities in his own.

We may, at last, be close to some sort of an explanation for the renovating strength that Wordsworth found he could draw from the memory of moments of dereliction—the renewed upsurge of Imagination that he and Coleridge found in contemplating its suspension. As we have seen, the central experience of the *Immortality Ode* is Wordsworth's attempt to define his own mental state. Successive schemata are matched and modified until he is able to isolate those moments in his childhood that now enable him, in turn, to assimilate the ambiguities of mental growth and change. But in memory, as in all perception, such modifications only occur when the schema fails to match up to its object. Growth can *only* develop from the failure of existing schemata. Wordsworth reached back always to moments of dereliction, fear, and guilt because these were the moments that altered his way of seeing things. Mill, even though he never fully understood Wordsworth, learned from him to look back on his breakdown as the turning-point in his life. For both men, the memory of past failure was a part of their moral awareness of the present. Fear, guilt, irrational awe, could all be 'moral' experiences for Wordsworth because they extended his consciousness—made him capable of a more subtle discrimination. It was, for him, as for Coleridge, a logical extension of the idea of the Imagination.

6

Wordsworth and Coleridge
A Romanticism

In stressing how similar Wordsworth's and Coleridge's ideas were about their own poetic growth, it may seem that we have, up till now, been ignoring their very obvious differences. The reason for this is that I believe, as I have tried to show, that if we look at them together as a unity they offer a coherent whole greater than either of its parts. Each poet tends to illuminate the other. Reading Wordsworth tells us more about Coleridge, and vice versa. But I think, too, there is more to it than that. If, as I have argued, there is no such thing as 'Romanticism', but only a number of casually connected 'romanticisms', then the theory of Imagination held by Wordsworth and Coleridge together would constitute the centre, or core, of one such 'romanticism'. In suggesting this, I am suggesting that their differences are as important a part of this unity as their points of agreement. It may help us, perhaps, to take as an analogy the kind of incomplete ambiguity—such as Steinberg's hands—mentioned in the last chapter, where each needs the existence of its opposite to explain it. Wordsworth and Coleridge are, for us, essentially congruent not because they always agree, but because they developed between them a creative, but not necessarily consistent idea. Looking at the differences between them, is, in this sense, not finding cracks in the picture we have so far built up, but completing it.

There is a very good example of just this dialectic unity I have been outlining in Coleridge's poem to Wordsworth on the completion of *The Prelude*, on 7 January 1807—'Composed on the night after his recitation of a poem on the growth of an individual mind.' In view of later disagreements, it is interesting how well Coleridge understands his friend at this point:

Theme hard as high!
Of smiles spontaneous, and mysterious fears
(The first-born they of Reason and twin birth),
Of tides obedient to external force,
And currents self-determined, as might seem,
Or by some inner Power; of moments awful,
Now in thy inner life, and now abroad,
When power streamed from thee, and thy soul received
The light reflected, as a light bestowed—
Of fancies fair, and milder hours of youth,
Hyblean murmurs of poetic thought
Industrious in its joy, in vales and glens
Native or outland, lakes and famous hills.

The currents of Coleridge's own associative processes reveal themselves in the inversions, classical references, and in the almost Miltonic syntax. For him, Wordsworth is the new Milton, whose Great Work will illuminate the psychological state of man, as Milton's did the spiritual. Coleridge seems to have grasped the structure of *The Prelude* perfectly—and apparently at the first hearing. As a critical analysis of *The Prelude* it has never been improved on. Coleridge recognizes in the 'mysterious fears' and 'smiles spontaneous' the twin sources of Wordsworth's mental growth—together the first offspring of 'Reason'. Now it is possible that he is using the word here in its eighteenth-century sense (i.e.: that both the smiles and the fears have an intellectual basis) but it makes far better sense to take 'reason' in its later Coleridgean meaning—in contrast with 'understanding'. Taken thus, 'Reason' is the organ of spiritual knowledge (as against the practical or empirical 'understanding')—the 'smiles spontaneous' and 'mysterious fears' would then be both qualities of spiritual intuition. We shall have more to say about this inter-dependence of the psychological and the spiritual later. Coleridge goes on to strike the balance between external influences and internal self-determination with extraordinary precision by his distinction in the imagery between 'tides' and 'currents'. To the casual onlooker it is the externally-motivated tides that seem to be the important movement of the sea; but in the long run such a surface oscillation has only a very minor effect on the direction of flow of the deep inner-directed currents. He sees *The Prelude* to be constructed of an alternation of such outward and inward movements—unified explicitly by the moments of awe:

> Now in thy inner life, and now abroad,
> When power streamed from thee, and thy soul received
> The light reflected, as a light bestowed—

In this image Coleridge summarizes what we have seen as the essence of Wordsworth's attitude to nature in his early poems. The direct parallel, and possibly the verbal inspiration of this image is, of course, in Book II of the 1805 *Prelude*, lines 387–93. In particular:

> An auxiliar light
> Came from my mind which on the setting sun
> Bestow'd new splendour...

This is *not* just the familiar image of the mirror and the lamp. In spite of Meyer Abrams's book of this title, the image of nature as a *passive* mirror to the mind is hardly ever used by either Wordsworth or Coleridge. The characteristic of their 'romanticism' is, as we have stressed all the way along, a continuous mutually modifying interaction between external and internal worlds. Wordsworth, here, would hardly receive his own reflection as 'a light bestowed'. Rather—to synaesthetize the image— Coleridge is suggesting that Wordsworth's projection finds in nature an answering resonance that modifies his initial preceptive schemata, sharpening his powers of definition, and so enlarging ultimately his self-knowledge. Coleridge himself, of course, uses a very similar image in that of the Brocken-spectre. What is reflected is also subtly transmuted: we may indeed 'receive' from nature 'but what we give', but the man's shadow on the Brocken is enveloped in a 'glory'. The 'fair luminous cloud' may issue from the soul itself, but in nature it undergoes a modification so profound as to alter the soul's apprehension of itself. It is this affirmation of rapport with nature that, as Whitehead saw,[1] lay at the root of Wordsworth's assurance of 'value' in human experience. Coleridge, moreover, like Wordsworth, stresses that it is through the 'moments awful' that this

---

[1] *Science and the Modern World*, Ch. v.

change occurs, and that the 'fancies fair' and 'milder hours of youth' are less truly characteristic of the growing imagination, which depends more upon the intensity of the other, darker moments.

Writing here, Coleridge has very little doubt of the agreement between himself and Wordsworth—even though the expression may strike the reader as being typically Coleridgean:

> as I listened with a heart forlorn,
> The pulses of my being beat anew:
> And even as Life returns upon the drowned,
> Life's joy rekindling roused a throng of pains—
> Keen pangs of Love, awakening as a babe
> Turbulent, with an outcry in the heart;
> And fears self-willed, that shunned the eye of Hope;
> And Hope that scarce would know itself from Fear;
> Sense of past Youth, and Manhood come in vain,
> And Genius given, and Knowledge won in vain;
> And all which I had culled in wood-walks wild,
> And all which patient toil had reared, and all,
> Commune with thee had opened out—but flowers
> Strewed on my course, and borne upon my bier
> In the same coffin, for the self-same grave!

One critic has quoted this passage as an example of Coleridge's self-pitying sense of the contrast between Wordsworth's 'self-sufficiency as an individual and his awareness of the disorganisation of his own personality'.[1] Certainly this is true, but in context the passage strikes the reader in a rather different perspective. The self-pitying backward glance at his own lack of a comparable poetic achievement is the by-product of an upsurge of new life in response to Wordsworth's poem: the beating of the 'pulses of his being' cause pins-and-needles...Nor is it accidental, I think, that this fit of self-pity and depression should be associated with the 'rekindling' of 'life's joy'. Joy, we recall, is the concomitant of perception and feeling. Coleridge gives us another image of this sympathetic upsurge a few lines later on:

> My soul lay passive, by thy various strain
> Driven as in surges now beneath the stars,

---

[1] G. Yarlott, *Coleridge and the Abyssinian Maid* (Methuen, 1967), p. 1.

With momentary stars of my own birth,
Fair constellated foam, still darting off
Into the darkness; now a tranquil sea,
Out spread and bright, yet swelling to the moon.

This is one of the most fantastic images of a mental state ever produced by Coleridge. It is as if he feels his mind to be the inert but living immensity of a tropical ocean—across which Wordsworth is steering like a ship. It is like an extraordinary inversion of the experience of the Ancient Mariner. Instead of the water-snakes we find, where the ship's bow ploughs through the waves, phosphorescent flashes are thrown off into the darkness of the sea—reproducing in microcosm for a moment the real stars overhead. Wordsworth is going somewhere—sailing purposefully to a destination—while Coleridge is not; yet by this very passivity he gains a kind of negative capability: he is capable of responding to Wordsworth in a manner that Wordsworth cannot do to him. Looked at with hindsight, this comparison between the two friends' poetic powers on that January night in 1807 is rather more double-edged than I think Yarlott is willing to allow. It is a comparison that will form the theme of this chapter. There is a great deal of evidence to suggest that this very lack of inner certainty and self-sufficiency that so depressed Coleridge, opened for him the possibility of an eventual growth that was denied to Wordsworth. In his poem, Coleridge sees Wordsworth as

thenceforth calm and sure
From the dread watch-tower of man's absolute self.

Once so fortified, however, any possibility of further creative development would seem to be very severely curtailed. Clearly such an implication is most unlikely to have been in any sense conscious in Coleridge's mind after hearing *The Prelude* read aloud by his friend—but it is possible for the imagery to betray a deeper awareness of Wordsworth's state than his conscious mind could permit. The real paradox of Wordsworth's development in *The Prelude* is that he seems to have drawn such strength from his memories of fear and awe that he became immured for ever from any repetition of similar experiences—as his fellow-poet was not. There is no doubt, I think, from Wordsworth's

Preface to *The Excursion*, that he felt his calmness and assurance to be signs of maturity. Such a maturity, however, was one that seemed to preclude, by its very definition, the possibility of further modification from experience.

I think we find the very centre of this contrast between Wordsworth and Coleridge in the group of poems which includes the *Immortality Ode*, the published version of *Dejection*, and Wordsworth's reply, *Resolution and Independence*. The unity of this group, as a dialogue, is quite remarkable. As in Coleridge's later poem on *The Prelude*, both poets are agreed about the organic connection between mental growth and poetic development. Creativity is seen as both the cause the the product of growth. The three main poems mentioned are themselves simultaneously reviews of past development, and actual stages of present growth. The original vague sense of loss that we found Wordsworth attempting to define in the *Immortality Ode* is taken through a series of progressively finer and more delicate discriminations foreshadowing with uncanny accuracy the future development of each poet. The dialogue begins with Coleridge's poem of October 1800, *The Mad Monk*.[1] Stanza II goes like this:

> There was a time when earth, and sea, and skies,
> The bright green vale, and forest's dark recess,
> With all things, lay before mine eyes
> In steady loveliness:
> But now I feel, on earth's uneasy scene,
> Such sorrows as will never cease;—
> I only ask for peace;
> If I must live to know that such a time has been!

This is taken up by Wordsworth for the opening of the *Immortality Ode*, and is used by him as the initial schema from which he can move towards a more precise analysis of his own sense of loss, and of its relation to his development.

> There was a time when meadow, grove, and stream,
> The earth, and every common sight,
>   To me did seem
> Apparelled in celestial light.

[1] G. Whalley, *Coleridge, Sarah Hutchinson, and the Asra Poems* (Routledge, 1955), pp. 128–9.

The glory and the freshness of a dream.
It is not now as it hath been of yore;—
    Turn wheresoe'er I may,
    By night or day,
The things which I have seen I now can see no more.

It is fascinating to see how even such an apparently personal record as the *Immortality Ode* needs a previous literary schema before its intense individual emotion can find a form. From the analogy we have been suggesting all the way through with the visual arts, this is in fact very much what one would expect. Gombrich, for instance, in a paper on 'Imagery and Art in the Romantic Period'[1] criticizes very strongly the popular idea of originality in art:

The original genius who 'paints what he sees' and creates new forms but of nothing is a Romantic myth. Even the greatest artist—and he more than the others—needs an idiom to work in. Only tradition, such as he finds it, can provide him with the raw material of imagery which he needs to represent an event or a 'fragment of nature'.

Where Wordsworth borrowed his original schema from a minor poem of Coleridge's, we now find Coleridge borrowing it back— receiving in this way 'the light reflected, as a light bestowed'. The two versions of *Dejection* differ little at this point:

    There was a time when, though my path was rough,
    This joy within me dallied with distress,
    And all misfortunes were but as the stuff
    Whence Fancy made me dreams of happiness:
    For hope grew round me like a twining vine,
    And fruits, and foliage, not my own, seemed mine.
    But now afflictions bow me down to earth:
    Nor care I that they rob me of my mirth;
        But oh! each visitation
    Suspends what nature gave me at my birth,
    My shaping spirit of Imagination.

Now it is the turn of Wordsworth's schema to be taken up and found wanting by Coleridge. Like Wordsworth, he had at one time been able to make misfortunes the raw material of future happiness. In *Biographia Literaria* he wrote of the *Immortality Ode*:

[1] In *Meditations on a Hobby Horse* (Phaidon, 1965).

the ode was intended for such readers only as had been accustomed to watch the flux and reflux of their inmost nature, to venture at times into the twilight realms of consciousness, and to feel a deep interest in modes of inmost being...[1]

This is above all Coleridge's characteristic activity, and it is from just such introspection on Wordsworth's poem that this passage of *Dejection* grows. Just as Wordsworth refines, by repeated discrimination, a definition of his own personal feeling of loss from the lament of the Mad Monk, so here Coleridge defines his own feelings by contrasting them with Wordsworth's. We can even follow the shift of words by which it is done. The joy of childhood remembered, which, for Wordsworth, now had 'the glory and the freshness of a dream', suggests to Coleridge a stage at one remove further from reality: 'happiness' has become a *dream* of Fancy. There is a real ambiguity here: did 'Fancy' make Coleridge imagine—falsely—that he *was* happy? or did it offer him an unrealized hope of happiness in the future? The effect of this uncertainty is to question Wordsworth's original schema very closely: just how illusory is this childhood gleam? Is it possible that if we could actually return to that state we might find it was in fact a hope for the future? A confidence that all *would* be well? But the agent of this ambiguous dream for Coleridge is 'Fancy', which is specifically contrasted only a few lines further on with 'Imagination'. Even if we did not have other evidence, this would be enough to suggest that by 1802 Coleridge's study of Wordsworth's poetry had reached the point of formulating a distinction between Fancy and Imagination substantially the same as that advanced thirteen years later in the *Biographia*. Coleridge has tried Wordsworth's schema in the twilight realms of his own consciousness. The characteristic of Fancy is its aggregating power—its mechanism—its putting together things not organically connected:

> And fruits, and foliage, not my own, seemed mine.

If this is the shallow Hartleianism that Coleridge has just thrown off, it is noticeable that the mainspring of this aggregating power is essentially the same as the well-spring of the Imagina-

[1] Vol. II, Ch. XXII, p. 120.

tion—Joy. As I have suggested, I think we must look to the Methodist revival to find the origins of the full creative force of this word for Coleridge. It is not the absence of 'mirth' that worries him now, but, as he explains in the earlier unpublished version of *Dejection* to Sarah Hutchinson,

> my coarse domestic life has known
> No habits of heart-nursing Sympathy,
> No Griefs but such as dull and deaden me,
> No mutual mild Enjoyments of its own,
> No Hopes of its own Vintage...

This footnote to his beloved Asra is a highly significant modification of the argument used by Wordsworth in the *Immortality Ode*. There is some problem over dates here, as to which came first. We know that the *Ode* was written in two halves, with a gap of some years in the middle. The first section finished with the unanswered question:

> Whither is fled the visionary gleam?
> Where is it now, the glory and the dream?

De Selincourt challenges Wordsworth's own dating of the *Ode* at 1803–6, and puts it instead at 1802–4.[1] If Wordsworth's own dating is accurate, the whole poem is a reply to *Dejection*; if (as I have assumed for the purposes of this argument) De Selincourt is correct, however, and the first part of the *Ode* was written before Coleridge wrote *Dejection*, then Coleridge's poem lies in time between the two halves of the *Ode*. In either case, Wordsworth's final affirmation of strength from the memory of childhood moments of guilt and fear is a *reply* to Coleridge's lament that isolation suspended his Imagination. Wordsworth's assertion that isolation can be a source of strength seems to have been triggered off by Coleridge.

Coleridge's position is complex. In *The Ancient Mariner* insight and new development grows out of an experience of utter dereliction and loss. But for Coleridge, not *all* such experiences are restorative. The distinction is between these, and those griefs 'such as dull and deaden' the Imagination. What then is

[1] *Poetical Works of Wordsworth*, Vol. IV, pp. 463–5.

the essential difference between such moments? Clearly, for Coleridge, it lies between those which, through affliction, assert our community with our fellow-creatures, be they water-snakes or men, and those which only increase the isolation of the individual. In both endings of *Dejection* it is in the act of blessing the 'Lady'—Asra—that Coleridge's own joy is finally restored. The opposite of joy, for Coleridge, is *isolation*. When he complains of 'no mutual mild enjoyments' in his loveless marriage, it is not the lack of those domestic pleasures that breaks him, but the desperate feeling that nothing, not even the most trivial pleasures, can be *shared* with his wife.

As we have seen, Wordsworth counters this with his massive assertion of the strength that comes from solitary endurance in the second half of the *Ode*, and in the character of the old Leech-gatherer in *Resolution and Independence*. To label such a fundamental cleavage as this in terms of 'character' or 'personality' begs the question. The poet's character, as it affects the poems, is the poet. A biographer of both poets makes the interesting observation: 'Wordsworth, except when an uprush of the imagination swept away all the merely mundane, was essentially moral, and a moralist: Coleridge was sinful, suffering and religious.'[1] This is, I think, a very fruitful distinction. So far from being merely an accident of character, this contrast represents a polarity that was to haunt the whole course of this particular romanticism. In Wordsworth the power of poetic creation seems almost always to well up from within him, whereas in Coleridge it seems usually to come from establishing a rapport with the external world—through recognizing a kinship with other creatures, or from the rising wind in the æolian harp.

We must frame this distinction with some care. Often it would seem to be Wordsworth who has this rapport rather than Coleridge. If we take, for instance, Wordsworth's *Daffodils* we can see how his sense of dislocation and loneliness is healed by his vision of the daffodils in the wind on the shore of Ullswater. The movement in Wordsworth's description is from, at first sight, a 'fluttering crowd', to a perception of order and har-

[1] H. M. Margoliouth, *Wordsworth and Coleridge 1795–1834* (Oxford, 1953), p. 176.

mony as 'a dancing host'.[1] The value of the daffodils lies purely in the didactic function Wordsworth has given them. It is the familiar process of abstracting a moral from nature for later contemplation as a memory. The flowers are merely, in this sense, an anodyne against depression. Wordsworth is not, it seems to me, recognizing any innate kinship between himself and the daffodils in the way that the Ancient Mariner does in the water-snakes.

The choice that seems to have faced both Wordsworth and Coleridge at a certain stage of their development was a moral one—whose outcome was to affect the whole structure of their imaginative development. In the case of Wordsworth, the difficulty of finding out how exactly he did come to envisage the Imagination is considerably aggravated by his ambivalent position between two epochs of thought. His criticism, even when it appears to be echoing Coleridge's, retains always an oddly eighteenth-century flavour—in particular of what Lovejoy has called 'Uniformitarianism': the belief behind his theory of poetry and poetic diction that men everywhere are really very much alike, and that one can, therefore, appeal to the educated for a common consensus of informed opinion. In contrast, as we have seen, his poetry reveals a much sharper and more highly developed power of discrimination. In his Preface to the poems of 1815, for example, he still seems to be thinking of the Imagination as an agent for modifying images by comparisons:

These processes of imagination are carried on either by conferring additional properties upon an object, or abstracting from it those which it actually possesses, and thus enabling it to re-act upon the mind which hath performed the process, like a new existence.[2]

As an example of what he means by this, he goes on to cite the description of the Leech-gatherer:

> As a huge stone is sometimes seen to lie
> Couched on the bald top of an eminence,
> Wonder to all who do the same espy
> By what means it could thither come, and whence,
> So that it seems a thing endued with sense,

[1] Durrant, 'Imagination and Life—Wordsworth's "The Daffodils"', *Theoria*.
[2] *Wordsworth's Literary Criticism*, ed. N. C. Smith (Oxford, 1905), p. 159.

> Like a sea-beast crawled forth, which on a shelf
> Of rock or sand reposeth, there to sun himself.
> Such seemed this Man; not all alive or dead
> Nor all asleep, in his extreme old age.

Wordsworth explains what is happening in this stanza as follows:

In these images, the conferring, the abstracting, and the modiying powers of the Imagination, immediately and mediately acting, are all brought into conjunction. The stone is endowed with something of the power of life to approximate it to the sea-beast; and the sea-beast stripped of some of its vital qualities to assimilate it to the stone; which intermediate image is thus treated for the purpose of bringing the original image, that of the stone, to a nearer resemblance to the figure and condition of the aged Man; who is divested of so much of the indications of life and motion as to bring him to the point where the two objects unite and coalesce in just comparison.[1]

Elsewhere, this would be interesting; here, what staggers the reader is the way in which Wordsworth has narrowed down the Imagination to a technique of image-formation. He has completely sidestepped the main question of the imaginative structure of the poem—of which the formation of images is an organic part—and is being, in the case of *Resolution and Independence*, less than fair to himself: as we shall see in a moment. More than a decade before this Preface was written, we have seen how Wordsworth's Imagination in the *Immortality Ode* had taken over the much more radical and architectural rôle of re-organizing the whole perspective of his memory. It is in this stark discrepancy between poetic practice and theory that Coleridge's criticism of Wordsworth begins. It is against the background of this description of the Imagination by Wordsworth that Coleridge, two years later in *Biographia Literaria*, reacts by trying to describe his Imagination simultaneously as a fact of physics, a psychological process, *and* a metaphysical phenomenon.

The first hint of trouble between them comes almost immediately after the poetic dialogue to which we have been referring. On 26 October 1803 Coleridge recorded in his notebook:

[1] *Ibid.*

A most unpleasant Dispute with W. & Hazlitt Wednesday after-
noon...—I spoke, I fear too contemptuously—but they spoke so
irreverently so malignantly of the Divine Wisdom, that it overset me.
Hazlitt how easily roused to Rage & Hatred, self-projected/but who
shall find the Force that can drag him up out of the Depth into one
expression of Kindness—into the shewing of one Gleam of the Light
of Love on his Countenance—Peace be with *him*!—But *thou*, dearest
Wordsworth—and what if Ray, Durham, Paley, have carried the
observation of the aptitudes of Things too far, too habitually—into
Pedantry?—O how many worse Pedantries! how few so harmless with
so much efficient Good!—Dear William, pardon Pedantry in others &
avoid it in yourself, instead of scoffing & Reviling at Pedantry in good
men in a good cause & *becoming* a Pedant yourself in a bad cause—
even by that very act becoming one!—But surely to look at the super-
ficies of Objects for the purpose of taking Delight in their Beauty, &
sympathy with their real or imagined Life, is as deleterious to the
Health & manhood of Intellect, as always to be peering & unravelling
Contrivances may be to the simplicity of the affections, the grandeur &
unity of the Imagination.—O dearest William! Would Ray, or
Durham, have spoken of God as you spoke of Nature?[1]

It is not easy to see precisely what this dispute, with its accusa-
tion, and counter accusations of pedantry, was about from this
note. Clearly the division which Coleridge felt so deeply was
over an attitude to nature in Wordsworth that, if allowed un-
checked, could (his friend suspected) permanently damage the
whole structure of his imaginative perception of the world, and
consequently his poetry. What, then, did this 'pedantry' consist in? It was, we are told, twofold: firstly, to look at the
'superfices of objects' for the express purpose of delighting in
their beauty, and reading into them a pathetic fallacy, and,
secondly, 'peering and unravelling Contrivancies', which are
inimical to the 'grandeur and unity of the Imagination'.
Coleridge, it seems, is arguing that Wordsworth is attempting
to apply too rigid a moral utilitarianism to nature. One thinks
again of Wordsworth in *The Daffodils*. He is less concerned
to feel his inter-dependence with nature than he is to find in it
an immediate value, or 'message' for him. The 'sermons in
stones' may be, as we have seen, very much more than the
'trite reflections of morality' that he turns aside from in Book XI

---

[1] *Anima Poetae*, p. 35.

of *The Prelude*, but they are essentially of the same kind: it seems
to me here that it is his whole attempt to *use* nature as therapy—
the very element that appealed so strongly to John Stuart Mill
—that is being so sharply criticized by Coleridge.

We may perhaps see better what I believe Coleridge means
about his friend if we look at the way the two poets react to
nature in the group of poems under discussion. There is, for
instance, in the *Immortality Ode* very little detailed observation
of nature. It is not Wordsworth's response, but his lack of it,
that is the central experience. When Coleridge comes, in *Dejection*, to reply to Wordsworth's statement of the sense of loss
that afflicts them both ('There was a time when...') the
difference is immediately felt. Where Wordsworth starts with
a generalization about the past, Coleridge begins by way of a
most detailed description of the present:

> Well! If the Bard was weather-wise, who made
> The grand old Ballad of Sir Patrick Spence,
> This night, so tranquil now, will not go hence
> Unroused by winds, that ply a busier trade
> Than those which mould yon cloud in lazy flakes...

He is giving his poem a specific local setting in time and place.
It is the evening of 4 August 1802, and there is a storm brewing.
By the first line we have picked up his ruminative and allusive
mood. Coleridge is not trying to read into nature a particular
message, but rather to establish a rapport with it *as it is*. Almost
casually, he uses the schemata of the storm-signs from the
The Ballad of Sir Patrick Spens to 'read' the weather, and in
doing so suggests a parallel between it, and the way his own
mind is already imperceptibly moving. While his own mood
follows the course of the storm to its climax, before dying away
to a new serenity, Coleridge does not make any real attempt to
project his own feelings into the storm—the deliberate projective fantasy of the storm's din in Stanza vii, first as a battle, and
then as a little child lost, emphasizes by contrast how much the
poem as a whole eschews the pathetic fallacy. What Coleridge
wants from the storm is not a 'message' but a sympathetic
revival of his own creative Imagination:

> Those sounds which oft have raised me, whilst they awed,
> And send my soul abroad,

Might now perhaps their wonted impulse give,
Might startle this dull pain, and make it move and live!

Hugh Sykes Davies has pointed out how the word 'impulse' is
used consistently by Wordsworth in a sense analogous to that
of the seventeenth-century philosophers. For Wordsworth, he
writes, 'it meant not an inexplicable eddy *within* the human
spirit, but a movement stirred in it from *without*, as an influence
upon the individual of some force in the outer universe.'[1] The
only context where Coleridge uses the word in this sense is here,
in *Dejection*. This was something Coleridge had learnt from
Wordsworth: it is yet another facet of the interplay between
man and nature, and between man and man, for which Coleridge
was constantly seeking new and more satisfactory images. What
is so striking, is that in *Dejection* there is already a sense in
which he has learnt from Wordsworth, and gone beyond him, to
a point where Wordsworth would not, or could not follow him—
to receive the light reflected as a light bestowed. The immediate
result is curious: in spite of a much deeper pessimism, Coleridge's
realization of the present in contrast to the past is so much firmer
than Wordsworth's in the *Ode* that it is at once clear that the
loss he is complaining of is *not* one of visual perception:

> I see them all so excellently fair,
> I see, not feel, how beautiful they are.

Coleridge is here putting his finger on the precise difference
between himself and his friend. Wordsworth had written in the
Ode:

> My heart is at your festival,
> My head hath its coronal,
> The fulness of your bliss, I feel—I feel it all...

What Wordsworth felt was threatened was not 'feeling', or
sight, but the 'visionary gleam': a sense of *meaning* in its most
literal form. His philosophic recovery is marked by his new
ability to find thoughts 'too deep for tears' in the meanest
flower. Coleridge, on the other hand, never looked for *thoughts*
in nature. He felt his whole imaginative intercourse with the

---

[1] 'Wordsworth and the Empirical Philosophers', *The English Mind*, ed. Watson
(Cambridge, 1964), p. 155.

created world—his whole capacity for open response—to be threatened, and it is *this* threat that drives him further into the problem of Imagination and value.

> I may not hope from outward forms to win
> The passion and the life, whose fountains are within.

In the response Coleridge is talking about there is no contradiction between laborious re-working and spontaneity. In the poem to Wordsworth on first hearing *The Prelude* the image of the breaking wave:

> My soul lay passive, by thy various strain
> Driven as in surges now beneath the stars,
> With momentary stars of my own birth,
> Fair constellated foam, still darting off
> Into the darkness...

is taken, almost to the word, from Satyrane's First Letter, published first in *The Friend*, and then in *Biographia Literaria*.[1]

A beautiful white cloud of Foam at momentary intervals coursed by the side of the Vessel with a Roar, and little stars of flame danced and sparkled and went out in it: and every now and then light detachments of this white cloud-like foam dashed off from the vessel's side, each with its own small constellation, over the sea, and scoured out of sight like a Tartar Troop over a wilderness.

Clearly, whatever Coleridge meant by 'Pedantry', he did not refer it to the construction of perceptions. It is not merely that he is taking as an image for his feeling the memory of a particular observation of foam at sea, but he is harking back verbally to a previous literary schema. Coleridge's 'spontaneous' response can immediately be analysed in terms of 'making and matching'.

Simultaneously, we have a glimpse of the enormous importance that he attaches to detailed observation. His notebooks and poems alike are full of the most minutely detailed descriptions of nature.[2] Few comparisons are more symptomatic of this

---

[1] See note by E. H. Coleridge, *Poems of S.T.C.*, p. 408.

[2] Humphry House (*Coleridge:* Clark Lectures, 1951–2 (Hart-Davies, 1953)) notes the similarity between Coleridge and Gerard Manley Hopkins in a number of places, and advances the suggestion that Hopkins may have had access to the *Notebooks* during his Oxford friendship with E. H. Coleridge.

difference between Wordsworth and Coleridge than the contrast between this sense of 'inscape' in *Dejection* and the way Words-worth opens *Resolution and Independence*:

> There was a roaring in the wind all night;
> The rain came heavily and fell in floods;
> But now the sun is rising calm and bright;
> The birds are singing in the distant woods:
> Over his own sweet voice the stock-dove broods;
> The jay makes answer as the magpie chatters;
> And all the air is filled with pleasant noise of waters.

It is the morning after the storm; a symbolic sequel to the storm that had raged for Coleridge in *Dejection*. But the effect is as deliberately diffused and generalized as Coleridge's was intense and particular. It could be any morning after any storm, for Wordsworth (for all his dislike of Johnson as a critic) is answering Coleridge's individual problem with a general truth. The jays and the stock-dove are named, but only as sound-effects to the prevailing mood. One bird stands for the species. In the next stanza we encounter the hare:

> All things that love the sun are out of doors:
> The sky rejoices in the morning's birth;
> The grass is bright with rain-drops;—on the moors
> The hare is running races in her mirth;
> And with her feet she from the plashy earth
> Raises a mist; that, glittering in the sun,
> Runs with her all the way, wherever she doth run.

So vivid is the description that we are not immediately aware of its ambiguity: is this, like the stock-dove, one hare standing for many, or is this one particular hare? Is it, in other words, an exquisitely realized detail of the landscape of the mind brought momentarily into focus as an example of the joyous resurgence of nature after the storm, or is it a solitary individual, a counter-part to the solitary poet himself, or the aged Leech-gatherer, to be contrasted with his environment? The animal, as an un-thinking child of nature, is drawing clouds of glory from the earth at every bound; can the poet do the same, or is he (after the experience of the *Immortality Ode*) separated by the mystery of human growth from this unreflecting abandoned joy? In the next stanza the ambiguity is resolved at the level of the narrative: evidently it is now an individual hare—but the gulf between the general and the particular has been spanned rhetorically, and the tension between unity and dissent has already been subliminally suggested. The way for Wordsworth's own polarity of mood has now been prepared:

> But, as it sometimes chanceth, from the sight
> Of joy in minds that can no farther go,
> As high as we have mounted in delight
> In our dejection do we sink as low,
> To me that morning did it happen so;
> And fears, and fancies, thick upon me came;
> Dim sadness—and blind thoughts, I knew not, nor could name.

As in the *Immortality Ode*, the scene of apparent pastoral bliss hides a deeply disturbing note. The movement of the poem is towards a discrimination and clarification of what causes this disturbance. Wordsworth shifts our attention from the outside world to his own inner world, echoing Coleridge's own desperate discovery in *Dejection*:

> By our own spirits are we deified:
> We poets in our youth begin in gladness;
> But thereof comes in the end despondency and madness.

The self-sufficiency of this 'deification'—both like, and unlike Coleridge's 'glory, enveloping the earth'—is ominous, perhaps, but does not warrant the latter's charge of 'pedantry'. Nature and the mind are unified, in poetry as in perception, by an imaginative act that finds an answering resonance in moors and waters to the tensions of the poet.

But it seems to me that at this point the poem falls into two. Wordsworth is rescued from his dilemma by outside intervention of a peculiarly ambiguous kind:

> Now, whether it were by peculiar grace,
> A leading from above, a something given,
> Yet it befel, that, in this lonely place,
> When I with these untoward thoughts had striven,
> Beside a pool bare to the eye of heaven
> I saw a man before me unawares...

164

There is a visionary and supernatural quality to the aged Leech-gatherer that marks him off from the world of the stock-dove. What overwhelms Wordsworth about him is a feeling of *intervention* in the natural order:

> the whole body of the man did seem
> Like one whom I had met with in a dream;
> Or like a man from some far region sent,
> To give me human strength, by apt admonishment.

Simultaneously, something dramatic has happened to the natural scenery. The sunshine and the woods have vanished. In their place is a world of 'bare pools' in lonesome places on the 'weary moors'. This is the scenery of the visionary dreariness of *The Prelude*; scenery that we have learned, paradoxically, to associate with the restoration of the Imagination. There is, of course, a simple naturalistic explanation for all this: Wordsworth has left the lush lakeland valley and climbed up on to the bare and peaty shoulder of the fells. But even in this there is a topographical symbolism. Moses-like, the poet has climbed from the world of the senses to the austerity of the naked spirit. Yet there is still another side to this abrupt climatic change. Wordsworth was initially at one with nature. Then, in the midst of harmony, came doubts and perplexities. Now, with the strange, almost supernatural meeting with the Leech-gatherer, he encounters an image of resolute opposition to a hostile environment. If Wordsworth is to emulate the heroism of the Leech-gatherer he so much admires, he must take up employment 'hazardous and wearisome' fighting inhospitable desolation for ever-diminishing returns. The paradox is that it is just this hopeless heroism that seems to offer him a way through the perplexities that had originally troubled him:

> My former thoughts returned: the fear that kills;
> And hope that is unwilling to be fed;
> Cold, pain, and labour, and all fleshly ills;
> And mighty poets in their misery dead.
> Perplexed, and longing to be comforted
> My question eagerly did I renew...

But what was 'perplexing' Wordsworth was a quite specific worry: his possible poetic decline. What if his 'summer mood'

were to end? Chatterton, 'the marvellous boy' had died young;
Burns, 'he who followed the plough', was a peasant primitive
whose development was no guide to Wordsworth's own; and—
the unspoken fear—Coleridge, the one poet against whom
Wordsworth could measure himself, had written *Dejection*:

> ...thereof comes in the end despondency and madness.

I do not think we can understand why the hopeless heroic stoicism of the old Leech-gatherer seemed so attractive to Wordsworth unless we can first see why he felt he *must* reject his
previous openness and receptivity to nature. His answer—and it
is hard to read it as *not* addressed to Coleridge—seems to be:
'That way lies madness!' The other alternative—which we must
more and more identify with Coleridge—that of struggling at
an ever-increasing cost to assert kinship with the created world,
was, for Wordsworth, an even more terrifying prospect. The
Leech-gathererer's magnificent resolution was for him the lesser
of the two evils.

> and when he ended,
> I could have laughed myself to scorn to find
> In that decrepit man so firm a mind.
> 'God,' said I, 'be my help and stay secure;
> I'll think of the leech-gatherer on the lonely moor!'

What is noticeable to us is that in making this choice there has
already been a distinct hardening of sensibility. The message
now is one of struggle, not of understanding. To that extent
he has already left behind the world of the *Immortality Ode*:

> To me the meanest flower that blows can give
> Thoughts that do often lie too deep for tears.

Instead the painful process of gathering an ever-declining
number of leeches is certainly a very ambiguous image of poetic
creation. We are reminded irresistebly of Coleridge's charge of
pedantry, 'deleterious to the grandeur and unity of the Imagination' in its 'peering and unravelling Contrivances'. If Wordsworth is really throwing in his lot with the Leech-gatherer, then
surely Coleridge is right. Wordsworth's own definition of
'Imagination' in his Preface of 1815, and his choice of examples

from *Resolution and Independence* which we have already looked at, suggest a logical continuation of his attempt to build a poetic structure that would tame and didacticize nature without correspondingly modifying the creating mind of the poet.

Coleridge's reference to 'pedantry' in his friend's attitude to nature dates from 1803. It is, I suspect, a part of the tension between them that was at first to prove so creative, and finally, so destructive. The poetic dialogue we have been examining continued spasmodically from 1800 until Coleridge's poem to Wordsworth on the completion of *The Prelude* in 1807. It spans in time, and is largely responsible for much of their best work. Each seemed capable during these years of providing the other with schemata to react against, and to work from. Yet they had been drifting apart well before Coleridge's trip to Malta in 1804. The tragic-comic quarrel between them in 1810 only illustrates how far apart these opposing characteristics had carried them.

The actual story is quickly told. The Wordsworths, who had suffered Coleridge at Grasmere throughout most of the crises attendant on the production of *The Friend* during 1809–10, had become understandably tired of the lack of discipline, the evasiveness, the self-pity and self-deception that accompanied Coleridge's opium-addiction, and now seemed inseparable from his method of working. Dorothy Wordsworth's letter of 12 April 1810 to Catherine Clarkson gives us a grim picture of Coleridge in the Wordsworth household at this time.

As to Coleridge, if I thought I should distress you, I would say nothing about him; but I hope that you are sufficiently prepared for the worst. We have no hope of him... If he were not under our roof, he would be just as much the slave of stimulants as ever; and his whole time and thoughts (except when he is reading and he reads a great deal), are employed in deceiving himself, and seeking to deceive others. He will tell me that he has been writing, that he *has* written, half a Friend; when I *know* that he has not written a single line. This habit pervades all his words and actions, and you feel perpetually new hollowness and emptiness. Burn this letter, I entreat you...[1]

In May 1810 Coleridge left Grasmere and settled at Greta Hall, Keswick, for the summer. By October he had decided to seek

[1] *Letters*, 1806–11, pp. 362–3.

medical attention in Edinburgh for his drug-addiction. Hearing of this, the Basil Montagues, who were staying with the Wordsworths, persuaded Coleridge instead to accompany them back to London and to live in their Soho house under the attention of their physician, Anthony Carlisle. Wordsworth at once intervened. He warned Basil Montague against the plan, stressing how impossible it was to live with Coleridge in his present state. Nothing was said to Coleridge at the time, but on their arrival in London Montague seems to have repeated Wordsworth's words in a manner that put the worst possible light on them. We do not know exactly what Wordsworth had said, nor Montague's accuracy in repeating it, but the expressions recorded by Crabb Robinson are sufficient to show how shattered Coleridge must have been. 'Wordsworth *has commissioned* me to tell you, first, that he has no Hope of you...' Coleridge had 'for years past' been 'an ABSOLUTE NUISANCE in the Family'; he was a '*rotten drunkard*', 'rotting out his entrails by intemperance'. Heart-broken, Coleridge retired to a hotel. He did not communicate with the Wordsworths at all, and it was not until the following May that the first rumours of what had happened reached Grasmere. For eighteen months there was complete silence between the two poets. Wordsworth when he heard from Southey what he was supposed to have said and Montague to have repeated, declared that Coleridge had invented it as a pretext to break with him 'and to furnish himself with a ready excuse for all his failures in duty to himself and others'. Coleridge waited in vain for an explanation. In April 1812 Wordsworth arrived in London and matters came to a head. His first reaction to the gossip circulating about the quarrel was to propose that Coleridge should 'stand trial' in the presence of Montague and himself, with Josiah Wedgwood as referee. This Coleridge indignantly refused. On 4 May he wrote to Wordsworth who refused to open the letter until he received assurances that it contained nothing but 'a naked statement' of what Coleridge alleged Montague to have said. Between Coleridge's sense of an utterly unjust betrayal and Wordsworth's high-handedness it is probable that even then no reconciliation would have been possible without the good offices of Crabb Robinson. The meeting and reconciliation was finally effected. They even went for a walk on Hampstead Heath together. But the restoration of their friendship was not the old collaboration. Coleridge noted: 'A Reconciliation has taken place—but the *Feeling*...can never return. All outward actions, all inward wishes, all Thoughts & Admirations, will be the same—*are* the same—but—aye there remains an immedicable *But*.'[1] Each had shown his characteristic vice. Coleridge, a weakness and self-pity that was to alienate many of his one-time friends just as it had alienated the Wordsworths and Sarah Hutchinson. In the same letter that Dorothy had complained of his addiction, she went on:

do not think that it is his love for Sara which has stopped him in his work...his love for her is no more than a fanciful dream. Otherwise he would prove it by a desire to make her happy. No! He likes to have her about him as his own, as one devoted to him, but when she stood in the way of other gratifications it was all over...

Wordsworth, on the other hand had been both insensitive, priggish, and above all, ruthless in his dealings with Coleridge. He had been exasperated to a point where he could ignore his friend's greatest need—the assurance of his own friendship. No one was more aware of his weaknesses than Coleridge. At the time of writing *Dejection* in October 1802 he had noted:

The unspeakable comfort to a good man's mind, nay, even to a criminal, to be *understood*—to have some one that understands one—and who does not feel that, on earth, no one does? The hope of this, always more or less disappointed, gives the passion to friendship.[2]

For Coleridge openness was finally incompatible with strength. Wordsworth, drawing strength from the memories of past isolation, husbanded his inward resources at the expense of the present. Each choice demanded the inclusion of its opposite if it was to prove a way of growth and not a dead end. Separated, neither poet seemed capable of sustaining what they had managed together.

Speaking of William in a letter to Dorothy Wordsworth in 1826 Crabb Robinson wrote:

it gives me real pain when I think that some future commentator may possibly hereafter write—'This great poet survived to the fifth

---

[1] *Letters*, Vol. III. pp. 406–7.
[2] *Anima Poetae*, p. 24.

decennary of the nineteenth Century, but he appears to have dyed in the year 1814 as far as life consisted in an active sympathy with the temporary welfare of his fellow creatures...'[1]

To us, such an insight may appear prophetic. Yet the evidence was plainly there for those contemporaries with eyes to see. Coleridge himself had hinted at it in 1807 when he described his friend

thenceforth calm and sure
From the dread watch-tower of man's absolute self.

In contrast to the increasing self-sufficiency of Wordsworth, at the centre of a household of three adoring women, Coleridge's loneliness was increasing. He was now tortured by a sense of failure. He had failed in his marriage, in his love for Sarah Hutchinson, and even in his friendships he seemed to have been betrayed. He was conscious above all of having failed to live up to his own great gifts—and to Wordsworth. Yet the fruits of their collaboration—the greatest literary collaboration in the language—were not yet over. Out of this sense of failure, out of their only partially-healed estrangement was to grow one more great joint work: *Biographia Literaria*.

George Whalley has demonstrated in his essay on 'The Integrity of "Biographia Literaria"' the closely-woven integral texture, centring not on Coleridge's own work, but primarily on Wordsworth's.[2] Yet even Whalley, it seems to me, does not lay sufficient stress on this central paradox: that the account of Coleridge's literary development should be mainly concerned with the work of another poet. The structure of the argument, so long dismissed as non-existent by critics, was, I suspect, mis-understood just because of the difficulty of accepting this fact. The account of Coleridge's own development in the early chapters from Hartelian mechanism to a formulation of the Imagination is simultaneously a criticism of Wordsworth's theory of association ('indistinct in outline, and encumbered by the doctrine of Hartley')[2] and of the inadequacy of the theory of Imagination that Wordsworth had advanced in his 1815 Pre-

---

[1] *Correspondence of Crabb Robinson with the Wordsworth Circle*, ed. E. J. Morley (Oxford, 1927), p. 153.
[2] In *Essays and Studies* (1953).

face. As early as 29 July 1802 Coleridge had written to Southey concerning Wordsworth:

I rather suspect that somewhere or other there is a radical difference in our theoretical opinions respecting poetry; this I shall endeavour to go to the bottom of, and, acting the arbitrator between the old school and the new school, hope to lay down some plain and perspicuous, though not superficial canons of criticism respecting poetry.

The foundations of the *Biographia* were being laid at the time of *Dejection* and the *Immortality Ode*. I think, moreover, that the early sections, up to the famous pronouncement on Imagination in Chapter XIII have an even closer relationship to Wordsworth than Whalley suggests. In one of the best critical essays that was to appear on Coleridge during the nineteenth century, F. J. A. Hort (*Cambridge Essays*, 1856) comments on his over-riding need to account for the greatness of Wordsworth's work in some other terms than the description Wordsworth himself was prepared to give of it. This Coleridge at last found himself able to do in 1816. The lengthy philosophical disquisition of Chapter XII, the 'Chapter of Requests', is performing a twofold function considerably more significant than the 'sung and snuffled... om-m-mject—sum-m-mject' metaphysical mumblings that was all Carlyle could find in Coleridge's philosophy.[1] Carlyle's incomprehension was typical of much of his generation. Yet what Coleridge was endeavouring to do was not something metaphysical at all, but practical and immediately relevant to his main argument. The central passage of the very tortuous and involved discussion in Chapter XII is leading up to the theory of Imagination to be expounded in the next chapter by dealing with the question of the 'reality' of our sense-perceptions. He is trying to establish on a sound philosophical basis that the Imagination is *neither* a quality imposed on the passive mind by an 'objective' natural world, as in Hartelian associationism, *nor* an emanation from the mind that imposes itself upon the passive cypher of an unknowable external world. Coleridge's argument is designed to show that his new concept of the Imagination does, in fact, give a strong philosophical foundation for the old common-sense notion of perception:

[1] *Life of James Stirling* (Chapman and Hall, 1893), Ch. VII.

The realism common to all mankind is far elder and lies infinitely deeper than this hypothetical explanation of perceptions, an explanation skimmed from the mere surface of mechanical philosophy. It is the table itself, which the man of common sense believes himself to see, not the phantom of a table, from which he may argumentatively deduce the reality of a table, which he does not see. If to destroy the reality of all, that we actually behold, be idealism, what can be more egregiously so, than the system of modern metaphysics, which banishes us to a land of shadows, surrounds us with apparitions, and distinguishes truth from illusion only by the majority of those who dream the same dream? '*I* asserted that the world was mad,' exclaimed poor Lee, 'and the world said, that I was mad, and confound them, they outvoted me.'[1]

What he and Wordsworth had felt, and attempted to communicate: a 'deep impression of certain inherent and indestructible qualities of the human mind, and likewise of certain powers in the great and permanent objects that act upon it, which are equally inherent and indestructible', corresponded both with the common sense-experience of mankind, and, for Coleridge, bridged the hitherto unbridgeable gap between mechanism and idealism. Even where his argument in this chapter is obscure (as it frequently is) what communicates itself to the reader is his feeling of sheer philosophical excitement. He has glimpsed, and is pursuing, the intellectual framework for that razor-edge equilibrium between projection and reception that he had already found that night in 1807 when Wordsworth first read him *The Prelude*:

> When power streamed from thee, and thy soul received
> The light reflected as a light bestowed...

This, as we have seen, is the essential characteristic of the Imagination in both poets. It failed when Coleridge lost the power, and Wordsworth the receptivity. What Coleridge has unerringly put his finger on in Chapter xii of *Biographia Literaria* is the fundamental difference between the Wordsworth of *The Prelude* and the Wordsworth of *Resolution and Independence*. It was this change in Wordsworth, as much as his own loss of creative power, that led Coleridge to his final formulation

[1] Vol. i, p. 179.

of what he meant by 'the Imagination'. The strongest argument for considering the two poets as a single 'romanticism' is the way that in the *Biographia*—the romanticism's manifesto—the examination of Wordsworth's Imagination illuminated Coleridge's own, and vice versa. *Biographia Literaria* is, in effect, the story of Wordsworth's and Coleridge's inter-dependence during their creative years.

In following his conception of the Imagination through Wordsworth's work, Coleridge deliberately rejected the whole system of neo-Hartleian classification with which Wordsworth had encumbered his 1815 *Poems*, and firmly re-interpreted the entire canon. To call certain poems 'Poems of the Imagination' was as irrelevant and misleading as it was to treat Wordsworth's work as naive and primitive. But Coleridge's warning was to be largely ignored by his own century:

the supposed characteristics of Mr. Wordsworth's poetry, whether admired or reprobated; whether they are simplicity or simpleness; faithful adherence to essential nature, or wilful selections from human nature of its meanest forms and under the least attractive associations; are as little the real characteristics of his poetry at large, as of his genius and the constitution of his mind.[1]

Wordsworth, in spite of his eminently un-philosophic mind, was for Coleridge primarily to be seen as a 'philosophic' poet. Without appreciating what Coleridge meant by his warning, we are in danger of missing the implications of the image of the swan with which he follows it:

In short...his only disease is the being out of his element; like the swan, that, having amused himself, for a while, with crushing the weeds on the river's bank, soon returns to his own majestic movements on its reflecting and sustaining surface.[2]

Coleridge's symbols are rarely, if ever, single-barrelled. The transformation of the ungainly flat-footed waddlings of the swan on the bank (note the weeds!) to the grandeur of its motion on the water, is a superb image of the contrast between Wordsworth's critical theory and the best of his poetry. The

---

[1] Vol. ii, p. 95.
[2] *Ibid.* pp. 96–7.

image is almost barbed. The picture of the swan riding on its own perfect reflection in the still water at its most facile suggests all the egotistic sublimity of Wordsworth's best work. More significantly, perhaps, it illustrates the relation between the poet's mind and the imaginative grasp of nature in its own image better than many chapters of 'sum-m-mjects and om-m-mjects'. But the water does more than reflect: it sustains the swan. The same nature that allows the imagination to find its own reflection upholds and supports it. We have already seen how Wordsworth himself uses the contrast of depth and reflection in water as a symbol of the mind; Coleridge, whether or not influenced by Schelling's symbolism of water for the unconscious,[1] has taken this and added to it a further quality of water: its passive buoyancy. Once again we are brought back to the inseparability of man from his environment; the inter-penetration of the poet and nature.

It is, in fact, in images like this that we can follow the course of Coleridge's real development long after the passing of what is usually compartmentalized as his 'poetic' period. Two American critics, J. A. Appleyard and J. D. Boulger, have both suggested that after 1816 there was an abrupt change in Coleridge's interests from poetry to philosophy.[2] Yet if we look closely it is difficult to find evidence to support this. Coleridge's prose-writing remains dense and 'poetic'. Even at its most apparently abstract, the real thread of Coleridge's argument is to be found, time and again, in the closely-packed images—often to the detriment of the 'philosophy'. Underneath there is a continuous pattern of development. Without Wordsworth the romanticism was truncated. Coleridge alone was a different kind of writer. But the astonishing thing about Coleridge's later philosophy is not its contrast with his earlier poetry, but, as we shall see in the next chapter, its essential continuity.

---

[1] For the pre-Jungian intuitions of Richter and Schelling see Abrams, *Mirror and Lamp*, pp. 211–12.

[2] Appleyard, *Coleridge's Philosophy of Literature;* Boulger, *Coleridge as Religious Thinker.*

7
Symbol and Growth

Coleridge, to many people, and often have I heard the complaint, seemed to wander; and he seemed to wander the most when, in fact, his resistance to the wandering instinct was greatest—viz., when the compass, and huge circuit by which his illustrations moved travelled farthest into remote regions before they began to revolve. Long before this coming round commenced most people had lost him, and naturally enough supposed that he had lost himself. They continued to admire the separate beauty of the thoughts, but did not see their relations to the dominant theme. Had the conversation been thrown upon paper, it might have been easy to trace the continuity of the links; just as in Bishop Berkley's *Siris*, from a pedestal so low and abject, so culinary, as Tar Water, the method of preparing it, and its medicinal effects, the dissertation ascends, like Jacob's ladder, by just gradations, into the Heaven of Heavens and the throne of the Trinity. But Heaven is there connected with earth by the Homeric chain of gold; and, being subject to steady examination, it is easy to trace the links; whereas, in conversation, the loss of a single word may cause the whole cohesion to disappear from view. However, I can assert, upon my long and intimate knowledge of Coleridge's mind, that logic the most severe was as inalienable from his modes of thinking as grammar from his language.

De Quincey, *Reminiscences of the English Lake Poets*

Coleridge helped to teach his century wherein the genuine super-humanness of Christianity really lay. Moreover, he taught this before the main attacks of the higher criticism and of science were launched, so that when the crisis came (in the middle of the century in England) the defensive positions were already laid down. If, throughout the century of biblical criticism and scientific agnosticism, Christianity held its ground, contrary to the expectations of many; if it did this by discarding its pseudo-foundations in historical, prophetic, natural, or miraculous 'evidences', and by discovering a firmer foundation in the specific religious experience, in man's need for a God who comes to meet and to redeem him; if this is so (and I believe that it is), then the debt of modern theology to Coleridge is very considerable.

Basil Willey, *Nineteenth Century Studies*

Few judgements on Coleridge may seem to have less connection with each other than these two well-known tributes, the one (somewhat back-handed), to his method of discourse, the other, to his major religious achievement. Yet in crude juxtaposition like this they point to a further aspect of him. Basil Willey himself seems to be echoing De Quincey when he observes that Coleridge 'was one of that rare class of minds which cannot contemplate any one thing without becoming aware of its relation to everything else'. It is, moreover, certainly true that this 'myriad-mindedness' of Coleridge, this power to perceive a vast complex of simultaneous relationships, underlay both his incredible circumambient method of holding forth, and his most influential religious insight. But there is a deeper link between the hidden but severe logic of Coleridge's conversation and his attempt to ground Christianity in specific religious experience. It is this deeper continuity that is the subject of this chapter. The 'defensive positions' of inward religious experience are themselves the product of a particular view not so much of religion, but primarily of the human mind; a view which succeeded in bringing together both the inwardness of religious experience and his recognition of his own apparently tortuous and rambling associative logic. Coleridge saw the human mind itself as essentially a myth-making and symbolizing structure. We can see the movement of his thought from his earliest poems through his literary criticism and political pamphleteering to his final philosophic and religious position as the history of his attempt to produce a satisfactory formulation for this basically intuitive concept of the mind.

As we mentioned at the end of the last chapter, it seems to be widely accepted, either explicitly or implicitly, in recent critical studies of Coleridge's later thought that, whatever continuities of approach may be traced between his early work and his later religious studies, there is a change of interest so radical as to amount to a discontinuity. Father J. A. Appleyard in *Coleridge's Philosophy of Literature* sees it as occurring sometime soon after the publication of *Biographia Literaria* in 1816. Elaborating on what René Wellek has called the 'fatal dualism' of Coleridge's philosophy, James D. Boulger in *Coleridge as Religious Thinker* concludes that ' ... the communion of man and Nature which had

been so central to the early poetry broke apart completely in his
Christian thinking, leaving a wide chasm between spirit and
Nature.'[1] Basing his argument on this interpretation of such
late poems as *Limbo, Ne Plus Ultra,* and *Coeli Enarrant,* Boulger
goes on to explain the Brocken-spectre of *Constancy to an Ideal
Object* as Coleridge's realization that man's highest nature is
'only the self-generating illusion of the rustic'. This is the
position with which we started in the first chapter. All the evidence we have seen in the course of this book suggests that such
an interpretation of the 'image with a glory round its head' is
based upon a misunderstanding of the ambiguity that Coleridge
saw as fundamental to the Imagination. It seems to me that
Boulger is here following I. A. Richards in attributing to
Coleridge a concept of the Imagination which involves 'the active
projection of the mind upon the objects of Nature, leading to the
interpenetration and fusion of all things'.[2] As we have seen one
of the very curious effects of this kind of crude 'projectionism'
when applied to the delicate interplay of Coleridge's theory of
perception is to make it seem much more 'mystical' than it
actually was. Coleridge is often complex, and frequently obscure;
he is never 'mystical' in this sense. Clearly, such poems as
Self Knowledge and *Ne Plus Ultra are* profoundly pessimistic,
and do draw the sharpest barrier between 'man's futility and his
hope of divine grace', but it seems to me that we must draw the
very clearest distinction between these very 'Calvinist' and
other-worldly poems, and a second group, including *Limbo* and
Coeli Enarrant, in which the gulf is not set between man and
God, but man and nature. *Coeli Enarrant* is worth quoting in its
entirety:

> The stars that wont to start, as on a chace,
> Mid twinkling insult on Heaven's darkened face,
> Like a conven'd conspiracy of spies
> Wink at each other with confiding eyes!
> Turn from the portent—all is blank on high,
> No constellations alphabet the sky:
> The Heavens one large Black Letter only shew,
> And as a child beneath its master's blow

[1] P. 206.
[2] *Ibid.* p. 210.

Shrills out at once its task and its affright—
The groaning world now learns to read aright,
And with its Voice of Voices cries out, O!

Boulger explains that here 'the image of the darkened sky
divides the "groaning world" of sin and physical evil from God.
Man reads in anguish the black-letter starless sky as an "O" corresponding to his own pain and alienation.'[1] But *is* this what the
poem actually says? The stars are surely visible and twinkling—
but their twinkling is an 'insult' to the dark sky. They are, Coleridge seems to be suggesting, secretive and hostile, alienated *both*
from their setting and from man, the beholder. They wink only at
each other. Coleridge's complaint is, in fact, the familiar one from
Dejection: 'I see, not feel, how beautiful they are.' The unifying
power of Imagination that links Coleridge to the created world is
suspended, leaving him imprisoned within himself, and only
capable of projection—without response. It is not that there are
no stars in the sky, but there are no *constellations*. He cannot
'read' the stars in the sky as a meaningful pattern; he can only
project the woe of his own isolation, and see them as isolated
hostile entities. Heaven now resembles Hell. So far then from
revealing an abrupt change in Coleridge's relationship to
nature, *Coeli Enarrant* turns out to be one of the most explicit
statements of a conflict that had been going on in him since *The
Ancient Mariner*. Though it may have religious implications,
there is nothing 'mystical' in this failure of the Imagination:
what he is describing is a psychological state.

There is a second cause of this kind of misunderstanding,
however, which is no less fundamental than the failure we have
seen here to grasp what Coleridge meant by the Imagination.
It involves a misreading of what he was trying to do, among
other places, in the poem *Limbo* (to which we shall return), and
in his prose philosophical work, *Aids to Reflection*. It is significant that most of the critics who have attempted to tackle the
problems presented by *Aids to Reflection* have, like René
Wellek, Boulger, and Appleyard, come to Coleridge by way
of Kant and German philosophy, and, not unnaturally, tend to
see him as an eclectic and unsystematic pseudo-*naturphilosopher*.

---

[1] *Ibid.* p. 205.

The result of this kind of approach is a polarization. Either, like Wellek, we have to dismiss Coleridge as only of secondary importance and marginal interest, or we must perform industrious and inconclusive feats of apologetic like Appleyard and Boulger. There is, however, another possible approach to these late works which has proved far more rewarding. Graham Hough, for instance, following Basil Willey, and remaining carefully uncommitted as to the feasibility of the attempt, argues in his discussion of Coleridge's influence on the Victorians that:

The aim of Coleridge's religious writing is to show that all the central doctrines of Christianity, all the sacraments and traditional devotional observances, are deducible, with the aid of revelation, from the constitution of the human mind itself.[1]

In referring us back to the 'constitution of the human mind', it is important to notice that Hough is in fact stressing the continuity between Coleridge's late religious thought and his earlier poetry and criticism. The Coleridge of *Aids to Reflection* can, I believe, best be understood not in the light of say Kant, but in the light of his own previous development. There is an interesting passage in a letter to J. H. Green (13 December 1817) which has not, perhaps, in this connection, been given the prominence it deserves.

My own opinion of the German Philosophers does not greatly differ from your's—much in several of them is unintelligible to me, and much more unsatisfactory. But I make a division—I reject Kant's *stoic* principle, as false, unnatural, and even immoral, where in his Critik der Practischen Vernun(f)t he treats the affections as indifferent in ethics, and would persuade us that a man who disliking, and without any feeling of love for, Virtue yet *acted* virtuously, because and only because it was his Duty, is more worthy of our esteem, than the man whose affections were aidant to, and congruous with, his conscience. For it would imply little less than that things not the Objects of the moral Will or under it's controul were yet indispensible to it's due practical direction. In other words, it would subvert his own System.—Likewise, his remarks on PRAYER in his RELIGION innerhalb d.r.V. are crass, nay vulgar; and as superficial even in psychology as they are low in taste.—But with these exceptions I reverence Immanuel Kant

[1] Graham Hough, 'Coleridge and the Victorians', from *The English Mind* (Cambridge, 1964), p. 181.

with my whole heart and soul; and believe him to be the only Philosopher, for *all men* who have the power of thinking.[1]

The final affirmation of reverence should not blind us to the
nature of Coleridge's criticisms of Kant. He thought at first that
the *Critique of Pure Reason* had not merely shown him where he
parted company with the English empiricists, but also enabled
him to come full circle and re-affirm on better psychological
grounds the same conclusions that had first made such an
impression on him in Hartley—namely, that religious faith and
psychological insight must ultimately be compatible since they
really reflect each other. Kant, of course, did not offer him this,
in the last resort, any more than Hartley. As a result, we find
him here criticizing the *Critique of Practical Reason* on the same
intuitive psychological grounds that had led him to break with
Hartley. Kant's view of religion, we observe, is attacked not on
theological, but on *psychological* grounds. Paradoxically, the
'fatal dualism' of thought that Wellek sees at the root of his
philosophical 'failure', was the result of his dissatisfaction with
Kant's account of experience. Coleridge was prepared to be
unsystematic and eclectic because he obstinately refused to omit
what he felt to be vital areas of his experience from the total
synthesis. Emotions were, for him, essential ingredients of
ethics. It was not so much a 'dualism', as a desire to demonstrate
the *unity* of our mental processes that prevented his forming a
systematic philosophical structure. We can see just how great is
the continuity with Coleridge's previous thought in this instance. He is criticizing the elevation of 'Duty' over 'affections'
not only because it implied to him a maiming of the whole
person, and a denial of his own conviction that true 'morality'
involved a spontaneous love of others, but also because of his
conception of 'Reason'. We recall how Wordsworth, writing
in the 'Letter to Mathetes' in *The Friend*, uses 'reason' in a
strongly Coleridgean sense when he described the youth's simultaneous awareness of his moral and spiritual existence as he
watches the dying candle. Emotions, Wordsworth argued,
properly based, are grounded not in the senses but in the intellect, and lead on directly to the society of 'Reason'. The
sequence of development seems to be: 'intellect'—'emotions'

[1] *Letters*, Vol. IV, pp. 791–2.

—'reason'. Though it transcends emotion, 'reason' is nevertheless an *emotional* faculty. So here, I think, Coleridge is outraged by Kant not merely for neglecting the whole man (a cardinal sin in itself), but also because he has failed to see that ethics will necessarily answer an emotional need. It is ethics themselves that Coleridge feels that Kant is threatening to undermine.

Nor is this an isolated example. We cannot understand what it was that Coleridge was trying to establish about the mind in *Aids to Reflection* without constant reference to his previous poetic and critical development. The whole structure depends on it. Even, for example, the fact that the title itself is an elaborate pun should serve as a warning. *Aids to Reflection* is avowedly a manual to enable university students to replace a decayed philosophical empiricism, and theological 'Paleyism', by an improved idealist basis of thought. But the title at once makes the connection between 'reflection' as a mode of thought, and 'reflection' as the action of a mirror. Thought, Coleridge argues, must flow out of 'reflection' or tend to it. 'Thought' is defined as:

The voluntary reproduction in our own minds of those states of consciousness, or...of those inward experiences, to which, as to his best and most authentic documents, the teacher of moral or religious truth refers us.[1]

Man, made in God's image as a living and creative soul, is at his *proper* activity ('each according to its kind') when acting as a mirror to God's enlightenment. But this Divine illumination is not a vision, but a 'state of consciousness' or an 'inward experience'. It is, Coleridge argues, from these that all true 'thought' must begin. He seems to be referring here to something very like Kant's 'noumena'. According to Kant, the ideas of 'God', 'Self', 'Freedom', 'Immortality', and 'Moral Duty' cannot be known cognitively (that is, that we cannot reach them by our own unaided logical reasoning), but are direct reflections in our souls of their Divine originator. Coleridge was paraphrasing Kant when he described them like this in *The Friend*:

God created man in His own image...He gave us conscience—that law of conscience, which in the power, and as the indwelling word, of a

[1] *Aids to Reflection*, p. 4.

holy and omnipotent legislator commands us—from among the numerous ideas mathematical and philosophical, which the reason by the necessity of its own excellence creates for itself, unconditionally commands us to attribute reality, and actual existence, to those ideas, and to those only, without which the conscience itself would be baseless and contradictory, to the ideas of soul, of free-will, of immortality, and of God![1]

According to Wellek, Coleridge is engaged in the futile game of trying to make Kant's regulative ideas constitutive, so that he can apply them directly and didactically in moral teaching. At the opposite pole, Boulger is prepared to defend this on the grounds that this was the way Coleridge could describe his own religious experience—an argument with some validity. Nevertheless, it seems to me that both arguments fall down over the utter futility of trying to decipher what Coleridge is doing with Kant—an exercise that tells us little about either Coleridge or Kant. In this case, moreover, I suspect it is a red-herring. Coleridge is, in fact, grappling with what is essentially an old *pre*-Kantian preoccupation.

The basic problem, as we saw in Chapter 2, arose for Coleridge when he attempted to view mental growth in organic rather than mechanistic terms. It is an enduring characteristic of his thought that throughout the rise and fall of his various 'systems' his long-term objectives scarcely wavered. Hartley's original model of human growth, as we have noticed, did include a crude vegetable analogy, and it was this original Hartleian concept that, in one form or another, continued to occupy Coleridge's attention in his struggles to produce a model of organic mental development that satisfied the requirements of his own introspective experience. So far, we have been investigating some of the implications of this line of thought, but it will not have escaped the reader's notice that the fundamental problem of *quality* or 'value' in experience—what John Stuart Mill saw as central to Wordsworth and Coleridge's romanticism —was hardly to be satisfactorily cleared up by a coherent philosophical system. Coleridge was well aware of this, and for the next thirty years after his rejection of Hartley much of his

---

[1] *The Friend* I, Essay 15, p. 67.

so-called 'philosophy' (in spite of the influence of Kant) continued, I believe, to pivot on this problem.

In the Introduction to *Aids to Reflection*, for example, Coleridge outlines in some detail a triad in human nature which is to form the ostensible structure of the book. I have summarized it briefly in a table, as follows:[1]

QUALITY (composition)		CHARACTERISTIC	MODE OF DEVELOPMENT
'Understanding'	{ sense and understanding	— Prudence	Mechanism
'Reason'	{ heart and conscience	— Morality	Organism
'Spiritual Mind'	{ will and reason	— Spirituality	'Spiritual organism' or 'Reflection'

Coleridge is not entirely consistent in the accounts he gives of this structure, sometimes suggesting that Morality is a hybrid born of mechanism and organism, or that true organism is only to be found on the spiritual plane. Nevertheless, the fantastic and impractical complications of the plan should be apparent. I instance it, however, for three very good reasons. The first is as a warning against taking Coleridge's stated plans too literally (Boulger finds Coleridge's arrangement 'baffling'—as well he might!). The second is that we are quickly struck by how much more this looks like a re-vamped Hartleianism (with Hartley's original seven stages from Sense to Theopathy now reduced to

---

[1] The table is a composite one, constructed from references throughout the *Aids*. See, in particular, Aphorism XXXII (p. 24):

'It may be an additional aid to Reflection, to distinguish the three kinds severally, according to the faculty to which each corresponds, the faculty or part of our human nature which is more particularly its organ. Thus: the prudential corresponds to the sense and the understanding; the moral to the heart and conscience; the spiritual to the will and reason, i.e., to the finite will reduced to harmony with, and in subordination to, the reason, as a ray from that true light which is both reason and will, universal reason and will absolute.'

Coleridge is at his least convincing when he is writing, as here, in terms of faculty-psychology—especially since, while ostensibly using a Kantian framework, he often seems to be talking of these faculties as if they were Hartleian stages. Against this apparent rigidity must be set his continual awareness of the inadequacy of such a framework. See, in particular, Aphorism CIV (p. 178):

'Christianity is not a Theory, or a Speculation, but a *Life*. Not a *Philosophy* of Life, but a Life and a Living Process... TRY IT.'

three) than like anything to be found in German transcendental philosophy. The third is even more revealing. The centre of interest, here, is not in any sense other-wordly, or even more than marginally 'idealist', but very firmly psychological. Coleridge has attempted to use Kant's Two Worlds to produce a scheme that will explain his own mental development. *All* organized matter is now seen as subject to the laws of mechanism, and perceived by the understanding. The higher will and spirituality are transcendent, and reason and morality are seen as the characteristic human attributes, linking man organically both with the realm of organized matter on the one hand, and the spiritual life of the heavenly host on the other. Growth is achieved according to its own peculiar mode at each level. How we are to try and disentangle the strands of Hartley, Kant, and Neo-Platonism from this amazing hotch-potch is anybody's guess! What we must do, instead, is to cut through this curious framework (which Coleridge, typically, makes only the most formal attempt to adhere to) and try and discover how these elements are used to mask the enduring preoccupations of Coleridge's life.

Underlying it all, as we have suggested, is the need to produce a model to replace that of the organic growth of a seed, without the unwelcome deterministic associations. Coleridge was led by this need to experiment with a whole series of analogues for the power of an organized pattern to reproduce itself, or to repeat its structure, without actual contact. Magnets and iron-filings,[1] the compass-needle (as an image of the will),[2] and the harmony of music are all made use of at various times. But paramount in his thought—and in conjunction with the theory of the Imagination as the prime instrument of perception—we find the symbol of the mirror. But as we have already seen in the lines to Wordsworth

---

[1] In this analogy, each iron-filing, while under the influence of the magnet, is itself a little magnet. It does not respond 'passively', but in aligning itself along the greater magnet's lines of force it is proportionally identical in structure and influence to the original. An idea can thus be like such a field of force, creating in the mind an identical alignment to the original. See, for instance, *Aids to Reflection*, p. 59, footnote. For the link in Coleridge's mind between light and magnetism, see *Table Talk*, 20 July 1827.

[2] *Aids to Reflection*, p. 19.

When power streamed from thee, and thy soul received
The light reflected, as a light bestowed...

Coleridge uses the image of the mirror in a very special sense. In the 'Introductory Aphorisms' of *Aids to Reflection* he clarifies his use of the image still further by means of his distinction between 'thought' and 'attention'.

In ATTENTION, we keep the mind *passive*: in THOUGHT we rouse it into activity. In the former, we submit to an impression—we keep the mind steady in order to *receive* the stamp. In the latter, we seek to *imitate* the artist, while we ourselves make a copy or duplicate of his work.[1]

The unspoken image behind this account is quite clear. In using the image of a reflecting mirror, Coleridge is determined to clear it of all passive and mechanistic associations. Behind the idea of 'reflection' there is a theory of imitation analogous to that of artistic 'mimesis'. In his essay 'On Poesy or Art' Coleridge had already clarified just what he meant by artistic 'imitation'.

philosophically we understand that in all imitation two elements must coexist, and not only coexist, but must be perceived as coexisting. These two constituent elements are likeness and unlikeness, or sameness and difference, and in all genuine creations of art there must be a union of these disparates. The artist may take his point of view where he pleases, provided that the desired effect be perceptibly produced,—that there be likeness in the difference, difference in the likeness, and a reconcilement of both in one.[2]

We recall that, according to Coleridge, thought either flows out of reflection, or tends to it. This process of artistic reproduction is turned inwards to what Coleridge defines as the 'authentic documents' of certain 'states of consciousness'. In other words, in 'reflection' our attention is fixed on certain inward experiences to be found, say, in literature, art, or even religion, which are to be re-created in our own minds not as mere copies, but having the same relation to the original experience as say a contemporary landscape painting by Constable had to life. From its original meaning of 'bent backwards', Coleridge has altered

[1] *Ibid.* p. 4, footnote.
[2] *Biographia Literaria*, Vol. II, p. 256.

the meaning of 'reflection' via the concept of a mirror and its image until it is a counterpart to Wordsworth's 'contemplation'—emotion recollected in tranquillity. Where he goes beyond Wordsworth, however, is in the second meaning he attaches to the word. These original experiences—the original 'authentic documents' of the mind—in turn reflect the greater reality that is beyond us. In bending backwards into introspection we are at the same time apprehending the spiritual truths of Christianity. Coleridge uses here, in another brilliant image, the idea of a star reflected in the bottom of a well.[1] Thus the power of 'reflection', or, as he describes it more fully, the power of 'reflective self-consciousness', is, in effect, the human power of *response* to either nature or to God.

To complete the new definition, he also shows us its opposite: the parody of reflection where man sees only himself:

And shall man alone stoop? Shall his pursuits and desires, the *reflections* of his inward life, be like the reflected Image of a Tree on the edge of a Pool, that grows downwards, and seeks a mock heaven in the unstable element beneath it, in neighbourhood with the slim water-weeds and the oozy bottom-grass that are yet better than itself and more noble, in as far as Substances that appear as Shadows are preferable to Shadows mistaken for Substance![2]

It is here, I think, with this definition of reflection, and of its false likeness, that we are given a glimpse of the basic model of the mind that Coleridge had been struggling to articulate ever since *The Friend*: namely, that the mind's operation is not primarily associative, or logical, or dialectical, nor even transcendental—but *symbolic*.

Now though (for good reasons) Coleridge was never able fully to show to his own satisfaction how the mind, so conceived, might actually work, he did devote considerable care to defining what he meant by a symbol. Whereas an allegory was, for him, merely mechanical substitution, a symbol was organically linked with the thing for which it stood:

a symbol...is characterized by a translucence of the special in the individual, or of the general in the special, or of the universal in the

---

[1] *Aids to Reflection*, p. 15, footnote.
[2] *Ibid.* p. 99.

general; above all by the translucence of the eternal in and through the temporal. It always partakes of the reality which it renders intelligible; and while it enunciates the whole, abides itself as a living part of that unity of which it is the representative.[1]

Once again Coleridge finds himself trying to find an analogy for the way in which an organized structure may repeat itself, not in a mechanical or determinate, but in a living (that is, organic) manner. A symbol is only a part of the greater whole it reveals, but it *implies* the totality. The way in which it does this he attempts to describe by the idea of 'translucence'. In a symbol, he suggests, the material and temporal becomes as it were a *lens* whereby we can bring into focus for a moment the eternal abstraction of which it is a fractional and incomplete part. By insisting that a symbol was above all a living part of the unity it represents, Coleridge was able to perform the astonishing feat of bringing together his Platonism and his knowledge of optical science. As we have seen in looking at his theory of perception, apprehension of the world around is built up by an active and imaginative interplay between projection and reception. Coleridge's frequent affirmations of 'One Life' were neither part of a Hartleian phase, nor mystical or metaphysical leaps, but a factual description of how he believed the mind worked. That is to say, it re-created in itself the pattern of the events and experiences of which it partook—not necessarily the events themselves, but a structure hidden beneath them, and implicit throughout. Poetry is thus the direct and natural medium of the mind's activity. It perceives hidden and alogical connections, seeing and symbolizing one thing in terms of another to suggest new aspects of each. He would have agreed with—and to some extent anticipated—that modern school of thought that sees man as a myth-making animal.[2] In this scheme of things events are not apprehended in isolation, but, as we have seen in the case of visual perception and memory, are inseparable from their mode of acquisition, their interpretation and history for the person concerned. That poetic perception was the normal activity of the mind, Coleridge had long been satisfied; what was infinitely

[1] *The Statesman's Manual,* 'Works', ed. Shedd, Vol. I, p. 437.
[2] See, for instance, Susan K. Langer, *Philosophy in a New Key* (3rd ed. Harvard, 1957).

harder to show was that the function of the Imagination in perception typified the entire working of the mind in every form of moral and religious experience. To this end his original intuitive distinction between mechanism and organism, so successfully used in defining 'Fancy' and 'Imagination', was rigorously re-applied to 'Understanding' and 'Reason', and to 'Attention' and 'Thought'—though with much less evident success.

Coleridge's system of scriptural interpretation, which was to have such an influence on people like Julius Hare and F. D. Maurice, was thus not an isolated insight that happened to prove opportune to the nineteenth century. It was an integral part of his whole structure of psychological and symbolic thought. At its centre is an insight not into the scriptures, but into the human mind. As early as 1816, in *The Statesman's Manual*, and within a few lines of his definition of a symbol, we find him writing like this about biblical stories:

In the Scriptures they are the living educts of the imagination; of that reconciling and mediatory power, which incorporating the reason in images of sense, and organising (as it were) the flux of the senses by the permanence and self-circling energies of the reason, gives birth to a system of symbols, harmonious in themselves, and consubstantial with the truths of which they are the conductors.[1]

This, in essence, is the line of argument Coleridge was to take in his *Confessions of an Inquiring Spirit*. Here, however, it is grounded not in biblical criticism but in the symbolizing activities of the mind. To Coleridge, the scriptures were, in effect, 'reflection' in his own sense of the word. Theirs is a presentational mode, rather than a discursive one. The truths they mediate symbolically to us are, at one and the same time, attributes of God, and to be found in our own psychic structure.

The reason why Coleridge made the mirror—in his sense of reflection—the organizing image of *Aids to Reflection* may now be apparent. In *The Friend* he had aleady begun to elaborate the first of his long series of mirror-analogies to illustrate the distinction between 'reason' and 'understanding'. Poetically, it is interesting to notice, he has no difficulty in avoiding the dualism to which his philosophy exposes him.

[1] P. 436.

We will add one other illustration to prevent any misconception, as if we were dividing the human soul into different essences, or ideal persons. In this piece of steel I acknowledge the properties of hardness, brittleness, high polish, and the capability of forming a mirror. I find all these likewise in the plate glass of a friend's carriage; but in addition to all these, I find the quality of transparancy, or the power of transmitting as well as of reflecting the rays of light. The application is obvious.[1]

Coleridge is not seeking primarily a philosophic formulation for his distinction between 'reason' and 'understanding', but a *poetic* one. It must satisfy the mind at all levels, symbolizing its own function by both reflecting (in a plain mechanistic sense) and transmitting (that is, being transluccnt[2])—revealing the mind's own operations to itself, and putting intellectual perception in an analogous relation to visual. The passage is extraordinarily interesting since it allows us to see, as it were in construction, the still more complex and symbolic idea of Reflection that he was to advance in its completed form some fifteen years later. Here, the original analogue of the mind's power to reproduce structures is divided into two modes: the mirror (which is the mechanical 'understanding') and the glass (the organic 'reason'). The natural world we perceive through the mirror of Understanding. As he puts it in a note elsewhere:

We understand nature just as if, at a distance, we looked at the image of a person in a looking-glass, plainly and fervently discoursing, yet what he uttered we could decipher only by the motion of his lips or by his micn.[3]

To understand *what* is being said we need the aid of Reason. The Reason does not use a separate power of apprehension, however, but the same perceptions as the Understanding: both reflecting and seeing through in the same act—incorporating Understanding, and at the same time transcending it to form a new 'simplicity'.[4] In *Aids to Reflection* it is very noticeable that Coleridge

---

[1] 'First Landing-Place', Essay 5, p. 97.
[2] Coleridge uses the two words as almost synonymous: i.e. 'transmit' in its original sense of 'to carry across'.
[3] *Anima Poetae*, p. 232.
[4] I am using the word here in the same sense as Martin Foss (*The Idea of Perfection in the Western World* (Princeton, 1946)). The 'simple' he defines (p. 49) as

consistently treats the reflecting power of Reason as simultaneously a power of response to God *and* to the natural world.

It seems to me, here, that we can see something of why Coleridge had such difficulty in trying to formulate his intuitive conception of the symbolizing action of the mind—as well as why he was so convinced of its truth. His images, appealing directly to the poetic and presentational mode of apprehension, are immediately revealing; their explanations—necessarily discursive—are strikingly less so. The distinction between Reason and Understanding was never as successful as the earlier one between Fancy and Imagination. Coleridge's whole concept of Reflection, as a power of response that, at the same time, symbolizes what it is responding to, is a poetic image and *not* a philosophic structure. It can only be properly understood, I think, if we stop thinking of his religious thought in *Aids to Reflection* as discontinuous with his earlier poetic insights. The one is founded directly on the other. In 1805, for example, while discussing the Roman Catholic doctrine of Faith and Works, in Malta, he had made the following observations:

No actions should be distinctly described but such as manifestly tend to awaken the heart to efficient feeling, whether of fear or of love— actions that, falling back on the fountain, keep it full, or clear out the mud from its pipes, and make it play in its abundance, shining in that purity in which, at once, the purity and the light in each the cause of the other, the light purifying, and the purified receiving and reflecting the light, sending it off to others; not, like a polished mirror, by reflection from itself, but by transmission through itself.[1]

In the sentence immediately preceding this passage, Coleridge had been attacking the rigid compartmentalization of Faith, as an 'intellectual conviction', and Works, as a 'material action'. In so doing, he was upholding precisely the same view of the mind that he found himself trying to elaborate in *Aids to Reflection* almost twenty years later. He was criticizing Roman

---

transcending all division, but in doing so, keeping the divisibility within the frame of its concept—the phenomenon when the whole is greater than the sum of its parts.

[1] *Anima Poetae*, p. 124; *Notebooks*, Vol. II, 7 Feb. 1805, 2435.

Catholic dogma for failing to see that the *least* important aspect of good works is their material effect. As a symbol of faith, each individual act is indeed a true part of that faith, but its real significance is its power of 'transmission' by which it reflects the greater whole of which it is a minute part, and, at the same time, enables man to see through it ('the translucence of the eternal in and through the temporal') and focus upon the reality of the faith behind it. The process by which the 'purity and the light is each the cause of the other' is exactly analogous to the activity of the Imagination in perception—we think, yet again, of the Brocken-spectre. Equally, each action, seen in this way, is an affirmation of Value in human life in the sense that John Stuart Mill desired it. The heart is awakened to 'efficient feeling', and the whole man is brought into the response. Lastly, and most important of all, each action is seen and weighed not in isolation, but as a stage in growth.

It is this connection between the symbolic value of the mind's response in Reflection, and the process of mental growth, that Coleridge returns to now as his central concern in *Aids to Reflection*. Behind all the struggles to avoid a philosophic dualism between spirit and matter, the Kantian, and pseudo-Kantian distinctions, is Coleridge's desire to demonstrate a mode of growth which was as 'poetic', in its comprehension of the whole man, as was Wordsworth's and his own during their closest days at Nether Stowey, but unlike theirs, dependent on something more stable than the human love and appreciation that Coleridge himself so desperately needed, and less inclined in isolation towards the 'tower' of self-sufficiency than Wordsworth's egotism. This personal stability Coleridge saw in Christianity—purged of Paleyan 'Evidences' and firmly grounded in the witness of inner experience. For him, the Christian Faith had become the unifying and esemplastic power by which the growing mind might apprehend and foster its own development. Reflection was inseparable from growth. Whereas a plant grew unreflectively, the growth of the human mind was a growth of 'reflective self-consciousness', and, therefore, by definition must be internally fostered. Combining his two key images of the mirror and the organism, he begins Aphorism xvii with the statement:

A REFLECTING mind is not a flower that grows wild.[1]

These two images run like a *leitmotif* throughout the book; they carry in conjunction Coleridge's idea of growth.

There is, thus from the start a tension in *Aids to Reflection* between the ostensible and the actual structure. The book seems to have started in Coleridge's mind as a Life and critical introduction to Archbishop Leighton;[2] in his final Introduction, however, Coleridge lays down no less than four main aims for the work:

(1) To direct the Reader's attention to the value of the Science of Words...

(2) To establish the *distinct* characters of Prudence, Morality, and Religion...

(3) To substantiate and set forth at large the momentous distinction between REASON and Understanding.

(4) To exhibit a full and consistent Scheme of the Christian dispensation and more largely of all the *peculiar* doctrines of the Christian Faith...[3]

But like the tripartite view of man outlined earlier, so little does Coleridge adhere to this scheme in practice that Boulger, in his attempt to defend *Aids to Reflection* as a philosophical work, is forced to admit at the outset:

It is not an easy book to read or to understand. Polemic and cross-purpose in organisation account for the zig-zag movement of the

---

[1] *Aids to Reflection*, p. 9.

[2] On 18 January 1822 Coleridge wrote to John Murray, his publisher:

'Briefly, then, I feel strongly persuaded, perhaps because I strongly wish it, that the Beauties of Archbishop Leighton, selected and methodized, with a (better) Life of the Author, that is, a biographical and critical introduction as Preface, and Notes, would make not only a useful but an interesting POCKET VOLUME...' (*Letters*, ed. Griggs, Vol. II, p. 717).

A second letter on 8 August 1823 gives an elaborated version:

'Now the Volume, I have prepared, will be best described to you by the proposed Table—

Aids to Reflection: or Beauties and Characteristics of Archbishop Leighton, extracted from his various writings, and arranged on a principle of connection under the three Heads, of 1. Philosophical and Miscellaneous. 2. Moral and Prudential. 3. Spiritual—with a Life of Leighton and a critique on his writings, and opinions—with notes throughout by the Editor.' *Unpublished Letters*, Vol. I, p. 315)

See also Boulger, *Coleridge as Religious Thinker*, p. 7.

[3] *Aids to Reflection*, Author's Preface, pp. xiii–xv.

thought, and for the seeming inconsistency in the form...its two structural principles of organisation are intricate without being clear. Coleridge's division into Introductory, Prudential Moral and Religious, and Spiritual aphorisms, unintentionally belies the importance and number of the religious issues considered; nor does it co-ordinate the numerous allusions to contemporary religious figures and problems.[1]

Frankly bewildered by the multiplicity of structures Coleridge offers the reader, Boulger finally asks 'Is there, then, any organisation in the baffling arrangement which resulted from the merger of the 'Beauties of Archbishop Leighton' with the 'Moral, Prudential, and Spiritual aphorisms?' It is clear that Boulger himself has done much valuable work on the origins and form of the *Aids*, and within his terms of reference one cannot do more than he does. Yet the end result is only to grope after structural fragments. One feels instinctively that it is the method which is at fault. Coleridge is not to be tied down in this manner. We must look, for instance, to where there does exist a coherent substructure of *nodal* images and symbols, which guide the reader across the main divisions of the book following Coleridge's own personal preoccupations. They are to be found in footnotes as often as in the main text—where Coleridge has started a hare which has crossed abruptly into another field of interest. If we follow these, even at the expense of the main argument, we follow the way in which his own mind was working, until suddenly (if we are lucky) we share De Quincey's experience: a glimpse of the all-embracing unity and logic of Coleridge's thinking. It is in this counterpoint that we find emerging certain dominant strains of imagery.

The first is seen in the traditional Christian symbol of the pilgrim:

Awakened by the cock-crow (a sermon, a calamity, a sick-bed, or a providential escape) the Christian pilgrim sets out in the morning twilight, while yet the truth (the perfect law of liberty) is below the horizon. Certain necessary *consequences* of his past life and his present undertaking will be *seen* by the refraction of its light...[2]

Here we have a fascinating example of the conflict of avowed aim and actual interests that runs throughout *Aids to Reflection*.

[1] *Coleridge as Religious Thinker*, pp. 5–6.
[2] *Aids to Reflection*, p. 19.

This is ostensibly an allegory: he even gives us bracketed explanations, in case we should miss his point. Yet Coleridge despised allegories. In the Appendix to *The Statesman's Manual* he contrasts allegory with symbol in terms of mechanism and organism, Fancy and Imagination—as

but a translation of abstract notions into a picture-language, which is itself nothing but an abstraction from objects of the senses; the principle being more worthless even than its phantom proxy, both alike insubstantial, and the former shapeless to boot.[1]

No less astonishing than this inconsistency is the avowed theology: what is Coleridge, of all people, doing with dramatic *external* causes of conversion, rather than with the inward need? Are the 'calamity' or the 'providential escape' any more than Elijah's the Wind, the Earthquake, and the Fire?—equivalents for the will of Paley's 'Evidences' for the reason? And yet (to the reader who skims the sense of the passage rather than analysing its meaning) it is quite clear what Coleridge *is* doing. Juxtaposed here are two of his key images: that of light—this time mere twilight, 'refracted' only, as a first and as yet mechanical stage towards true Reflection; and that of Bunyan's Pilgrim, at the first stirrings of spiritual growth. But unlike Bunyan's Pilgrim, Coleridge's is not following a light beyond himself, but within. His progress towards God is a continual development of 'reflective self-consciousness'. This is something that seems to foreshadow, as it were in embryo, the major theological revolution of the twentieth century—the movement that was in Germany to lead eventually to Bonhoeffer and Tillich. Whereas previous Christian apologists, from St Paul onwards, had seen mental growth as a product of spiritual development, Coleridge, like Bonhoeffer after him, is inclined to see spiritual development as the product of mental growth. There are passages in *Aids to Reflection* that seem at times to contradict such a view (nor would Coleridge have necessarily have admitted this implication) but the whole tenor of his argument and images is clear.[2] Once again we are faced with

1 P. 437.
2 Take, for instance, Aphorism XIII (p. 7):
    'Never yet did there exist a full faith in the Divine Word (by whom *light*, as well as immortality, was brought into the world) which did not expand the

this curious Coleridgean conflict between what he is supposed to be saying, and how he is saying it.

Within this conflict is developed a second strand. The cumulative experience of a lifetime of outward suffering, wrong-decisions, drug-addiction, and failure reveals itself now as an introspective insight into, and awareness of the depth, range, and subtlety of the mind. Coleridge demonstrates an awareness of the unconscious, not merely anticipating Jung in form, but based on similar premises of the symbolizing structure of our mental processes. We have already referred in passing to the image of the star reflected in the deep well of the mind, but the whole footnote is of extraordinary interest, tying up as it does this view of the unconscious with the theological revolution we have just mentioned:

The Greek word, *parakupsas*, signifies the incurvation or bending of the body in the act of *looking down into* : as, for instance, in the endeavour to see the reflected image of a star in the water at the bottom of a well. A more happy or forcible word could not have been chosen to express the nature and ultimate object of reflection, and to enforce the necessity of it, in order to discover the living fountain and springhead of the evidence of the Christian faith in the believer himself, and at the same time to point out the seat and region, where alone it is to be found. Quantum *sumus, scimus*. That which we find within ourselves, which is more than ourselves, and yet the ground of whatever is good and permanent therein, is the substance and life of all other knowledge.[1]

Another passage, already quoted in part in a previous chapter, is worth looking at in full:

If any reflecting mind be surprised that the aids of the Divine Spirit should be deeper than our Consciousness can reach, it must arise from the not having attended sufficiently to the nature and necessary limits of human Consciousness. For the same impossibility exists as to the

---

intellect, while it purified the heart; which did not multiply the aims and objects of the understanding, while it fixed and simplified those of the desires and passions.'

What is so noticeable about this (and kindred statements) is that even while he seems to be arguing that spiritual growth fosters intellectual development, his interest remains firmly centred on the intellectual development. The reason for this, of course, is that in the last resort Coleridge drew no real distinction between 'mental' and 'spiritual' (as in the German *geist*).

[1] *Aids to Reflection*, p. 15.

first acts and movements of our will—the farthest back our recollection can follow the traces, never leads us to the first footmark—the lowest depth that the light of our Consciousness can visit even with a doubtful Glimmering, is still at an unknown distance from the Ground: and so, indeed, must it be with all Truths, and all modes of Being that can neither be counted, coloured, or delineated.[1]

Lastly, and briefly, another observation that has appeared elsewhere: 'The Chamaeleon darkens in the shade of him who bends over it to ascertain its colours.'[2]

Against this background, the main objectives that Coleridge wished to achieve in *Aids to Reflection* are clear. Growth is a fundamental law equally of the natural and spiritual worlds. Man is a hybrid, stretched between the two, and his peculiar mode of growth is Reflection. The fury of Coleridge's onslaught on the unfortunate Archdeacon Paley follows from his realization that his emphasis on natural 'Evidences' for Christianity (to which Coleridge had no objection in themselves) was substituting no more than intellectual assent for what should be a dynamic process of development. In the last resort, it is Coleridge's permanent preoccupation with the conditions of growth that makes him stress the true inwardness of Christianity:

Hence I more than fear, the prevailing taste for Books of Natural Theology, Physico-Theology, Demonstrations of God from Nature, Evidences of Christianity, &, &, *Evidences* of Christianity! I am weary of the Word. Make a man feel the *want* of it; rouse him, if you can, to the self-knowledge of his *need* of it; and you may safely trust it to his own Evidence...[3]

The point that is so often missed in dealing with this quotation is how a man is to be made to 'feel the *want* of it'. On the one hand, Coleridge goes on, 'No man cometh to me, unless the Father lead him'; on the other hand, the Father's leading is not the divine intervention by miracle which some Evangelicals were prone to suppose when speaking of 'conversion'. Coleridge's own attitude is clear from the many marginal annotations he made to conversion accounts in Southey's *Life of Wesley*. These notes are sceptical to a degree; he is interested

[1] *Ibid.* p. 60.
[2] *Ibid.* p. 70.
[3] *Ibid.* p. 363.

always in the state of mind that produces a dramatic conversion—and in how long it lasts.[1] 'Need', we observe, is the product of 'self-knowledge' as far as Coleridge is concerned, or, to put it another way, Reflection *is* the leading of the Father. He who would find God must look inwards.

Similarly, what seems to me the key section of Coleridge's Preface to *Aids to Reflection* is not the outline of the 'plan', but a note at the very end.

But you are likewise born in a CHRISTIAN land: and Revelation has provided for you new subjects for reflection, and new treasures of knowledge, never to be unlocked by him who remains self-ignorant. Self-knowledge is the key to this casket; and by reflection alone can it be obtained. Reflect on your own thoughts, actions, circumstances, and —which will be of especial aid to you in forming a *habit* of reflection,— accustom yourself to reflect on the words you use, hear, or read, their birth, derivation and history. For if words are not THINGS, they are LIVING POWERS, by which the things of most importance to mankind are actuated, combined, and humanized.[2]

The last sentence is frequently quoted out of context. As a result it is often missed that what Coleridge is saying is that words are living powers *because* they are the tools of self-knowledge. Words have a psychological significance wider than their face value. They are, in Coleridge's sense of the word, *symbols* of the meaning they convey. They do not come down to us empty-handed, but carrying with them in their derivation and subsequent development the history of the development of human consciousness itself.

Ironically, this statement is a faint echo of Hartley's original concept of the association of words and ideas:

[1] Vol. II, p. 8. The footnote reads:
'What shall I say to these and other instances? Disbelieve the narrators? I cannot—I dare not. I seem to be assured that I should quench the ray, and paralyse the factual nerve, by which I have hitherto been able to discriminate veracity from falsehood, and deceit from delusion. Is then aught real, though subjectively real as the law of conscience? When I find an instance recorded by a philosopher of himself, he still continuing to be a philosopher—recorded by a man, who can give the distinctive marks by which he had satisfied himself that the experience was not explicable physiologically, nor psychologically,—I shall think it time to ask the question: till then, I shall find no more rational solution than that afforded by *disorder* of the nervous functions from mental causes...'
[2] P. xvii.

197

Since Words thus collect Ideas from various Quarters, unite them together, and transfer them both upon other Words, and upon foreign Objects, it is evident, that the Use of Words adds much to the number and Complexness of our Ideas, and it is the principal means by which we make our intellectual and moral Improvements.[1]

Between this, and *Aids to Reflection*, lies a major revolution in the history of ideas—yet, if an illustration were needed of Coleridge's assertion, we have it here: his own statement reveals its ancestry.

But here, too, we find again the dualism that has dogged Coleridge's attempt to formulate his concept of the mind at every stage. In *Biographia Literaria* he had attempted to draw a distinction between words and symbols in terms of Ideas: 'An IDEA, in the *highest* sense of that word, cannot be conveyed but by a *symbol*.'[2] We can see here why Coleridge had such great difficulty in saying what he meant by an Idea. As a poet he felt the full creative force of language; as a philosopher he desired an Idealist existence for ideas independent of language. From our present vantage-point, 140 years after, we can see how it was not so much the philosopher that destroyed the poet in Coleridge, but the poet that undermined the philosopher. In *Aids to Reflection* he is clearly thinking of ideas in terms of his old concept of organic unity. So far from existing in timeless abstract perfection, Plato's 'ideas' are made somehow *dynamic*—so that they are analogous to the seed that compounds within itself the whole history of its past and future growth at any given moment. As early as *The Statesman's Manual* we can see that Coleridge has begun to think of ideas in this way: 'But every living principle is actuated by an idea; and every idea is living, productive, partaketh of infinity, and (as Bacon has sublimely observed) containeth an endless power of semination.'[3] It is above all by the process of Reflection that words and ideas coalesce as symbols in the mind. Reflection, as Coleridge is attempting to demonstrate it, is the assimilation of a symbol. He here seems to be very close to the position of the modern liberal

---

[1] *Observations on Man*, Vol. i, p. 287.
[2] Vol. i, p. 100.
[3] P. 433.

theologian Paul Tillich. Assimilation of a symbol involves both consent and response. Tillich, we recall, writes:

Every symbol opens up a level of reality for which non-symbolic speaking is inadequate...but in order to do this, something else must be opened up—namely levels of the soul, levels of our interior reality. And they must correspond to the levels in exterior reality which are opened up by a symbol. So every symbol is two-edged. It opens up reality and it opens up the soul.[1]

For Coleridge, 'Self-knowledge is the key to this casket; and by reflection alone can it be obtained'. The similarity of 'opening' images in Coleridge and Tillich is not accidental. Both are trying to describe what they feel is a general law of human nature, and of psychology, but at the same time is something of an esoteric secret, which, for all its potential universality, is in fact known only to a few. Growth, for Coleridge, was an 'opening up' of consciousness through Reflection. What he was trying, vainly, to do in his *Aids to Reflection* was to formulate an explanation in Kantian terms for a process that he could, in reality, only predicate as a symbol. In other words, 'Reflection', as he attempts to describe it, is not a philosophic concept at all, but Coleridge's method of accounting for the symbolizing power he had experienced in himself, and which seemed to correspond to a phenomenon he had observed in his favourite 'creative' thinkers, from Plato to Archbishop Leighton. Though *Aids to Reflection* is in no sense 'poetry', its achievement, if it is to be measured at all must, I think, be conceived of as 'poetic'.

If this is true of *Aids to Reflection*—as I believe it is—then our whole approach to the late poems must be re-orientated. Coleridge was never anything but a poet—even when he was being unsuccessful as one. The prevailing critical orthodoxy is, I suspect, right in approaching the late poems through such prose works as the *Aids* and *Confessions of an Inquiring Spirit*, but in misinterpreting these, it has in many cases successfully prevented us from seeing what these poems are really about. We have already seen, for instance, how *Coeli Enarrant* depends

[1] *Theology of Culture*, pp. 56–7.

for its interpretation on Coleridge's ideas of perception. The same is true of two other poems put forward by Boulger as examples of the 'wide chasm between spirit and nature', *Limbo* and *Constancy to an Ideal Object*. While it is possible to trace such a 'chasm' in Coleridge's philosophy (though I do not think, as we have seen, that it is anywhere near as wide as is sometimes argued) we find in the actual poems the same phenomenon that we have noticed in his prose works of this period: that what he is apparently saying, and how he is saying it, seem to be at odds. As in the case of the concept of 'Reflection', he shows us a presentational unity that he cannot always defend discursively. In a sense, it is this tension that the late poems are about. We have already seen in the Introduction to this book how the whole image of the Brocken-spectre is far more ambiguous than a simple philosophical examination would suggest. Moreover, it is significant that *Constancy to an Ideal Object* has been classed with *Limbo*. The two poems, it seems to me, constitute a polarity: the one positive, the other negative. We have already seen how in the former poem, Coleridge symbolizes the paradox of creativity in its most ambiguous form: the Brocken-spectre.

> And art thou nothing? Such thou art, as when
> The woodman winding westward up the glen
> At wintry dawn, where o'er the sheep-track's maze
> The viewless snow-mist weaves a glist'ning haze,
> Sees full before him, gliding without tread,
> An image with a glory round its head;
> The enamoured rustic worships its fair hues,
> Nor knows he makes the shadow, he pursues!

It is the act of pursuit that creates the ideal object; again, a scriptural injunction, 'Seek, and ye shall find,' has been transformed by Coleridge into a psychological fact. The corresponding passage in *Limbo* goes like this:

> An Old Man with a steady look sublime,
> That stops his earthly task to watch the skies;
> But he is blind—a Statue hath such eyes;—
> Yet having moonward turn'd his face by chance,
> Gazes the orb with moon-like countenance,

With scant white hairs, with foretop bald and high,
He gazes still,—his eyeless face all eye;—
As 'twere an organ full of silent sight,
His whole face seemeth to rejoice in light!
Lip touching lip, all moveless, bust and limb—
He seems to gaze at that which seems to gaze on him!

Whereas the 'rustic', of *Constancy to an Ideal Object*, in following his ideal finds himself Reflecting, here, in Limbo, there is
total separation between man and nature, and between man and
God. Men shrink 'as Moles', like 'Nature's mute monks, live
mandrakes of the ground...', and exist in a state of alienation,
fearing light itself: 'the natural alien of their negative eye'. In
such a world there is no perception; the conditions which make
the Imagination possible do not exist. In the midst of this Limbo
is the old man with the 'foretop bald and high'—recognizably
Coleridge himself. He mirrors in exact replica that which he
cannot see; his 'moonward' face is itself 'moon-like', seeming
to gaze at 'that which seems to gaze on him'. This is the exact
opposite of the Reflection of the rustic. His projection was
dynamic and found itself invested with a 'glory' in nature; the
old man's 'reflection' is sterile and mechanical. Without the
modifying interplay between projection and receptivity he is
totally cut off: 'blind' in a meaningless void. He is like the piece
of polished steel described in *The Friend* which can reflect, but
without translucence. As a result there is no longer any possibility of development since he, Coleridge, is in a state of complete isolation. He goes on 'A lurid thought is growthless...'
but this is only a purgatorial suspension of his animating power;
what he fears is far worse: the philosophical paradox of 'positive negation'—for him the ultimate horror suggested by
Schelling. This, then, is the meaning of the title: 'Limbo' is the
state of sterile static isolation where projection is unanswered by
any resonance in nature—with fine irony, the very state that
I. A. Richards attributes to Coleridge as his normal imaginative
activity!

Just as the act of perception is fundamentally ambiguous in its
variety of interpretations, so too there is a kind of negative
ambiguity in this absence of the imagination. Everything, we
notice, exists in a world of 'seems'. The old man 'seems to

gaze', because without some kind of response from the external world he cannot properly define even his own activity; the moon 'seems to gaze on him', but similarly he has no means of finding out whether it is really so or not. This is the philosophic paradox which the poem is about. Coleridge here is taking Kant's doctrine of the unknowability of things-in-themselves to its logical conclusion.[1] With time and space attributes of the mind, external objects are, we recall, quite unknowable according to Kant. All we can ever know of them are their ambiguous appearances. For a long time it seemed that Coleridge's theory of perception could be reconciled with Kant's, but here in this poem Coleridge has reached Kant's limitations. The old man of the poem is Coleridge the pure Kantian philosopher—living in a world that is demonstrably unknowable. It is here that we can see the poem's polarity with *Constancy to an Ideal Object*, without which I do not believe it can be understood. In the second poem the old man's logical impasse is resolved not by philosophy, but by a poetic insight. The rustic knows no more of the external world than the white-haired philosopher—he is in a mist—but he is not troubled by the impasse of philosophy of which he knows nothing, instead he acts, he *creates*, and without understanding how he resolves the deadlock. His self-projection is thrown back by the 'viewless snow-mist' with 'a glory round its head'—and in pursuit he finds both growth and value. Reflection, opening up our consciousness, enables man to apprehend through symbols what cannot be known in any other way. Thus the question addressed to the spectral Ideal Object takes on a new significance beside the impasse of *Limbo*:

And art thou nothing?

For the white-haired old man, 'his eyeless face all eye', searching for philosophic truth, the answer can only be 'yes'. Coleridge makes it clear that his ideal is not one of Kant's *a priori* 'noumena', but a living human love, a thing of material involvement:

Yet still thou haunt'st me; and though well I see,
She is not thou, and only thou art she,
Still, still as though some dear embodied Good,

[1] *Critique of Pure Reason*, p. 54.

Some living Love before my eyes there stood
With answering look a ready ear to lend,
I mourn to thee and say—'Ah! loveliest friend!
That this the meed of all my toils might be,
To have a home, an English home, and thee!'
Van repetition! Home and Thou art one.
The peacefull'st cot, the moon shall shine upon,
Lulled by the thrush and wakened by the lark,
Without thee were but a becalmed bark,
Whose Helmsman on an ocean waste and wide
Sits mute and pale his mouldering bark beside.

His 'Ideal Object' is not an abstract concept, but is the creativity of the Imagination which manifests itself in our most everyday perceptions. Without it, even the beauty of nature is as terrifying as the sea on which the Ancient Mariner was becalmed. If, as seems very likely, the 'she' referred to here is Asra—Sarah Hutchinson—then the Ideal Object, though not to be identified with her, is glimpsed in the love and sympathy he might have found in a life with her. Without this loving sympathy his Imagination was barren. It was the misery of Coleridge's marriage that lay behind the failure of *Dejection*. In Asra the freeing of his Imagination can be actualized, perhaps personified as 'some dear embodied Good/Some living Love'. But this is a might-have-been. In the absence of the domestic happiness that Wordsworth was able to surround himself with, Coleridge is driven on to a further, more fundamental questioning of what it is that he has been in pursuit of. His answer is the disturbing ambiguity of the Brocken-spectre.

The vision to which he has remained constant throughout the agonizing dereliction of the Mariner's experience is that of the Imagination. The inter-penetration of man and nature which is both perception and creation. Only from this could spring that central affirmation of Value in human life that Mill found in Wordsworth's and in Coleridge's particular 'romanticism'. As Wordsworth put it in *The Prelude*:

such a Being lives,
An inmate of this *active* universe;
From nature largely he receives; nor so
Is satisfied, but largely gives again,

For feeling has to him imparted strength,
And powerful in all sentiments of grief,
Of exultation, fear, and joy, his mind,
Creates, creator and receiver both,
Working in alliance with the works
Which it beholds—Such, verily, is the first
Poetic spirit of our human life...
(Book ii, lines 265–76)

It is this total poetic vision of human integration that Coleridge followed throughout his life—even when he most conspicuously lacked it—and it is to this vision that *all* his work must be related, if it is to be properly understood. It is the reason why, in the last resort, and for all its usefulness, Kant's system, which left man only in Limbo, had to be abandoned by Coleridge. Only then was he free to retain it, as he had retained so many of Hartley's ideas, as a partial and philosophic answer to a problem that was not philosophic at all—but poetic.

We are now, perhaps, finally in a position to grasp the connection between the two quotations with which this chapter was prefaced. De Quincey spoke more truly than he seems to have realized in emphasizing the hidden but rigorous unity of Coleridge's thought. It pervades the whole of his life's work, linking his poetry to his theology in a surprisingly consistent progression of personal development. It is this, as much as his tiny group of great poems, that makes Coleridge at least co-equal with Wordsworth as one of the great poets of the English-speaking world. The religious position that he gave to the succeeding generation of the nineteenth century was only a part of this unified psychological insight. It was only one part of a campaign in his life-long war on systems of thought which compartmentalized the richness of human experience, or tried to see creativity as a thing separated from growth or Value.

Concise Bibliography

Place of Publication is London, except where otherwise stated

PRIMARY SOURCES REFERRED TO

COLERIDGE, SAMUEL TAYLOR

Aids to Reflection. Grant, Edinburgh, 1905.
A New System of Education. Seventh of a series of lectures held at the White Lion Inn, Bristol, 18 November 1813. Reprinted from the *Bristol Gazette* in the *Athenaeum*, 13 March 1909.
Anima Poetae. Ed. E. H. Coleridge. Heinemann, 1895.
Biographia Literaria. Ed. J. Shawcross. Oxford, 1907.
Church and State. Ed. H. N. Coleridge. Pickering, 1839.
Confessions of an Inquiring Spirit. Ed. H. N. Coleridge. Pickering, 1849.
The Friend. Bohn, 1867. Also, not included in Bohn ed., Appendix 'B', *The Friend*, Vol. III, 1844.
Letters. Ed. E. L. Griggs. Oxford, 1956-9.
Notebooks. Ed. K. Coburn. 2 vols. Routledge, 1957-62.
'On Poesy or Art'. Contained in Vol. II, *Biographia Literaria*.
Philosophical Lectures. Ed. K. Coburn. Routledge, 1949.
Poems. Ed. E. H. Coleridge. Oxford, 1912.
Shakespeare Lectures. Text that of *Literary Remains*, ed. H. N. Coleridge, 1836. Ed. Rhys, Everyman, 1907.
Shakespearean Criticism. Ed. T. M. Raysor. 2nd ed., Everyman, 1960.
The Statesman's Manual. 'Works', ed. W. G. T. Shedd, Vol. I. New York, 1853.
Table Talk. Ed. H. N. Coleridge. Murray, 1852.
The Theory of Life. 'Misc. Aesthetic and Literary'. Bohn/Bell, 1892.

WORDSWORTH, WILLIAM

The Letters of William and Dorothy Wordsworth. Ed. E. De Selincourt. Oxford, 1935-41.
Literary Criticism. Ed. N. C. Smith. Oxford, 1905.
Poetical Works. Ed. E. De Selincourt. 5 vols. Oxford, 1940-9.
The Prelude (1805). Ed. E. De Selincourt. Oxford, 1933.

CONCISE BIBLIOGRAPHY

USEFUL SECONDARY SOURCES

BOOKS

Abrams, Meyer H. *The Mirror and the Lamp*. Oxford, New York, 1958.

Appleyard, J. A. *Coleridge's Philosophy of Literature*. Harvard, 1965.

Barfield, Owen, *History in English Words*. Faber, 1962.

Beatty, A. *William Wordsworth*. University of Wisconsin Studies, Madison, 1922.

Beer, John B. *Coleridge the Visionary*. Chatto, 1959.

Berkeley, G. *A New Theory of Vision, Etc*. Everyman, 1910.

Boulger, J. D. *Coleridge as Religious Thinker*. Yale, 1961.

Carlyle, Thomas. *Life of James Stirling*. Chapman and Hall, 1893.

Coveney, Peter. *The Image of Childhood*. Revised ed. Peregrine, Penguin Books, 1967.

Deschamps, Paul. *La Formation de la Pensée de Coleridge*. Didier, Paris, 1964.

De Quincey, Thomas. *Reminiscences of the English Lake Poets*. Everyman, 1961.

Ehrenzweig, Anton. *The Hidden Order of Art*. Weidenfeld and Nicolson, 1967.

Eliot, T. S. *The Use of Poetry and the Use of Criticism*. Faber, 1933. *Selected Essays*, 3rd ed. Faber, 1951.

Empson, William. *Seven Types of Ambiguity*. 2nd Ed. Peregrine, Penguin Books, 1961.

Ewing, A. C. *A Short Commentary on Kant's Critique of Pure Reason*. Methuen, 1938.

Foss, Martin. *The Idea of Perfection in the Western World*. Princeton, 1946.

Gerard, Alexander. *Essay on Genius*. 1774.

Gill, F. C. *The Romantic Movement and Methodism*. Epworth, 1937.

Gombrich, E. G. *Art and Illusion*. Phaidon, 1960.

Hanson, Lawrence. *The Life of Samuel Taylor Coleridge*. Allen and Unwin, 1938.

Hartley, David. *Observations on Man, his Frame, his Duties, and his Expectations*. 1749.

Haydon, Benjamin. *Autobiography*. Ed. Elwin. Macdonald, 1950. *Correspondence and Table Talk*. Chatto, 1876.

Helmholtz, A. A. *The Indebtedness of Samuel Taylor Coleridge to A. W. Schlegel*. Madison, 1907.

House, Humphry. *Coleridge*: Clark Lectures, 1951–2. Hart-Davis, 1953.

206

CONCISE BIBLIOGRAPHY

Hume, David. *Enquiry Concerning Human Understanding*. 1777.
  Treatise on Human Nature. 1739.
James, D. G. *Scepticism and Poetry*. Allen and Unwin, 1937.
Kant, Immanuel. *Critique of Pure Reason*, trans. N. Kemp Smith.
  Macmillan, 1920; abridged ed., 1934.
Laing, R. D. *The Divided Self*. Pelican, Penguin Books, 1965.
Langer, Susan K. *Philosophy in a New Key*. 3rd ed. Harvard, 1957.
Leavis, F. R. *Revaluation*. Chatto, 1936.
Lovejoy, A. O. *The Great Chain of Being*. Harvard, 1936.
Lowes, Livingstone. *The Road to Xanadu*. Houghton Mifflin, New
  York, 1930.
Mackenzie, Gordon. *Organic Unity in Coleridge*. University of Cali-
  fornia Publications in English. Vol. vii, Berkeley, 1939.
Manning, B. L. *The Hymns of Wesley and Watts*. Epworth, 1942.
Margoliouth, H. M. *Wordsworth and Coleridge 1795–1834*. Oxford,
  1953.
Mill, J. S. *Autobiography*. World's Classics, Oxford, 1924.
  Bentham and Coleridge. Ed. Leavis. Chatto, 1950.
Nicolson, Marjorie. *Newton Demands the Muse*. Archon Books,
  Hamden, Connecticut, 1963.
Priestley, Joseph. *Disquisitions on Matter and Spirit*. 'Theological and
  Misc. Works', ed. Rutt, 1818.
  A Free Discussion of Materialism and Necessity. *Ibid.*
  Introductory Essays to Hartley's Theory of the Human Mind. *Ibid.*
Ramsey, I. T. *Models and Mystery*. Oxford, 1964.
  Religious Language. S.C.M., 1957.
Richards, I. A. *Coleridge on Imagination*. Kegan Paul, 1934.
Robinson, Crabb. *Correspondence of Crabb Robinson with the
  Wordsworth Circle*. Ed. E. J. Morley. Oxford, 1927.
Salveson, Christopher. *The Landscape of Memory*. Arnold, 1965.
Schlegel, A. W. *Lectures on Dramatic Art and Literature*, trans. Black,
  1815.
Smith, Norman Kemp. *Commentary on Kant's Critique of Pure Reason*.
  Macmillan, 1923.
Snyder, Alice. *Coleridge on Logic and Learning*. Yale, 1929.
Southey, Robert. *Life of Wesley*. Ed. C. C. Southey, with notes by
  S. T. Coleridge. 1858.
Tillich, Paul. *Theology of Culture*. Oxford, New York, 1959.
Tucker, Abraham (pen-name, Edward Search). *The Light of Nature
  Pursued*. 1768.
Walsh, William. *Coleridge*. Chatto, 1967.

CONCISE BIBLIOGRAPHY

Watson, George. *Coleridge the Poet.* Routledge, 1966.

Wellek, René. *Immanuel Kant in England.* Princeton, 1931.

Wesley, Charles. *Short Hymns on Select Passages of the Holy Scriptures.* 1796.

Whalley, George. *Coleridge, Sarah Hutchinson, and the Asra Poems.* Routledge, 1955.

Whitehead, Alfred North. *Science and the Modern World.* Mentor Books, New York, 1948.

Willey, Basil. *The Eighteenth Century Background.* Chatto, 1940. *Nineteenth Century Studies.* Chatto, 1949.

Williams, Raymond. *The Long Revolution.* Chatto, 1961.

Wordsworth, Dorothy. *Journals.* Ed. E. De Selincourt. 2 vols. Macmillan, 1941.

Yarlott, Geoffrey. *Coleridge and the Abyssinian Maid.* Methuen, 1967.

Young, Edward. *Conjectures on Original Composition.* 1759.

ARTICLES

Arnold, Matthew. 'Wordsworth'. *The Portable Matthew Arnold*, ed. Trilling. Viking, New York, 1949.

Coburn, Kathleen. 'The Interpenetration of Man and Nature'. Warton Lecture. *Proceedings of the British Academy.* 1963.

Davies, Hugh Sykes. 'Wordsworth and the Empirical Philosophers'. *The English Mind*, ed. Watson, Cambridge, 1964.

Durrant, G. H. 'Imagination and Life—Wordsworth's "The Daffodils"'. *Theoria* (Journal of Studies of Arts Faculty, Natal University), No. 19. October 1962.

Emmet, Dorothy. 'Coleridge on the Growth of the Mind'. *Bulletin of the George Rylands Library*, Vol. 34, No. 2. Manchester, March 1952.

Gay, John. 'Dissertation Concerning the Fundamental Principles of Virtue and Morality'. Preface to Law's translation of Archbishop King's *Essay on the Origin of Evil.* 1732.

Gombrich, E. H. 'Imagery and Art in the Romantic Period'. *Meditations on a Hobby Horse.* Phaidon, 1965.

Harding, D. W. 'The Theme of the Ancient Mariner'. *Scrutiny*, IX, 1941.

Hort, F. J. A. 'Coleridge'. *Cambridge Essays*, Vol. II. Parker, 1856.

Hough, Graham, 'Coleridge and the Victorians'. *The English Mind.* Cambridge, 1964.

James, D. G. 'Kant's Influence on Wordsworth and Coleridge'. *The Listener*, 31 August 1950.

CONCISE BIBLIOGRAPHY

'Wordsworth and Tennyson'. Warton Lecture. *Proceedings of the British Academy*, Vol. xxxvi. 1950.

Knights, L. C. 'Idea and Symbol: Some Hints from Coleridge'. *Further Explorations*. Chatto, 1965.

'Taming the Albatross' (review of J. A. Appleyard's *Coleridge's Philosophy of Literature*). *New York Review of Books*, 26 May 1966.

Lea, F. A. 'Carlyle and the French Revolution'. *The Listener*, 17 September 1964.

Leslie, Margaret E. 'The Political Thought of Joseph Priestley', unpublished Ph.D. Thesis, Cambridge University Library. Appendix on Hartley.

Lovejoy, A. O. 'Coleridge and Kant's Two Worlds'. *Essays in the History of Ideas*. John Hopkins Press, 1948.

'On the Discrimination of Romanticisms'. *Ibid.*

Mill, John Stuart. 'Two Kinds of Poetry'. *Mill's Essays on Literature and Society*, ed. Schneewind. Collier-Macmillan, New York, 1965.

'What is Poetry?' *Ibid.*

Pater, Walter. 'Coleridge'. *Appreciations*. Macmillan, 1928.

Richards, I. A. 'Coleridge's Minor Poems'. Freeman Lecture. Montana State University, 1960.

Salingar, L. G. 'Coleridge—Poet and Philosopher'. *Pelican Guide to English Literature*, Vol. v. Penguin Books, 1957.

Trilling, Lionel. 'The Immortality Ode'. *The Liberal Imagination*. Secker and Warburg, 1951.

Warren, Robert Penn. 'A Poem of Pure Imagination'. *Selected Essays*. Eyre and Spottiswoode, 1964.

Whalley, George. 'The Integrity of "Biographia Literaria"'. *Essays and Studies*. 1953.

Index

INDEX

187–8, 194, 198; *Table Talk*, 184 n.;
Theory of Life, 64, 101; *To William Wordsworth*, 43, 73, 147–52, 172
Constable, John, 90 n., 185
Coveney, Peter, 1 n.
Cretan paradox, 129

Dante, 114
Davies, Hugh Sykes, 161
De Quincey, Thomas, 143, 175–6, 193, 204
De Selincourt, 137, 155
Durrant, G. H., 18 n., 157 n.

Ehrenzweig, Anton, 125–6, 131
Eliot, T. S., 44–5, 118–19
Emmet, Dorothy, 50 n., 108–9, 113
Empson, William, 69, 89, 95–6, 100 n., 123, 125, 131, 137–8, 141
Ewing, A. C., 27 n., 91 n.

Fenwick, Miss., 134
Fichte, J. G., 28, 71, 78
Flower, its use as a symbol, 15–18
Foss, Martin, 189
French Revolution, 31, 88
Frye, Northrop, 144 n.

Garland, Robert, 121
Gay, The Reverend John, 50–1, 56, 83, 103
Gerard, Alexander, 27, 82, 84
Gill, F. C., 106
Godwin, William, 53, 88
Gombrich, E. H.: *Art and Illusion*, 42–3, 45, 72, 90 n., 121–2, 124–5, 128–31; *Meditations on a Hobby Horse*, 153
Grasmere, 167, 168
Gray, Thomas, 114
Green, J. H., 179
Greta Hall, Keswick, 167

Hanson, Lawrence, 79 n.
Harding, D. W., 48 n., 124 n.
Hare, Julius, 3, 188
Hartley, David, 14, 19, 20, 27, 28, 31, 33–4, 35, 41, 44, 46–68, 70–3, 74, 79–80, 81, 82, 83, 85, 91–2, 103, 107, 108, 141, 154, 170, 171, 173, 180, 182–4, 187, 197–8, 204
Haydon, Benjamin, 9–10
Hazlitt, William, 81, 159

Herbert, George, 103
Hopkins, Gerard Manley, 14, 162 n.; *It Was a Hard Thing*, 13
Hort, F. J. A., 3 n., 86 n., 171
Hough, Graham, 179
House, Humphry, 162 n., 171
Hume, David, 51–2
Huntington, Countess of, 103
Hutchison, Sarah (Asra), 155, 156, 169, 170, 203

Imagination (principal refs. only), 2, 10–13, 19, 27–9, 36–42, 67–8, 71–94, 95–102, 110, 115–17, 146, 154–62, 170–4, 177–8, 201–4; Addison on, 7–8; Akenside, 8–9; Gerard, 82; Kant, 27, 74–8; J. S. Mill, 36–7; Tucker, 81–2

James, D. G., 32 n., 74–6, 88–9
John (Gospel), 106
Johnson, Samuel, 163
Jung, C. G., 195

Kant, Immanuel, 19, 20, 26, 27, 46, 56–7, 71, 74–80, 91, 108, 179–84, 191, 199, 202, 204
Keats, John, 4, 10, 73; *La Belle Dame Sans Merci*, 8
King, William (Archbishop of Dublin), 50
Knights, L. C., 15, 35 n., 48 n.

Laing, R. D., 34
Lange, Ernst, 105
Langer, Susan K., 187 n.
Law, Edmund (Bishop of Carlisle), 50
Lawrence, Sir William, 64
Leavis, F. R., 96 n.
Leighton, Robert (Archbishop of Glasgow), 192–3, 199
Leslie, M. E., 61 n.
Locke, John: 'Essay Concerning Human Understanding', 6–7, 'Lockean' philosophy, 11, 12, 33, 40, 44, 50, 54, 65, 70, 81, 85
Lovejoy, A. O.: on Coleridge and Kant, 56–7; on 'the history of ideas', 28; on preformation, 63; on Romanticism, 1–2, 27 n.; on 'Uniformitarianism', 157
Lyrical Ballads, 10

212

INDEX

213

INDEX